W9-AST-733

Verdura

The Life and Work of a Master Jeweler

Sept. 19/03

Happy Birthday Sue!
I hope you will enjoy our book —
(it took 12 years to research.)
all best wishes —
WARD

VERDURA

THE LIFE AND WORK OF A MASTER JEWELER

Patricia Corbett
Introduction by Amy Fine Collins

Harry N. Abrams, Inc., Publishers

The first Verdura design I remember seeing, a bold shiny gold star brooch encrusted with diamonds, wasn't actually by Verdura—it was a copy. I realized this in 1965 when, over a lunch of jellied aspic in Dallas with opera diva and movie star, Lily Pons, I saw the real thing. I was appraising her collection. Mme. Pons was surprised that I, the 24 year old newly appointed head of Sotheby's USA jewelry division, had never heard of "the fabulous Duke Fulco di Verdura"!

From then on, I kept a lookout for Fulco's elegant, flattering and highly original jewels. I left the auction business to start my own firm in 1973, the same year Duke di Verdura retired to London. I dreamed that one day I would acquire his company and vast archive of jewelry designs. Verdura's long-time associate and then owner of Verdura Inc., Joseph Alfano, finally agreed to sell me the firm in 1985.

This book, eleven years in the making, not only portrays the life and work of the talented Sicilian Duke; it is a social history of the twentieth century. From his privileged childhood in Palermo, to his eight-year stint with Coco Chanel in Paris, to the opening of his Fifth Avenue salon with the backing of his dear friend Cole Porter, Verdura unfolds; a complex, cultured and wickedly funny man of his time.

I wish to thank the Verdura staff, past and present, with special thanks to Maria Kelleher Williams for her devotion to everything at Verdura; my friend and CEO, Larry Freedman, for his advice and for keeping the numbers straight with the help of John Fonte; Melissa Kuba for her meticulous and beautiful work in creating today's Verdura jewels; our gifted author, Patricia Corbett, Stanley Baron, editor *par excellence*; Babs Simpson, friend of Fulco; Tom Parr, dear friend of Fulco and continuous supporter of this project; Harry Fane, our keeper of the flame "across the pond"; and my family, daughter India, son Nico and especially my wife, Judith, for continuous encouragement and help even when I thought this would never come to fruition. Lastly, and most importantly, my gratitude to our patrons, without whose support none of this would have come to pass.

WARD LANDRIGAN   *New York 2002*

Library of Congress Control Number 2002108383
ISBN 0-8109-3529-5

Copyright © 2002 Thames & Hudson Ltd, London
Text copyright © 2002 Patricia Corbett
Introduction copyright © 2002 Amy Fine Collins

Published in 2002 by Harry N. Abrams, Incorporated, New York
All Rights Reserved. No part of the contents of this book may be reproduced without the written permission of the publisher.

Printed and bound in Singapore
10 9 8 7 6 5 4 3 2 1

Harry N. Abrams
100 Fifth Avenue
New York, New York 10011
www.abramsbooks.com

Abrams is a subsidiary of

LA MARTINIÈRE
G R O U P E

Contents

Half-title A lily of the valley brooch, set with pendant pearls, diamonds, and green enamel leaves, *c.* 1960.

Title Verdura's drawing for a cabochon emerald scarf necklace made in the early 1940s for Dorothy Hirschon (the first Mrs. William S. Paley).

Opposite and above Two Maltese cross cuff bracelets, one of Verdura's signature designs.

INTRODUCTION BY AMY FINE COLLINS

AS THE CHAOTIC, aggressive excesses of turn of the century fashion recede into obsolescence, the serenely romantic jewelry of Fulco Santostefano della Cerda, Duke of Verdura is once again looking very fresh and timely. Auction prices for his civilized, nature-based designs are climbing, sales at the Verdura shops in New York, Palm Beach, and London are brisk, and the Verdura name, which briefly had fallen into obscurity, is now recognized among cognoscenti as a signifier of rarefied glamor. Verdura's cosmopolitan sensibility has been absorbed by a new, ascendant generation of jewelers who readily acknowledge the refined influence of the Sicilian master.

Brought up in the languid, cultivated world of the Palermo aristocracy memorialized by his cousin, novelist Prince Giuseppe di Lampedusa, in *The Leopard,* Fulco, from an early age, was an aesthete with a facility for drawing. Finding the inbred Palermo society 'a little narrow' (according to his friend Prince Jean-Louis de Faucigny-Lucinge) and his pockets a little empty, Fulco left his ancestral Sicilian home in the mid 1920s with vague plans of becoming a painter in Paris. For the young nobleman poverty proved to be "a heaven-sent grace," said Faucigny-Lucinge. With the help of Linda and Cole Porter (whom he had first encountered in 1919 during their honeymoon stopover in Palermo), Fulco landed a position at Chanel—first as a textile designer, then as a jeweler. "Chanel was the most chic woman I ever met," Fulco declared, and "the first person ever to take me seriously." In collaboration with the couturiere, he developed a suavely naturalistic style of jewelry that displaced the reigning hard-edged, slick, abstract 1920s Deco taste.

"Fulco came into Chanel's life at the end of her Grand Duke Dmitri period," explains veteran *Harper's Bazaar* and *Vogue* fashion editor Babs Simpson, a Verdura intimate and client. "Chanel and Fulco were responding to that Russian feeling for extravagance, of barbaric color and enormous scale, stones being thrown around like nothing. Never, never at Boivin or at Cartier, who were all about serious diamonds and platinum, would you ever have seen tourmalines next to diamonds, or settings of gold."

Verdura's organic but urbane aesthetic closely paralleled tendencies in the Parisian avant-garde of the 1930s. Disillusioned with industrialism, artists by the beginning of the decade had begun exploring the more unruly, irregular shapes of nature, particularly of the sea. Former cubist Ozenfant began painting mermaids, Man Ray photographed sea horses, while Picasso assembled beachcomber sculptures. In 1928 Fulco's friend, Count Etienne de Beaumont, hosted his eccentric Sea Ball, and around 1930 the architect and ébeniste Emilio Terry planned a house in the form of a nautilus shell. The surrealists Dalí, Masson, and Magritte were especially attracted to aquatic motifs— partly because the ocean depths served as a metaphor for the unfathomable unconscious but also because in marine fauna they found creepy-looking organisms that could playfully suggest the primordial, slimy origins of life. More preoccupied with worldly existence, the neo-Romantics Christian Bérard, Eugene Berman, and Pavel Tchelichew rejected the avant-garde altogether, instituting in its place a retro vogue for lyrical symbolic figuration. "There was a kind of osmosis between Society, and artists and writers," Faucigny-Lucinge reminisced. "Those Paris years no doubt helped Fulco's development and artistic formation."

A necklace of graduated aquamarines, totaling 553 carats, connected with diamond ribbons.

Verdura broke from this heady milieu in 1934 when he sailed for America. Not only was he fleeing Chanel—whom he had begun to find a little 'scary,' Simpson says—he was also on a mission to distance himself from his dissolute Old World friends. Working first for the jeweler Paul Flato in Hollywood (Fulco designed Katharine Hepburn's adornments for *The Philadelphia Story*), he next migrated East because, he asserted, "Movie people like to wear things from New York." In 1939 he opened his Manhattan business, which he ran until he retired in 1973.

Verdura quickly discovered that his work appealed as much to Park Avenue patricians as to Hollywood royalty. "His clientele was very rich and sophisticated," Babs Simpson says. "But one didn't buy Fulco's jewelry the way you'd buy bonds, as an investment. They were less expensive and more fun than that—like baubles, or toys."

Diana Vreeland wore his dynamically bold Maltese-cross cuffs, and Averell Harriman presented his fiancée Pamela with a ring composed of an emerald insouciantly embedded in black enamel. Playwright Clare Boothe Luce in 1941 accepted from Jock Whitney a pearl-tasseled brooch depicting the doubled masks of tragedy and comedy, and Linda Porter, in a more flagrantly theatrical spirit, commissioned a cigarette case for the opening of each of her prolific husband's shows. "Every time Linda gave Fulco a free hand to do something novel and amusing," Simpson says. "His ideas were lovely, no one ever rejected them." One of his more outlandishly clever conceits was the tiara he concocted for Betsey Whitney in 1955 after her husband was appointed American ambassador to the Court of St James. Instead of the usual fussy diadem bristling with heraldic emblems, he conjured up an Indian chief's headdress, all in gold and veined with diamonds. "That was so typical of him," Simpson says. "He adored American Indians, and always had his book of Edward Curtis's photographs of them around." For Whitney's exquisite sister Babe Paley, Fulco made a baroque-pearl swan with black enameled legs, each encircled with a delicate diamond ankle bracelet. The Duchess of Windsor also brought her snobbish cachet to Fulco's wares; his mabé pearls latticed in gold were identification badges for both of them. And Fulco, in

turn, facilitated her process of self-creation. "Verdura alone," the photographer Horst said, "knew how to make her a Duchess."

Meanwhile, inside the recherché Colony Restaurant, the uniform for the ladies who lunched was "Hattie Carnegie's suits with the little collar, brightened with a clever brooch from Fulco," Babs Simpson recalls. "A popular one was the big bunch of violets, made of cabochon amethysts and emerald leaves"—a beguiling trinket originally conceived for Betsey Whitney. (Fulco even appeared in a 1944 *Life* magazine spread on the Colony, consorting with an array of café society notables, including Myrna Loy, Kitty Carlisle, Princess Natasha Paley, and Elsa Maxwell). And when it came time to reapply lipstick and powder one's nose, out of the crocodile handbags came his "lovely little clamshell compacts—real ones picked up at the beach, rimmed in gold."

A compelling reason for the sensational success of Verdura's designs was that they were ingeniously calculated to flatter the wearer. Earrings undulated to complement the convolutions of an earlobe, rings seductively followed the phalanges of a finger, and necklaces gracefully traced the anatomy of the throat. Likewise, his supple handheld objects—compacts or lighters—rested sensually in the palm. Understanding that the jewelry was as becoming against a backdrop of fabric as of skin, women displayed Fulco's cunning treasures in way we no longer think of: on belts, hat bands, glove cuffs, furs or, to judge from a 1940s photo of Paulette Goddard, on beach-cabana outfits.

Shells like the one with which the starlet embellished her bathing costume had for Fulco the charm of throwaway chic. Determined to downplay glitz (flashy gems were to him like wearing "checks around one's neck"), he incorporated fascinating but inexpensive found objects—specimen rocks and purple scallop shells from the American Museum of Natural History, pebbles gathered during Fire Island weekends—into his designs. He then transformed these mundane items by studding them with precious stones or wrapping them in gold netting. On one pin a golden escargot body slithers through a perfect, sapphire-topped snail shell. On another, meandering diamonds and emeralds mimic the effect of foamy seaweed clinging to a mollusc. His gold 'nautical ropes' (based on his complete knowledge of sailors' knots) are twisted into elaborate necklaces or looped around cabochon clusters. So understated was his treatment of gems that the irregular, cascading emeralds in one necklace—caught by a gold mariner's knot—could easily pass for sea glass. "The important point about Fulco," Simpson says, "is that he has an aristocrat's attitude—his jewelry, like him, was totally unpretentious."

If Fulco's eye was steeped in contemporary art and natural history, it was also conversant with art history. His pearl-bodied Baroque dolphins, Raphaelesque putti, diamond Hokusai waves, and rococo acanthus leaves only hint at the vast range of his erudition. Among his friends (interchangeable with his clients), he was known as *le petit Larousse roulant*—the walking dictionary. "Fulco Verdura was a man of much culture and knowledge in many directions," wrote Prince Faucigny-Lucinge, "and always made me think of Renaissance men such as Benuto Cellini or Jean de Bologna." Decorator Billy Baldwin admired Fulco's apartment as "obviously the residence of a person of great intelligence and wide interests…. Books on architecture and decoration, history, music…were the heart of the place."

Though an expatriate who adored the fact that "there was no past for me" in America, he regularly mined the rich lode of his patrician Sicilian background, especially through his subtle references to classical mythology and the Church. In his asymmetrical diamond and gold 'Pleiades' brooches (named for Atlas's seven daughters who metamorphosed into the constellation), four stars twinkle on one shoulder and three on the other. Flaming hearts, symbols of religious fervor, appear time and again, enameled or engorged with nuggety cabochons. Fulco's hearts, however, were probably also infused with a more private, secular meaning. "Fulco was a man who had 'crushes' on people of either sex," Faucigny-Lucinge recollected, "and this rather ruled his life." Airborne feathery diamond wings—some bearing aloft pearl drops—could suggest either Icarus or the Archangel Michael, and even the signature Verdura scallop shell was an emblem worn by Christian pilgrims on route to St

James's tomb in Spain. Of course the scallop shell also conjures up imagery associated with the birth of Venus, as well as, perhaps, of Fulco's own. The jeweler, it seems, entered the world at his family's Villa Niscemi in a narrow room illuminated in all four corners by plaster seashell sconces. Less personal and perhaps more typical of the period are Verdura's nostalgic references to colonial exoticism, at a time when the British and French Empires were rapidly shrinking. (Another of Etienne de Beaumont's fancy-dress parties was his 1930 Colonial Ball.) Blackamoors dangle from bow eardrops, a rhinoceros lumbers beneath a ruby obelisk and 18th-century Moghul ivory chess figurines are converted into bejeweled brooches.

Like no one else's objects, Fulco's seem to possess an *élan vital*. They swell with life, sometimes to the point of bursting. A peridot pomegranate (ancient symbol of the Passion) explodes, exposing ruby seeds within. Blackamoors embrace, ecclesiastical tassels swing, cornucopia spew their contents, and Jovian lightning bolts crackle. By contrast, other designers' work looks flat, inert.

Verdura's thousands of miniature tempera-on-vellum sketches reveal that these astonishingly animate effects were meticulously planned right from the start. Ward Landrigan, the former Sotheby's jewelry head who took over the Verdura firm in 1985, has now painstakingly restored the company's design albums. At the New York Verdura showroom customers can view not only these diminutive archival masterpieces, but also Fulco's equally accomplished landscapes, figure studies, and still lifes, which are on display among the jewelry vitrines.

While the old guard remains faithful to Verdura, a new, well-informed, and stylish clientele—attracted by serendipitous, one-of-a-kind vintage estate pieces as well as by the changing inventory of new objects—has now found its way to the 12th floor door at 745 Fifth Avenue. The appeal of Verdura to the younger customers, some of them children and grandchildren of Fulco's original patrons, is the jewelry's ideal balance between restraint and flamboyance, sophistication and accessibility. Says Babs Simpson, "Fulco's references to nature, culture, and religion keep his work classic. But without question he was a revolutionary, the one who changed everything. Fulco made it all modern."

The Golden Conch...whosoever has seen it,
shall carry it in his heart forever.
-J. W. GOETHE

A brooch of diamonds and enamel
in the form of a conch shell.

Opposite A portrait of Verdura by
Horst, 1930.

IF THERE EXISTS such a phenomenon as geographical predestination, then surely it must have affected Verdura: the Italian jeweler famous for precious shell ornaments was born in 1899 on the cusp of the *Conca d'oro*. Palermo's Golden Conch is still the first sight to greet travelers approaching the Sicilian capital by sea. Suburban blight has recently dimmed its glory, but until not so very long ago the pearly-hued city seemed to rest upon a gilt-lipped shell of citrus groves, sheltered in the distance by a rosy crescent of limestone cliffs.

Almost every major civilization has left its imprint on Sicily, the largest island in the Mediterranean, as well as the most strategically located. After colonization by the Phoenicians, Greeks, and Carthaginians, Sicily fell to Rome during the Punic wars. Palermo was overrun by seafaring Vandals and Ostrogoths before the island became a prosperous Byzantine province. Soon after the Arab invasion of 831, Palermo rivaled Cordoba and Cairo as a major Islamic center of commerce and learning. A couple of centuries later, following the Norman Conquest in 1072, it ranked as one of the great cities of Christendom, second only to Constantinople. The Hauteville lords were succeeded by the Swabians; a courtly culture of extraordinary magnificence flourished under Emperor Frederick II (1194–1250), a poet, scholar, diplomat and philosopher known to his awestruck contemporaries as *Stupor Mundi*, or Wonder of the World. Then came the Angevin rulers, later supplanted by the Aragonese who ushered in three centuries of Spanish dominion. The Kingdom of the Two Sicilies, established by the Bourbons in 1734, linked Sicily and Naples until 1860. That was the year in which Garibaldi and his Thousand swarmed over the island, annexing it to the new Kingdom of Italy governed by Victor Emmanuel II of Savoy.

Despite the political travail and bloodshed that accompanied the Unification of Italy, by the last quarter of the century Palermo boasted an international reputation as the most luxurious resort in the land. Almost miraculously, its *ancien régime* splendor had been preserved intact, enhanced rather than overshadowed by the recently acquired wealth of the bourgeoisie. At the heart of the *beau monde* was the nobility of Spanish origin, into which fresh blood had been infused by the Bourbon and Savoy aristocracies. A few select foreign families—the Whitakers, English makers of sweet Marsala wine, and the Boston Gardners, whose fortune

came from sulfur mining—had been assimilated through marriage. The Florio dynasty of fabulously rich shipping magnates and industrialists occupied a unique category, proving as extravagant in their private affairs as they were enterprising in business. Sicilians maintained that Palermo ranked as "the Southern subsidiary" of Paris: a glamorous year-round flurry of balls, fêtes and musicales organized in ancestral *palazzi* as well as at various social clubs, of which the Circolo Bellini was the most exclusive. The usual outdoor events—from hunts and horse races to regattas—were promoted by half a dozen well-equipped sports associations. There were even enough diehard Anglophiles to support a cricket team. A state-of-the-art luxury hotel, the Villa Igiea, was managed according to the precepts of César Ritz. J. P. Morgan's *Corsair*, Cornelius Vanderbilt's *Vara*, Rothschild schooners, the yachts of Theodore Roosevelt, Anna Gould and Sir Thomas Lipton, were frequently sighted in the harbor.

Such an aura of opulence held understandable appeal for royalty. Extended Palermitan sojourns first became fashionable among crowned heads in 1845, when Tsar Nicholas I rented a villa on the edge of town for his consumptive wife Alexandra, whose doctors had prescribed the "temperate and transparent air of the *Conca d'oro*." During the *belle époque*, the royal tourist roster lengthened to include Kaiser Wilhelm II, King Edward VII and Queen Alexandra, the former French Empress Eugénie, Frederick Augustus III of Saxony, Archduke Franz Ferdinand of Austria, Leopold II of the Belgians, Oscar II of Sweden and Norway, Queen Wilhelmina of Holland, Queen Amelia of Portugal. The most exotic visitor was doubtless Paramandra Maha Chulalongkorn of Siam, who created a sensation as he promenaded through town trailed by six of his progeny and a retinue of eighteen courtiers.

Palermo was not merely a glorious holiday destination for those who could afford it: there reigned an aesthetic fervor that attracted artists and performers of the highest caliber. *Stile liberty*, the sunny Italian version of Art Nouveau, flourished in Palermo. The authoritative British Arts and Crafts periodical *Studio* praised the Sicilian Ernesto Basile, the nation's most versatile practitioner, as "an architect of great learning and taste, essentially modern, inexhaustibly inventive, many-sided but thorough." Ducrot, a local firm specializing in interior decoration and furniture design, was hailed as "a perfect centre of applied art." Palermo also enjoyed world-class theater: Sarah Bernhardt starred in *La Dame aux Camélias*, Eleonora Duse performed in the premiere of D'Annunzio's *La Gioconda*. The portraitist Boldini came to capture the likenesses of Queen Elena's Sicilian ladies-in-waiting, while Renoir depicted Wagner during his stay at the Hotel des Palmes, at work on *Parsifal*. Puccini and Leoncavallo were lionized, as were Edmond Rostand, Jules Verne and Guy de Maupassant. Although polite society snubbed Oscar Wilde, he was enchanted by the *Conca d'oro*, which reminded him of Marvell's "golden lamps in a green night."

Opposite A street scene in Palermo, Verdura's birthplace, in the early years of the twentieth century.

This was the privileged universe—soon to vanish—into which Verdura was born. His full name was Fulco Santostefano, to which two titles were attached: Marchese di Murata la Cerda and Duca di Verdura. The Santostefanos, of old Spanish stock, acquired their dukedom through marriage. The marquisate was granted by Felipe IV in the seventeenth century in recognition of the family's descent from Blanche of Castile and Leon, still at that time designated as *la Cerda*, the sow, in royal circles. The daughter of the sainted French king Louis IX had produced two Infantes whose inconvenient claim to the throne was usurped by Sancho IV. The seat of Murata la Cerda was a fortified village perched high in the Madonie mountains; once advantageously situated along a major trade route linking Palermo to Messina, it is known today for its bumper artichoke crops.

For generations, Fulco's forebears had been active in public life. His maternal grandfather Prince Corrado Valguarnera di Niscemi was a senator of the realm, and his paternal great-great-grandfather Alessio Benso, Duca di Verdura, had been Praetor of Palermo. As mayor, his son Giulio Benso was responsible for installing the city's first gas-lamps and water mains. Fulco's father Giulio Santostefano della Cerda participated in several municipal governments. However, when Giulio first met his wife-to-be in 1893, he was still a colonel with the White Lancers of Novara, a regiment greatly feared throughout the peninsula—less for equestrian daring in battle than for a cavalier attitude towards the payment of bills. Giulio was tall and strikingly handsome, with sloe eyes, lustrous black hair and a smooth coppery complexion offset by his snowy uniform. He had inherited the violent Cerda temper: in Santostefano slang, *cerdiare* was synonymous with throwing a tantrum. One comically unsportsmanlike incident was covered in the press: after being disqualified in a 'Gentleman Riders' race, Giulio ranted at the judges until they relented and reversed their original decision against him; he then proceeded unblushingly to run the course in solitary splendor after all the other competitors had withdrawn in scornful protest. Though he was careless in most human relationships, his love of animals was unconditional: the image of "Father surrounded by his horses and dogs, dispensing justice in the streets of Palermo" made a vivid impression on Fulco. Giulio's charm, when he chose to turn it on, was equally redoubtable; though rarely expended in the family circle, it proved gratifyingly effective in other contexts. In a popularity contest, he received an avalanche of *voti di simpatia* or sympathy ballots (all in feminine script) and just as many negative votes (in manly scrawls). Reporting the results, a local society journal drew this conclusion: "As agreeable as you are to women, so shall you be disagreeable to men. O envy, o envy!" Having survived a number of duels, Giulio was regarded as an expert in matters of honor.

Giulio Santostefano was an unlikely match for the reserved

Verdura's mother, born Carolina
Valguarnera di Niscemi, in a
1901 photograph.

Carolina Valguarnera di Niscemi, also descended from Spanish
grandees who had settled in Sicily during the thirteenth century. In
later years, Carolina often professed regret at having missed her
vocation as a nun. In fact, she was bookish rather than prudish;
her children were to fill a notebook entitled *Dictons
Pornographiques d'une Femme d'Eglise* with her salacious
witticisms. Of meek demeanor and emphatic profile, Carolina
did not rate as a beauty, at least by the canons of the day. Her
figure, however, was willowy and her gaze gentle; her hands
were her best feature—smooth as ivory, and just as cold.

It was love at first sight, or so Carolina and Giulio proudly
insisted. Being second cousins constituted no obstacle: some degree of
consanguinity was difficult if not impossible to avoid in the upper
echelons of island society. A dowry was negotiated, which Carolina's
mother, the formidable Princess Maria, paid out of her own estate. The
wedding was celebrated on 30 March 1894, and eleven months later a
child was born—alas, a girl. Despite the promise implicit in her name,
Maria Felice's parents were not happy, nor indeed had they been since
their wedding night. The moment of truth came for Carolina when her
hitherto dashing cavalry officer appeared before her attired in nightshirt
and red slippers, spindly legs in evidence: she sensed instantly that she
was "not made for love." For his part, Giulio could never comprehend,
much less forgive, his bride for remaining so effortlessly unresponsive,
"like a piece of chicken."

Still, a male Cerda needed to be produced, and the couple
dutifully persevered. A little over a year later, a son was stillborn. Giulio
assured the devout Carolina that he had had the little body christened,
waggishly adding that he had named it—nothing else having sprung to
mind on such brief notice—Garibaldi. So ill-suited in every way were the
couple that an ingenious solution was devised that would neither offend
conventional morality nor disappoint the families' expectations. Carolina
was allowed to return home to her parents with little Maria Felice in tow,
but continued to pay conjugal visits to her estranged husband. Regular
sessions on the monstrous Louis XVI-style bed, which she referred to as
"the place of the crime," were ultimately rewarded. On 20 March 1898,
Carolina was delivered of the long-awaited Santostefano heir at her
parents' villa outside Palermo. Fulco was born in a crimson and gilt salon
beneath a medallion of Tobias and the Angel. Thereafter life continued as
before: Carolina and her mother took their customary cultural jaunts
through northern Italy, France, and Switzerland, while Giulio would
embark on Count Mazzarino's yacht for bachelor cruises in the Adriatic.

A welcome release for Carolina, life at Villa Niscemi was sheer
bliss for Maria Felice and Fulco. Located at the foot of Monte Pellegrino
and only a short distance from the Mondello beach, it was a country
residence built for comfort rather than show around a large squarish

courtyard. At the end of a long boxwood alley, the main façade was swathed in bougainvillea; its twin terraces seemed to beckon Fulco like "open, inviting hands." Within, the Villa presented a complete heraldic gallimaufry, "every available space...crawling with coronets, coats-of-arms, initials and mottoes." Hauteville, Hohenstauffen, Angevin, Aragonese, Savoy and Bourbon effigies ringed the Hall of the Kings of Sicily. In the Four Seasons Salon, a large fresco showed Charlemagne languidly bestowing a shield upon a rosy-cheeked Valguarnera knight; to Fulco, their figures appeared about as warlike as a pair of ballet dancers in tights. *Trompe-l'oeil* landscapes and architectural *capricci* abounded, with garlands inhabited by pasty cherubs and gaudy fowl, every niche and cornice accented with scalloped baroque shells. There was a Music Room, a Green Ballroom upholstered for some unfathomable reason in red velvet, and a cosy wood-paneled library lined with over 4,000 volumes—Greek and Latin classics, French literature from Racine to Bourget, Tauchnitz editions of Dickens, Thackeray, and Collins. The hub of life at Villa Niscemi was the Salon of Santa Rosalia, otherwise known as the Telephone Room, with its jigsaw puzzles, workbaskets, and tidily stacked issues of the *Revue des Deux Mondes*, the *Revue de Paris,* and the *Illustrated London News*. Elsewhere an eclectic jumble prevailed, featuring rococo sedan chairs, rusty armor, and potted palms amid tasseled poufs and green leather sofas, sprightly bentwood tables and gaily daubed rustic cabinets. Sturdy crewel-work curtains hung at the windows, patterned Chinese silk lined the walls. There were inlaid marble floors, good for roller skating, and polychrome majolica tiling, which was not.

Every day Fulco and Maria Felice "covered at least a mile coming and going from [their] rooms to the seats of nourishment, learning and cleanliness." But their special domain was the out-of-doors—not the tame Floretta, an ornamental parterre of jasmine, hibiscus, and magnolia in front of the Villa, but the wilder reaches of the picturesque Anglo-tropical park with its grotto, pond and *Kaffeehaus*. A door in the wall surrounding the estate gave them special access to the royal enclosure of La Favorita, a privilege first awarded the Niscemis by King Ferdinand I in 1799 in gratitude for their offer of land on which to construct a lodge. This turned out to be a turreted Chinoiserie-style pagoda, strung about with myriad tiny bells chiming softly in the breeze. When the House of Savoy inherited the Bourbon estates, the family's licence to trespass was graciously renewed.

At Villa Niscemi there were stables to inspect and a domestic menagerie to tend: a swan, a couple of donkeys, a ram, a mongoose, a cage of baboons, a chameleon, and a diarrhoeic marmoset called Shinshitrscaramangananusaiamahowa, or Shin for short. Dogs starred in many of Maria Felice and Fulco's capers. Mongrels were passed off as rare specimens of the 'English breed' and, on one memorable occasion,

Fulco with his sister Maria Felice, their nanny, and dogs.

Overleaf The elaborately decorated interior of the Villa Niscemi was the setting in which Fulco grew up.

pug milk was served to an unsuspecting nanny at tea-time. Miss Aileen Brennan, Miss Irene de Villiers, Miss Lilley, Miss Harriet Simpson Kay—none of Fulco's governesses lasted for long. A darling boy, but such a mercurial temperament: one minute he would be leaping about on the furniture, shrieking "I am a Hun of small stature" at the top of his lungs, and the very next he would be quite still, forlornly mumbling the phrase *"Bimbo disoccupato"* —unemployed child, *i.e.* with nothing to do. And that habit of letting him sleep with his mother and drink wine with his meals.... Still, the girls kept coming, from every outpost of the British Empire and in particular from Ireland, since it was essential that they be Catholic. House servants—all called Angelina or Peppino—were Italian, except for the cook. In Sicily, chefs were traditionally regarded as honorary Frenchmen, in recognition of their expertise in *haute cuisine*, and addressed as *monzù*, the local mispronunciation of *monsieur*. The Niscemi *monzù*, having trained briefly in London, was more adept at scrambling up such improbably named hybrid dishes as *mezzosposo* (mince-pie) and *strabbifuoddi* (strawberry fool).

This volatile company was governed by Granmamà, whose control became absolute after the death of Carolina's father in 1903. By then the aged princess was "a rather plump little lady in black with finely chiseled features under a halo of dazzling snow-white curls." There was no longer any trace of the luscious *baronessina* Maria Favara whose 1866 marriage to Prince Corrado had been decried as a misalliance. The Favara baronetcy was undistinguished, but the Favara fortune was conspicuous; it was probably amassed after the abolition of feudalism in 1812 by usurious but not illegal methods. Maria's father Don Vincenzo was scorned as a parvenu, yet unlike many of his critics, he (and his father before him) had obtained a university diploma, a signal accomplishment for the era, especially in Sicily. In his youth, he had traveled to Paris and London where he was close to the exiled Italian patriot Mazzini. In later years, Baron Favara appeared more circumspect in his political views, causing some to accuse him of opportunism.

Despite her lineage, no fault could be found with Maria Favara as a gorgeous sixteen-year-old. The very stuff of legend, she was immortalized a century later as Angelica Sedara, the heroine of *The Leopard*, the best-selling novel by Prince Giuseppe Tomasi di Lampedusa, who was Fulco's second cousin. Generously proportioned, Angelica had a creamy complexion and a wavy mane "the color of night"; her green eyes shone with a slightly cruel glint, as "unmoving as those of a statue."

Despite the embarrassment of a share-cropping grandfather who went by the name of Peppe 'Mmerda, or Joe Shit, Angelica was so voluptuous that even her "sheets must smell of paradise."

Handsome and impetuous, Prince Corrado was one of several individuals who inspired the character of Angelica's suitor, Prince Tancredi Falconeri. But while Tancredi was prompted to wed out of his class by a mixture of lust and necessity, Corrado could afford to do as he pleased. And whereas Tancredi was an incorrigible turncoat, Corrado was an idealist, imprisoned three times for his steadfast support of Garibaldi—once even at his own request, in order that he might suffer the same fate as his comrades.

Palermo eventually capitulated; the new Princess was not only irresistible, she was exemplary. After marriage, she returned to her studies, perfecting her mastery of French and German. She bore three daughters and two sons; when Enzo, the youngest, died suddenly at the age of twelve, she "lost her reason for many long months, and her faith forever." Often pointed out to visitors as one of city's emblematic "majestic maternal figures," the Princess was lauded in the press for her philanthropy: she was a patron of the Children's Hospital, of the Red Cross, of the Society for the Protection of Animals. A favorite project was the *Cucine economiche*, a string of soup kitchens operating in the city's most impoverished slums.

Fulco at the age of six.

Foreign travel was always Granmamà's great delight, and she indulged in it each year, touring the Continent for two months with her daughter and grandchildren. She drew up the itinerary, selecting destinations for their artistic merit: Bavaria for a tour of Mad Ludwig's castles, Vienna to hear Caruso in *Rigoletto*, or Munich during the Oktoberfest. Means of transport were various and precarious, from horse-drawn coach (the St Gothard Pass), to rented automobile (the Loire Valley). On one occasion, a special stop was made at Nice, where Fulco's grandfather Giuseppe Santostefano lived with his second wife Emma Morisot, who was distantly related to the Impressionist painter Berthe Morisot. As the widow of the genre painter Eugène Isabey, Emma had inherited a number of miniatures of "high-waisted ladies" executed by her father-in-law, Jean-Baptiste (1767–1855) at the court of Napoleon I and Empress Josephine. It was Mamà's goal to secure this special hoard for Fulco, and she brazenly informed her stepmother-in-law that her "dear little one loves all beautiful things, especially painting, and now all he talks about are these little marvels." The hint fell on deaf ears.

A family gathering at the Villa d'Este in 1909. Granmamà, the ruling matriarch of the family, is seated far left. Also at the table are Maria Felice, Fulco, and their mother.

Granmamà's other passion was music, and she eagerly befriended a number of famous singers, including the superb *tenore di forza* Francesco Tamagno, who had been Verdi's first Otello. When Fulco was seven years old, she took him to a matinée at the Teatro Massimo. Completed in 1897 by Basile, it ranked as Europe's third most important house after Vienna and Paris, in musical excellence as well as sheer grandeur. However, only a Palermitan born and bred could appreciate the hierarchical subtleties of the seating plan: the auditorium was a snob's inferno. The second tier of loges was the most desirable, being on a level with the Royal Box. Members of the professional classes were confined to the stalls, while minor officialdom was admitted to the first tier. The bourgeoisie was safely tucked away in the third tier. The fifth tier

The Teatro Massimo in Palermo,
where Fulco's lifelong interest in
opera began.

accommodated second-tier habitués in mourning and aristocrats too poor
to afford the second tier but too proud to be seen anywhere else. The
fourth tier was the worst of all, packed with rejects from every other
social sector.

The opera Fulco saw (from the second tier) was *Aida*, under the
baton of Tullio Serafin, then a promising maestro still in his twenties who
had been hired to conduct the entire season. It was an exceptional
production, to judge from the reviews, rapturous to the point of
incoherence: "grandiose and magnificent," "amazing beyond belief," this
Aida was "the most complete and triumphant success," eliciting a
continuous ovation that was interspersed with applause, more applause
and yet more applause; Fulco totally "lost his seven-year-old head."

A love of theatrics permeated every age and stratum of
Palermitan society. Adults staged elaborate *tableaux vivants*, preferably
with an eighteenth-century theme. At one memorable fancy dress ball,
the bewigged participants, caked in talcum from head to toe, posed as
life-sized Meissen shepherds and shepherdesses on large *rocaille* papier-
maché pedestals. While Carolina, a reluctant actress, was once persuaded
to play a Roman matron in *Herculaneum*, the limelight was Giulio's
natural element. So forceful was his *General Kléber with a Lady of the
Empire* that it was repeated twice by popular demand. In *The Difficult
Choice*, he rendered a convincing impersonation of a gentleman unable to
decide between a blond and a brunette.

Children, too, put on pantomimes among themselves, and for the
amusement of their elders. The raven-haired Maria Felice specialized in
Arab maidens. Thanks to a vast wardrobe of costumes, pompously
referred to as *panoplies*, Fulco could be cast as a zouave, a cowboy, a

foreign legionnaire, a dandified *incroyable* with 'cocker-spaniel wig', and bicorne; his befeathered Red Indian outfit was more Papageno than Native American. Because Granmamà disapproved of their rowdiness, most of these lively entertainments were mounted at Robert and Maude Whitaker's nearby Villa Sofia; their daughter Beatrice, nicknamed Boots, had her own play-cottage in the grounds. As the youngest, Fulco was frequently relegated to doing "voices off"; yet he was always prepared to recite *The Fatal Pancake*, a dramatic monologue that involved some skill in belching. Particularly well received was a French skit set in a Far West telegraph office that started with the intriguing lament: *"Ah, quelle vie que celle d'un employé télégraphique!"*

A major event on the Palermo social calendar was the Battle of Flowers, a spectacular pageant in which the aristocracy paraded through town in blossom-bedecked carriages, to the admiring cheers of the less fortunate citizenry. So lavish were these floats that special consignments of roses, violets and lilacs had to be shipped from as far away as Naples and Florence. On one occasion the Niscemi landaulet, blanketed with wisteria and pale pink carnations, passed the carriage of the German Emperor and Empress. Family legend soon had it that Fulco hurled a rose at the Kaiserin "with such violence that, when she passed again, she was holding a handkerchief to her face." He was later to regret that the flower had not been some heavier object, lobbed at her husband instead.

Dressing-up played an important part in Fulco's and Maria Felice's childhood. Here, Maria Felice poses as 'Tulipano' in a costume suggested by the book *Les Fleurs Animées* by Grandville. Fulco is pictured in his 'redskin' costume and as a French *incroyable* or dandy, 1907.

It was a matter of course that Donna Franca Florio, whether in a bower of bluebells, camellias, or red roses, would win all the accolades. Even in newspapers not owned by her husband, she was hailed as the Daughter of the Heavens, the Ornament of the Earth, the Glory of Springtime, the Queen of Flowers. "Why can't you be as beautiful as Franca Florio?" Fulco would whine to his mother. The Kaiser called her 'Star of Italy', while for D'Annunzio she was a "dusky, golden, aquiline and indolent" temptress. Everything about Donna Franca was exquisite, her possessions as well as her person: her jewels—in particular her resplendent diamond parures from Cartier—were the envy of many a queen. But it was common knowledge that each precious natural pearl on her long and perfectly matched strand stood for one of her husband's infidelities.

Fulco's boyhood was nothing if not predictable, and he relished its comforting repetitiousness: "the same unfolding of the seasons, the same reassuring familiar voices, Christmas, the days getting longer, Easter, May, June, sea-bathing at Mondello, the excitement of travelling and then coming home and being reunited with my beloved garden." The rare surprises were always happy. Once Giulio presented Fulco with

Fulco, far left, and friends at the beach at Mondello.

Fulco with his boyhood Somali
playmate, Abu-ba-ker.

A drawing by Verdura for a camel
brooch comprising a baroque pearl
and emeralds. It recalls the camel
that the Verdura family had received
many years before as a gift.

an exotic playmate, Abu-ba-ker, a chieftain's son from Italian Somaliland
—"tall, lithe, with perfect manners"—who spent a summer with the
Santostefanos at Villa Serradifalco, their property at Bagheria. Later
there was another less refined African gift: a camel that was dubbed
Moffo just before an outraged Granmamà compelled Giulio to remove it
from the Niscemi stables. Predictably, he donated the beast to an
attractive circus artiste who had caught his fancy. Years later, as Fulco and
Maria Felice were making their way down the rue de Rivoli one drizzly
autumn afternoon, they noticed a poster advertising a unique attraction
at the Cirque d'Hiver: *Moffus, le seul chameau musicien*. It had to be, it
must be, it was indeed their own Moffo. To Fulco's chagrin, there was not
the slightest glimmer of recognition: "He looked
through us with dead eyes and turned his head
away."

Reality hardly ever cast its shadow over Villa
Niscemi, although storm clouds were gathering over
Sicily. A rapidly dwindling group of landowners
continued to mismanage island resources, while
thousands of emigrants left each year for the New
World. In the refrain of a popular ballad, a youth
pleaded with his mother for the 100-lire transatlantic
fare: *Mamma mia, dammi cento lire, che in America
voglio andar*. Giulio Santostefano's well-intentioned
proposals concerning the local Society for the
Protection of Animals were met with scorn. One
journal published a list of laments addressed to the
nobleman by several unfortunates:

"Marchese della Cerda... must be jesting.
He wishes to protect the animals, he is moved by
the fate of the poor beasts? Oh, then why does
he slaughter them in our poor countryside when
he goes hunting?" A skylark.

"The Society will care for donkeys and dogs;
but who shall provide for us? Do we not lead
an unhappier life than the animals? What is the
Marchese della Cerda's opinion?" A street-sweeper.

The Mafia was an occult presence, whose long sensitive tentacles adroitly probed the island's discontent. When the Santostefanos ventured into the countryside, they were always escorted by a band of *campieri*, although Giulio reassuringly insisted that the armed horsemen were for show rather than protection. It was whispered, but never confirmed, that one of the Whitaker cousins had been abducted while riding with her groom near Monte Pellegrino and held for a miserable 100-lire ransom. And once, as Boots's mother was strolling in the garden, a small object flew over the wall and landed neatly at her feet. Bending down to retrieve it, she realized it was a severed hand—a warning.

Most unpleasantness was of the common bedchamber or drawing-room farce variety. When the Queen's married lady-in-waiting Countess Giulia Trigona di Sant'Elia was murdered in a cheap Roman hotel by her lover Baron Vincenzo Paternò del Cugno (both Palermitans, both distant relatives), a national scandal ensued, complete with public uproar and lurid magazine covers. Closer to home, there were rumors about one of the first families being addicted to the morphine their physician prescribed as a universal remedy: the butler who served after-dinner shots on a silver tray also filled a tiny syringe for the Pekingese. But for the most part, Fulco would listen "spellbound to the strange stories of the Marquis-of-this or the misconduct of Donna so-and-so, only to discover subsequently that one had died in the seaquake of 1789 and the other of cholera in 1836. Life was easy and protected then, and the past a living thing."

The most shattering experience Fulco had to face was enrolment in a state-run school at the age of eleven. After the first day when Mamà accompanied him to the Ginnasio Garibaldi in her carriage with liveried coachman and footman—"a grave mistake"—he insisted on being conveyed into town on the kitchen cart and returning home alone on the tram. English sailor suits were discarded, in favor of threadbare pullovers and trousers. Relatives were strictly prohibited from greeting him should they meet him in the company of schoolmates. In the classroom, he was just Fulco Santostefano; however, so unaccustomed was he to the simple formula, minus the Cerda and Verdura handles, that he often failed to respond when called. When he failed end of term examinations, he was transferred to another sterner institution, the Umberto I, and a brigade of home tutors was engaged to shore up the gaps in his education. When Mamà questioned one of these—a priest—about Fulco's scholastic aptitude, the candid cleric responded firmly: "No, *Signora Duchessa,* he is not intelligent, he is vivacious."

Vivacious indeed: the only lessons Fulco threw himself into wholeheartedly were the dancing classes organized on a rotating basis at the *palazzi* of his friends' parents. He waltzed and mazurka'd and polka'd; he tripped through the other steps in vogue at the time, the Season, the Washington Post, the Sir Roger de Coverley. Later, when the tango craze swept Italy, Fulco practiced in secret, since it was stigmatized as a "sensual and obscene dance which provokes giddiness and is the beginning of corruption." Even Pius X voiced his disapproval of the tango, vainly recommending in its stead the Furlana, a sort of rustic minuet. Undaunted, Fulco tangoed on.

Art was not taught at school, but Fulco's knowledge was growing prodigiously. He took his "first steps in that miraculous garden that is the Italian Renaissance" when he happened upon Eugène Müntz's monograph on Raphael on the bottom shelf of the hall bookcase. Fascinated by the gold medal embossed on the cover, representing "a young man with long curls and a tam-o'-shanter," he would sit on his bed turning the plates slowly "to see those noble serene faces looking back at me." Returning to the Continent each year, he began to develop preferences—for the Salon Carré at the Louvre, the Uffizi Tribuna and, above all, the Galleria Pitti, "a collection of pictures bought for themselves and not a collection of stamps catalogued in terms of countries and years." As a boy Fulco sketched tirelessly, inventing fantastical island kingdoms in minute topographical detail; his masterpiece in the genre was Table, the haunt of Le Baron d'Agneau, Châteaubriant, the Demoiselle de Caen, and Sir Loin. As his draughtsmanship improved, he began to realize also "that a pencil was a thing I could use to draw whatever I saw or whatever went through my mind."

There was little warning that the very foundations of Fulco's halcyon existence were about to be reduced to rubble. The first intimations came one spring day, as he and his mother were being driven back to Villa Niscemi. Taking his hands in hers, Carolina told him, very gently, that Granmamà was ill and that, if she died, the three Cerdas would have to leave the Villa and go live with father. There was more: Fulco should consider whether he might not like to attend boarding-school, perhaps La Quercia near Florence, or Mondragone the Jesuit *collegio* in Frascati—"if we can get you in." Then came a question, more horrific than any of the preceding statements of fact: "Have you ever thought of what you want to do when you grow up?" Fulco remembered his reaction: "I began to realize then that the world as I had always known it, my world, was going to disintegrate, evaporate or rather, which in a way was worse, fall into small pieces that could never be put together again." He tried hard to keep his chin from trembling, then burst into tears.

Thus was abruptly terminated the prospect of endless blue skies that Fulco had taken for granted. For her part, Maria Felice was deprived of long-cherished certainties, such as the grand outdoor ball that Granmamà had promised would mark her eighteenth birthday. One evening as brother and sister were walking in the garden, Maria Felice gestured towards the ornamental lamp posts among the pepper trees: "'They will never be lit now, there won't be any ball.' We hugged each other very hard and, hand in hand, went back to the house with the dogs."

After that, the situation deteriorated rapidly: "time seemed suspended, but was instead running out." Granmamà died a few months later, on 11 September 1912, and suddenly the villa was crawling with over-curious strangers, who examined registers, sifted receipts, winnowed through the archives. The word 'testament', then on everyone's lips but still unfamiliar to Fulco, would become the leitmotif of every family reunion thereafter. A letter from the Princess to her lawyer had been found among her papers. It read: "My will regarding the testament of which we spoke yesterday is as follows: I name my grandson Corrado Valguarnera as my universal heir, and his father my son Giuseppe Valguarnera e Favara Prince of Niscemi, as usufructuary of the available property." Dated 5 September 1906, and signed in full—Maria Favara, widowed Princess of Niscemi—the entire passage was set in quotation marks. Below, on the same sheet, the Princess had added a few lines, also dated: "Here are my ideas, or rather, my last will. In haste. Thanks as always, with regards and, as ever, highest esteem. Niscemi." The Princess's three daughters were devastated—none more so than Carolina, whose entire life had been spent in her mother's despotic yet apparently benevolent orbit. Although male primogeniture had long been abolished, she had expected the Princess to favor her only surviving son—never for a moment imagining that she and in particular Maria Felice and Fulco would be passed over entirely. Giuseppe Valguernera di Niscemi claimed his mother's note to be a legally valid will, and his sisters had no recourse but to take him to court.

Meanwhile, the four Santostefanos experienced the dubious novelty of family living. Over time, Giulio had become a guest in his own home: Carolina had agreed to cover any debts incurred as he frittered away his inheritance, in exchange for a share in and, eventually, full ownership of Palazzo Verdura. He was almost a figure of fun to his children, who referred to him as Giulietto, a diminutive more flippant than affectionate.

Living together did not mean sharing the same roof, for Palazzo

Verdura was not one but three separate *palazzi* plus a house, arranged haphazardly around a cluster of gardens and plunging 'moon wells', courtyards so deep and narrow that they never saw the light of day. To Fulco, impressed by the fact that it was built on the site of an old Arab cemetery, the rambling structure looked "more like a Kasbah than a palace." The atmosphere within was vaguely sepulchral: enfilades of darkened rooms were magnified in "smoky old mirrors like black crepuscular lakes." Luckily there were compensations for an inquisitive boy. Fulco's paternal great-grandfather and namesake, Fulcone Santostefano, had been an enthusiastic, if occasionally indiscriminate collector—of everything, from fossils and shells to Murano glass and incunabula. In the picture gallery, scenes of martyrs and hermits "indulging in their favourite pastime of hitting themselves with a stone or just gazing, half-naked, into space" were interspersed with other more suggestive canvases, of "disheveled females and lustful satyrs in a vortex of purple grapes and fractured watermelons." And beyond the Verdura portals lay all of Palermo, with its "palaces too vast, churches too golden, colossal arches leading to tiny gardens, giant staircases leading to nowhere...." Fulco was entranced by Palazzo Gangi's dizzying double-domed hall, the ballroom of Palazzo Valdina with a tiled floor exactly reproducing the ceiling decor, the baroque church interiors richly encrusted with *marmi mischi*, polished hardstone and marble meanders, the white-and-gilt stucco ornamentation by Serpotta that transformed chapels into frothy rococo theaters.

During the summer of 1915, glad tidings came at last for Carolina and her sisters: the Civil Court of Palermo had ruled against Princess Niscemi's male heirs, declaring that she had in effect died intestate. But their victory was short-lived; Corrado's crack defence team rallied and appealed the decision. A highly significant series of entries had been discovered in the Princess's account book, starting with "L. 3000 to Pasquale for tickets" on 5 September and continuing until 2 November 1906. The payments all related to the two-month trip she took that year with Carolina, Fulco and Maria Felice. Every step of their leisurely itinerary was painstakingly documented. After the outward passage from Palermo to Naples, the party stopped in Rome before progressing north to Milan and Como; the Swiss leg of the trip linking Lausanne, Berne, and Basle was followed by a circuitous route to Paris. The return journey took them back through Basle, the Italian Lakes, and Milan; a second Roman sojourn preceded the homeward cruise from Naples to Palermo. The Niscemi lawyers successfully argued that the Princess's letter constituted a valid epistolary draft for a will: it had been composed on the eve of her departure for a lengthy journey, potentially fraught—as was most travel at the time—with life-threatening perils. A settlement, favoring the claims of Giuseppe and Corrado, was reached out of court the night before the verdict.

Opposite Fulco in a sailor suit at the age of ten.

At this juncture, although Fulco was nearing the end of his course of study at Umberto I, all debate concerning his choice of profession became academic. There would be no money to support a diplomatic career, or even to send him in Uncle Alessino's footsteps to the Naval Academy at Leghorn. Circumstances now dictated that Fulco would enter the army, not as a glamorous White Lancer like his father, but as one of the tens of thousands underage recruits known as the *ragazzi del novantanove*. The "Boys of '99" were the seventeen-year-olds called up in desperation as Italian war losses began to mount during the second half of 1916. Fulco would later joke that he enlisted not out of any misguided sense of patriotism, but because he wanted to be an officer. Commissioned as a second lieutenant in the Alpine infantry, Fulco was promoted to lieutenant and assigned to the shock troops on the Isonzo front. On 24 October 1917, he was at Caporetto (now Kobarid in Slovenia), where the 14th Austro-German Army inflicted on Italy its most massive defeat ever: 40,000 casualties, 300,000 prisoners and a humiliating 70-mile retreat. Fulco sustained a serious shoulder injury, was discharged and sent home to recuperate. His beloved family, and Palermo, awaited him, but "the happy summer days" were truly over.

Three of Fulco's drawings revealing his love of animals: a Norwich terrier, a 'Christmas' rabbit, and a mouse with a necklace.

The brazen throat of war had ceased to roar,
All now was turned to jollity and game,
To luxury and riot, feast and dance.
- JOHN MILTON

A Blackamoor brooch with a large
cabochon emerald of 150 carats,
diamonds and enamel.

Opposite Fulco with his sister on the
beach at Mondello in 1923.

AS A WOUNDED INFANTRYMAN, Fulco was entitled to be cosseted like the
schoolboy he had been eleven months earlier—although it was tacitly
agreed that for him to return to the classroom would be pointless. Veteran
status had the added advantage of emancipating him from the role of
younger child, every aspect of whose existence was subject to maternal
overview and sisterly interference: always benevolent, sometimes
welcome, often exasperating. He was now free to choose his companions,
to buy his own books and records, even to travel alone.

Fulco was short of stature, a stocky body supported by well
muscled legs, toned not in a gym (as would have been the case today) but
on the ballroom floors of Europe. His head was on the large side, with a
rather long nose, and topped by an abundance of dark hair. In his mature
years he developed a distinctive gray streak which ran back from his
forehead, but this became less pronounced as age turned his hair gray.

When the war ended, the Palermo social whirl resumed with the
usual complement of monarchs: George V, Constantine and Sofia of
Greece with their three daughters, Queen Marie of Romania, and King
Alfonso of Spain. A welcome touch of native glamor was provided by
the younger generation of Italian royals. There was, first and foremost,
Crown Prince Umberto, who seemed—at least from a distance—to exude
the smooth charm of a matinee idol, but was known among the nobility
for his natural reserve and piety. Umberto's habit of leaving even the most
convivial parties in time for 6 a.m. mass provoked at least as much
comment as did his carefully publicized infatuation with a pretty music-
hall entertainer named Milly. In addition to the genuine appreciation of
the arts that sparked his friendship with Fulco, Umberto displayed a keen
sense of style. He personally designed the jeweled U-shaped tokens
bestowed upon the ladies of the court who captured his fancy; and when
nuptials were arranged with the Belgian Princess Marie José, he was
involved in every phase of the creation of her wedding gown. Had he not
been born to rule, the Prince of Piedmont might have made his mark in
fashion. His two handsome Aosta cousins exhibited a more
swashbuckling appeal: Amedeo, Duke of Apulia, in particular succeeded
in collecting a dazzling string of flirtations, including a dalliance with
Boots Whitaker—from which she never entirely recovered. The gilded
youth of Sicily, eager to show off the island's many natural and social
attractions, took each royal visit as an excuse to engage in a giddy round

of lightly chaperoned seaside picnics, romantic excursions to view the Greek ruins at Selinunte by moonlight, fancy-dress balls, and charity galas. Wanton dance-steps from abroad, such as the foxtrot and the shimmy, were performed with relish, provoking elders' spluttered indignation: "In my day, we only ever did such things in the dark."

These festive events shone all the more radiantly in the ambient gloom. The Great War and the disintegration of the Austro-Hungarian Empire had shattered *belle époque* complacency and a heightened awareness of life's transience seemed to grip the country. Those who could afford to, took their pleasures where they might; others, whose only recourse was the street, marched and protested. From 1918 to 1920, civil unrest shook Italy. Scarcely a week passed without strikes, arrests, or assassinations: the time would soon be ripe for Mussolini and Fascism.

For Fulco, however, it was an exhilarating season of self-discovery. Although his financial means were less than negligible, his needs were limited. He belonged to a coterie of young bibliophiles, two of whom were to achieve literary fame several decades later. One was Fulco's cousin, Prince Giuseppe Tomasi di Lampedusa, whose masterpiece *The Leopard* was published posthumously in 1958, in accordance with his deathbed wish: "Get the book printed...but not at my expense." His vision of Sicily as a feudal backwater where "everything must change in order for everything to remain the same" was highly controversial in political circles; but the romance of Angelica and Tancredi captured the entire nation's imagination. Pale, podgy, and tongue-tied as a child, Giuseppe had always been pitilessly mocked by Fulco for his fear of animals and obvious distaste for the great outdoors, despite their shared love of books. Lampedusa's unexpectedly impressive military record, featuring a daring escape in disguise after capture by the Austrians, gained him new respect among his peers. His nickname *il Mostro* came to refer more to his 'monstrous' fund of knowledge than to his unprepossessing physique.

The other writer-to-be was Lampedusa's cousin, Baron Lucio Piccolo di Calanovella. A polymath whose interests ranged from musical composition to philosophy to astronomy, he was to publish a volume of poetry in 1954, thanks to the support of Nobel laureate Eugenio Montale, impressed by a few smudged sheets that had been delivered to him despite insufficient postage. Piccolo's *Baroque Cantos* became an overnight prize-winning sensation. They portrayed a "unique Sicilian world—more precisely that of Palermo—which now finds itself on the verge of disappearance without having had the good fortune to be preserved in any art form...a world of baroque churches, of old convents, of souls suited to such places, whose lives have been spent leaving nary a trace." "The whispers of the shades" were clearly audible to Lucio, who reminded Fulco of one of Snow White's dwarves. He corresponded regularly with W. B. Yeats, drawing comparisons between the wee folk of

Ireland and Sicily's own elfin population. His brother Casimiro, likewise a champion of eccentricity, was mainly preoccupied with manifestations of the infinitesimally small. These phenomena fell into two categories: on the one hand, germs and microbes against which he battled, armed only with a flacon of disinfectant alcohol; and on the other, faeries whom he lovingly portrayed in elaborately detailed canvases. Thanks to the marvels of infrared lighting, Casimiro actually succeeded in photographing various wraiths. There was also a sister, Agata Giovanna. Despite countless evenings passed in the Piccolos' company, Fulco never actually set eyes on her, although upon occasion he heard her warble to her brothers from behind a shut door: "Mamà wants you." The reclusive trio shuttled between a family *palazzo* in town and a villa overlooking the sea at Capo d'Orlando, remarkable for its indoor aviary: a salon a-twitter with canaries, goldfinches, and the canary-goldfinches whose song they deemed sweetest of all. Ardent spiritualists, the Piccolo brothers were in constant communication with the denizens of the afterworld. Fulco refused to participate in their frequent seances, after once being chased up a flight of stairs by a particularly agile table.

On one matter alone these dilettanti agreed: that the man of letters in their midst was Fulco. His irreverent wit, his linguistic fluency, his exceptionally retentive memory, both verbal and visual, gave him the edge in all their discussions. A taste for contemporary French literature having replaced the Anglophilia of his boyhood, Fulco had become an avid collector of the works of Pierre Louÿs and Apollinaire. He was entranced by Paul Valéry's complex verse, his subtle analyses of Leonardo's method and the Italian Renaissance "qualities of clarity, order and harmony." By a curious genealogical coincidence, Valéry turned out to be a distant relation through marriage: his wife Julie, like Fulco's step-grandmother Emma, was related to Berthe Morisot.

Unlike Lampedusa and the Piccolos, Fulco also thrived outside the hothouse atmosphere of their clique. An alluring figure was Rasputin's supposed assassin Felix Youssoupov, who visited Sicily on several occasions with his wife Irina. In his bachelor days, the Prince enjoyed wearing gems from his mother's priceless collection, which included some of the French Crown Jewels; as a married man, he felt it more appropriate for these baubles to adorn his spouse. The Princess cultivated an exotic elegance: she often wore a turban and a single, large egg-shaped pearl dangling from one earlobe. When Fulco inquired about its pendant, Youssoupov airily explained that it had long since disappeared down Cleopatra's throat, dissolved in the goblet of vinegar she drank to Mark Antony's health. The truth was just as impressive, for the pearl was the famous 'Pellegrina' given by Philip IV of Spain to his daughter Maria Theresa upon her marriage in 1659 to Louis XIV.

It was also during this period that Fulco established an enduring friendship with the English author and connoisseur, Sacheverell Sitwell, whose family owned Montegufoni Castle in Tuscany. In appearance they made a comical pair since, at 6 feet 4 inches, Sachie Sitwell towered over the much shorter Fulco; temperamentally, however, they were ideally suited. "Their camaraderie was mainly about laughter," according to one observer, although both were formidably equipped with what Sachie's sister Edith termed "the power of retort." Although Fulco never warmed to any of Sachie's pet twentieth-century 'isms'—Cubism, Vorticism, and Futurism—both men delighted in the baroque and rococo, florid styles dismissed at the time as "vulgar beyond words." Sicily provided inspiration for Sitwell's revolutionary 1924 study, *Southern Baroque Art*. In Bagheria, he was spellbound by the "wizard-world" of Villa Palagonia with its eerie black-mirrored interiors, its tangled gardens ringed by a gigantic stone bestiary of half-animal, half-human grotesques.

Fulco was soon part of a fun-seeking yet fastidious crowd of "society gypsies", who determined that even in the shambles of postwar Europe it was "possible to travel while remaining aristocratic." He earnestly claimed in later years to have been "a real bum" engaged in riotous living—"the kind of thing you shudder at now"; in fact, wherever he went, Fulco could count on the hospitality of a network of well-placed friends and relatives. An uncle, Marchese Pietro Tomasi, was Italy's Ambassador to the Court of St James; his friends Gabriella and Andrea di Robilant were the brightest young couple in Venice—known to *cognoscenti* as the City of Beautiful Nonsense.

Scarcely out of her teens, Contessa Gabriella was already a celebrated hostess. D'Annunzio called her *la bella dogalina*, in homage to the doges in her husband Andy's family tree (the most illustrious being Alvise Mocenigo, who crushed the Turks at Lepanto in 1571). With a penchant for unconventional amusements, Gabriella rocked the ancestral Palazzo Mocenigo "down to its deepest timbers". The Grand Canal landmark with its ballroom decorated by Sansovino was the site of treasure hunts, "sailor parties" requiring naval costume, and "baby parties" at which infant attire was *de rigueur*. There were also *settecento* masquerades and a Diaghilev Ball, for which Serge Lifar obligingly choreographed a sylphide *pas-de-cinq* for Gabriella, the French socialite Princess Baba Faucigny-Lucinge, the Russian *émigrée* Princess Natalie Paley, and Princesses Marina and Elizabeth of Greece. At the cocktail hour, modern informality was the keynote: short muslin frocks and wide-brimmed straw hats for the ladies, open-necked linen shirts with rolled-up sleeves for the gentlemen.

When Gabriella first met Fulco, he was just "an unknown little Sicilian duke, accompanied by his sister"; but their ebullience proved irresistible. "No one could tell stories the way they did. They painted a picture of Sicily with such colorful brushstrokes, we felt we had already been there ourselves. Through their imitations, we became familiar with the island's most scabrous events and bizarre individuals." Unlike the

Elsa Maxwell, the professional
party-giver of the carefree 1920s
and 1930s, seated next to Nicky de
Gunzburg and Fulco.

staid old guard who retreated to their Palladian villas along the Brenta
canal to avoid the foreigners summering at the Lido, the Robilants
mingled happily with the international smart set. They even went so far
as to entertain people in 'trade', such as Coco Chanel and Jean Patou, in
their own home. Gabriella was especially intrigued by their streamlined
approach to dressmaking, a career she was unexpectedly to take up with
success a decade later.

On the Lido, the only place to stay was the Excelsior, with its
casino and terrace restaurant. Guests and well-heeled day trippers
congregated daily on the hotel strand; circumscribed by two rows of
cabanas, this beach was part open-air salon, part arena. Gossip-mongers
exchanged choice titbits, as the fashion-conscious sunbathed or exercised
under the guidance of a callisthenics instructor. As clothes became more
revealing, the body beautiful was recognized as a fashionable necessity.
Some women wore the fluttering silk beach pajamas that Chanel had
recently introduced at Biarritz; the men all sported short, tight trunks.
Both sexes draped themselves with colorful bead necklaces or strands of
natural pearls.

"It was in the early Twenties that something happened to the
Lido that changed it from a pleasantly smart Adriatic beach to a magnet
for the celebrities of two continents, perhaps the best known beach in all
the world," according to *Fortune* magazine. "Just what that something
was remains an argument. Some say it was nothing more complicated
than the world boom, some say Fascism. And some insist it was just plain
Elsa Maxwell." A public relations genius with a mysteriously effective
knack for making distinguished people act undistinguished, Maxwell

Cole Porter, the celebrated song writer, first met Fulco in 1919; they quickly became close friends. This portrait was taken in 1934 by Horst.

had been hired to enhance the resort's image. This she accomplished by diverting a stream of millionaires from the Côte d'Azur to the Serenissima. The most junior members of the American contingent were Margaret and Maud Kahn (Nin and Momo), grand-daughters of the influential New York financier and Metropolitan Opera benefactor Otto Kahn, who married John Ryan and Sir John Marriott. The unchallenged doyenne was Princess Jane Campbell di San Faustino, whose daughter Virginia had married an automobile industrialist from Turin, Edoardo Agnelli. A sharp-tongued New Jersey original who made no concessions to modes or meteorology, Princess Jane would drift across the hot sands in long flowing robes copied after the garb of Mary Queen of Scots, complete with ruff and wimple. In describing how small and close-knit a group it was, Fulco would tell the story of a young man who arrived in Venice determined to make his way in society. When he sat down at Florian's in the Piazza of San Marco, the Princess challenged him with the words, "Who asked you into the Piazza?"

New World talent was represented by Cole Porter, whom Fulco had met soon after his marriage to Linda Lee in 1919. Following a secret ceremony in a Paris registry, the "Boy with $1 Million" and the "Girl with $2 Million" had embarked on a protracted bridal trip, crisscrossing the Continent in a private railway car, their own staff in attendance. Their Sicilian sojourn was described many years later by Cole as "a dream that I remember so well…. This Palermo has so many beautiful examples of so many civilizations that one could see and see for months and months."

The Porters spent the summer of 1923 in Palazzo Barbaro. The fifteenth-century architectural gem where Henry James wrote *The Aspern Papers* seemed the perfect setting for Cole to compose his first and only serious score *Within the Quota*, commissioned by the Ballets Suédois. Instantly taken up by the Robilants, Cole could always be persuaded to play his sophisticated songs as their all-night revels faded into dawn. Gabriella remembered the restful moments when "he would sit down at the piano and turn his evanescent gaze toward us, looking at each one singly. His hands flew over the keyboard, and he accompanied his music with words so beautiful, so full of real life, that every listener made them his own."

The Venice season was in full swing when, on 31 August 1923, Fulco received word of his father's death; he arrived in Palermo only just in time for the funeral. A sense of unreality, rather than grief, overwhelmed him as he mounted the staircase of Palazzo Verdura, and heard the ancient porter Piddu ring the bell not thrice, as was customary to announce a family member, but four times—to signify the master of the household. "I realized it was for me." For some time Fulco and his father had been estranged: despite his own notorious indiscretions, Giulio had been outraged by the scandal that ensued when one of Fulco's companions, in a fit of jealousy, drew a gun on him at the Grand Hotel in Rome. Fulco finally felt free to steer his own course in life—whatever that might turn out to be. His mother had her charities and Maria Felice, his strongest tie to Palermo, had just become engaged and would be moving to the mainland.

Wit being no substitute for conventional beauty, Maria Felice had suffered as a girl for her strong features and swarthy complexion: one local rag printed unkind doggerel comparing her unfavorably to an inkspot and a bogey. Now, at the advanced age of twenty-eight, verging on spinsterhood, she found herself betrothed to one of the most eligible bachelors in all Europe—perhaps in the entire world. The heir of a prominent Piedmontese military family, Tommaso Lequio di Assaba was the equestrian gold medal winner at the 1920 Antwerp Olympics. With his beloved mare Trebecco, he then accomplished the unusual feat of taking the silver in 1924, and the bronze in 1928. Sighting Tom at the Palermo race course shortly after his first victory, Maria Felice had fallen desperately in love. Whenever she stayed with the Robilants at Alvisopoli, their estate near Trieste, she would beg to ride the most skittish nags in their stables, "heedless of danger, dreaming all the while of becoming an Amazon worthy of his love." Her fiancé closely resembled her father physically, as well as in his passion for animals and—as it later transpired—other women. Unlike Giulio, Tom cultivated an aloof, inscrutable demeanor that caused the extrovert Santostefanos to refer to him among themselves as the Sphinx. After their first encounter, Fulco sent his sister a card bearing one of his sharp caricatures: the calligraphic outline of a long aquiline nose, laconically inscribed, "I've met him."

The wedding was celebrated in 1925, after the appropriate mourning period had elapsed, in the private chapel of Palazzo Verdura. Out-of-town guests were intrigued by the characteristic Palermitan mélange of pomp and ruination. Prince Jean-Louis de Faucigny-Lucinge, a young Parisian banker who was one of Fulco's Venice acquaintances, noticed a number of empty jewelry cases exhibited among the wedding gifts. He warmed to Fulco's endearingly offbeat explanation: a kleptomaniac relative had been inspecting the display, and his manservant would doubtless return the missing items on the morrow. "How not to love someone who could reveal human miseries with such gaiety and nonchalance?"

Fulco was becoming a fixture of the lengthy Venice season, which ran from July through early September. At a Gods of the Seas Ball, he made his entrée as a Triton flautist, parading to the strains of the *Aida* March. He attended another fête as a bare-chested Faun. At a third soirée, he impersonated a mustachio'd Turkish warrior enamored of a damsel in captivity—a tulle-clad Lady Ashley, the former starlet Sylvia Hawkes who was to replace Mary Pickford as Mrs. Douglas Fairbanks.

Cole, too, had elected Venice as his summer headquarters. In 1924 the Porters moved to the more spacious Palazzo Papadopoli, a classical sixteenth-century edifice, where they kept open house for

Phantom Palace, a miniature painting by Verdura.

Bernard Berenson, Tallulah Bankhead, Duff and Diana Cooper, Emerald Cunard, George Gershwin. The following year they upgraded again, securing the splendid 200-room Palazzo Rezzonico with salons frescoed by Tiepolo. To Henry James, the palace had appeared "to [throw] itself upon the water with a peculiar florid assurance, a certain upward toss of its cornice which gives it the air of a rearing sea horse." Fulco attended the famous Red and White Ball which inaugurated the Porters' tenure: a dangerously flammable gathering of 300 paper-costumed socialites illuminated by 250,000 candles and torches.

In 1926 Cole launched the notorious Dance Boat with Andrea di Robilant. It was actually a *galleggiante*, a barge on which over a hundred guests could eat, drink, and cavort while being towed through the canals or out into the lagoon. Expressly imported from Paris, the nightclub hostess Bricktop did the honors of the Boat, with musical accompaniment courtesy of Leslie Hutchinson's jazz band from London. One Didymus Belcampus, a.k.a. the conductor Sir Thomas Beecham, commemorated the venture in a ballad:

> *Young King Cole*
> *– Sacred fury in his soul –*
> *Now blared all day at the sea.*
> *Each morn he'd syncopate,*
> *Every night he'd ululate*
> *To a grateful Italy.*

Below and opposite Fancy dress balls were a highlight of Parisian society during the 1920s and 1930s. Here, Verdura is a Turkish warrior saving a damsel in distress in the guise of Lady Ashley (later Mrs. Douglas Fairbanks).

Not everyone was equally euphoric. Diaghilev's secretary Boris Kochno complained peevishly of having to move from the Excelsior to the Hôtel des Bains to avoid the "fracas" and the "Negroes" involved in Cole's "idiotic night club." "They are teaching the 'Charleston' on the Lido Beach! It's dreadful! The gondoliers are threatening to massacre all the elderly American women here," he suggested hopefully.

Faucigny-Lucinge's mother-in-law, the Baroness Catherine d'Erlanger, held a fancy dress ball at the Fenice theater; while the attendance of Crown Prince Umberto constituted a social coup, it also meant that from a purely artistic point of view the event would be a disappointment since masks were forbidden in the presence of royalty. Cecil Beaton, a young free-lancer trying to break into professional photography, found the 'glitterati' he had come to portray insufferable. Although well pleased with his own costume, a page's tunic "that showed to full advantage my willowy figure," Beaton "hated being a nobody, while all these brainless fools were having such a triumph." Baba de Faucigny-Lucinge as Water—fitted out in "flowing armour made of hundreds of strips of tin and a casquette of florin-sized sequins"—was gorgeous but totally uncooperative. Beaton reserved special disapproval for the lovely Alice, Lady Wimborne, "in a crinoline of wheat sheaves

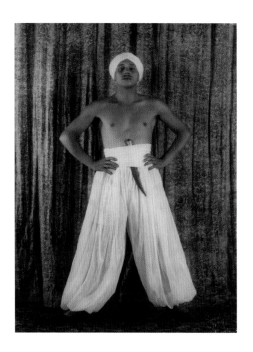

embroidered in gold. She wagged her hips, pranced about 'talking common', and shouted to the Duc de Verdura, 'Allo, dearie'."

Lady Wimborne was one of London's great hostesses and a generous yet discriminating patroness of musicians and composers. The company of younger men delighted Queen Alice, as she was called after her husband Ivor Guest was appointed Lord Lieutenant of Ireland. Before long, Verdura became one of her special friends.

Princess Jane di San Faustino's annual vaudeville production, benefiting a Tubercular Children's Hospital, was always staged in the Excelsior Hotel ballroom. The *New York Times* reported that "scions of proud old Italian houses, members of the British nobility and daughters of American magnates combined in a jazz revue which for swing and pep would yield place to no amateur show." As barmaids, Linda Porter and Lady Diana Cooper kept the champagne flowing. Prince Jagatjit Singh of Kapurthala played the ukelele and Elsa Maxwell in blond wig and bathing suit sang "Just a Lonely Little Lady on the Lido." The 'Duc de Verdura' was praised for leading a trio in a "most amusing eccentric dance." He also participated in the final Charleston chorus with the Robilants, the tenacious Lady Wimborne, and Baron Nicolas de Gunzburg, a White Russian who was to become a lifelong friend of Fulco's. They were rehearsed by Bricktop, who received terse instructions from the Princess on how to keep the rambunctious crew in line: "Cuss'em out." She did, and they adored her for it. At the end of the performance, when Andrea di Robilant surprised her with a birthday cake, Bricktop burst into tears; she was thirty-two years old and a long way from Harlem.

By comparison, the subsequent season might reasonably have been expected to be a letdown; in the event, it proved a total disaster. During one of Linda Porter's frequent absences, the police raided Palazzo Rezzonico; Cole was accused of entertaining a group of boys, including—or so it was rumored—the police chief's own son. The Porters were advised to leave town without delay. Before their departure, Linda took Fulco aside and gave him one of her legendary 'big shoves'. With the instinctive flair of a talent scout that made her so precious to Cole, she sensed the time had come for Fulco to tackle life seriously. He had often sketched with Cole, who, when in a splenetic mood, would weigh the advantages of abandoning his musical career for painting. Linda had been impressed by Fulco's ability to summarize a silhouette with a quick flourish of his pen, to render a landscape with a few lines and a splash of watercolor. Now she encouraged him to discover some means of exploiting this gift. The widest range of opportunities would be available to him in Paris, she thought, where art, literature, music, and fashion were interacting in an unprecedented, vital manner. Baba and Jean-Louis Faucigny-Lucinge, who agreed with Linda's diagnosis, unhesitatingly invited Fulco to stay with them. There were no unknown

A comical Verdura doodle, a reminder of 'djin' [gin] and "No" tonic.

quantities among the fifty or so 'right people' who then constituted international society. As Lifar once remarked: "In Paris, the people who [welcomed] me were the same ones I met in London, Rome or Venice—all capitals on that axis of triumphant worldliness."

Fulco vacillated: the idea of involving himself in some arts-related endeavor was attractive, but he was uncomfortable with the implicit prospect of supporting himself in that way. It was not customary for the Sicilian aristocracy to engage in professional activity of any sort. The situation had changed little since 1850, when a British commentator remarked that "the nobles will not become advocates or physicians or engage in trade or take orders, except with hopes of entering the higher orders." The apparent absence of competitive drive among the privileged classes was linked to conflicting concepts of respect and self-esteem. When Lampedusa was asked by a friend to write a few words in the visitors' album which other guests had already inscribed, he concentrated for a moment and then scribbled: "Too proud to compete."

However, Fulco was aware that for all his ducal ancestry, he was already something of a maverick in provincial Palermo, which he was starting to call *le bout du monde*—the world's end. In one of Lampedusa's short stories about the more obtuse elements in Sicilian society, there is a revealing vignette in which a certain "Marchese F"—perhaps Fulco himself—is scorned for being "aesthetical," a malapropism signifying 'aesthete', which was, of course, a delicate "euphemism for worse things." There was also a cautionary example, uncomfortably close to home, of the dire consequences of expatriation. A cousin of Fulco's grandfather Corrado, one of Lampedusa's great-uncles, Marchese Filomeno Tomasi della Torretta, had emigrated to England in 1861 at the age of twenty. Resisting all entreaties to return, he supported himself first as a circus clown, then as a clerk in a coal depot. When he ultimately became a gem dealer, the family gave a collective shudder that Fifi could be implicated in anything so crassly commercial.

Overleaf A pencil sketch by Verdura of kittens at play, and a brooch of the same subject in diamonds and a pearl, designed for Barbara (Babe) Cushing Mortimer Paley in 1955.

*Dancing is a rough attempt to apprehend
the rhythm of life.*
- GEORGE BERNARD SHAW

3 PARIS

A brooch of a hot air balloon set
with a large cabochon emerald and
caliber cut sapphires, *c.* 1960.

Opposite Verdura in the Napoleon
costume he wore for the '1799' ball
he gave in honor of the famous
lovers, Lord Nelson and Lady
Hamilton, at the Palazzo Verdura
in 1929.

AS THE FAUCIGNY-LUCINGES' guest in 1927, Fulco found himself at the heart of the youngest, most brilliant constellation in the Parisian social galaxy. Baba and Jean-Louis had married only four years earlier while they were still in their teens, despite parental misgivings on both sides. Now, aged twenty-three, Jean-Louis was taking his first steps in the world of high finance at Daniel Dreyfus & Company, after shelving plans for a career in diplomacy. It was considered good form for the husband of an heiress, no matter how blue his blood, to be involved in a lucrative activity.

Baba's family, the Erlangers, were prominent bankers of German origin, closely linked to the Foulds and the Rothschilds, and known for their patronage of the arts. They had prospered in France under Napoleon III, before settling in England where their barony was recognized. Although by Erlanger standards the Faucigny-Lucinges were merely well off, theirs was an ancient dynasty with impeccable bloodlines. In the eleventh century, the Faucigny-Lucinges had ruled over a small Alpine principality, and were connected through marriage to the House of Savoy as well as the French Bourbons.

"We were a young couple," Jean-Louis later recalled, "with a sense of curiosity and a taste for the company of artists, writers and musicians, combined with a liking for the parties and frivolities that embellish life." Their villa in the leafy residential quarter of Passy was a regular meeting place for the *haute bohème* of the capital. Although Baba did not have a traditional salon, or one special day of the week when she played hostess, almost every evening a group of friends would gather for a drink before going on to theater or dinner engagements. The Faucigny-Lucinge crowd included many of the artists who frequented *Le Boeuf sur le toit*, a popular nightclub whose name came from Milhaud's 1920 pantomime about a New York speakeasy called the 'Nothing Doing Bar'. To habitués, it was "the crossroads of destinies, the cradle of loves, the hearth of discord, the bellybutton of Paris"; outsiders viewed it somewhat warily as "a chic and comfortable Congo near the Place de la Concorde." The composer Georges Auric and his Austrian wife Nora, a painter, Jean and Valentine Hugo, both designers, the surrealist Salvador Dalí, the illustrator and scenographer Christian Bérard, Diaghilev's protégés Boris Kochno, and Serge Lifar all congregated there. In this unconventional, animated company, the hilariously wicked imitations that were Fulco's forte quickly "inspired liking—and a certain fear."

Baba's principal means of self-expression was fashion. With her elongated pallid visage and her dark almond-shaped eyes, she was often compared to a princess in a Persian miniature. To Bettina Ballard, an editor with American *Vogue*, it appeared that "her chic all stemmed from her head, her unsmiling strange oriental face, the hard almost shocking chic of a woman who, though not pretty, projected allure."

Baba sounded as special as she looked, her numerous bracelets, brooches, and necklaces tintinnabulating softly at her slightest gesture. She launched the fad for tiny evening hats, cocked turbans, sprays of feathers, a puff of black lace; or she would simply tie her hair back with a narrow silk bowknot. The idiosyncratic clothes she designed for herself were much admired and frequently copied. Yet her one foray into the garment business met with scant success: it turned out that there was little demand for Tyrolean beach attire.

Baba's lush Second Empire taste in interior design ran counter to the shiny, hard-edged Art Déco manner that was popular at the time. In the various Faucigny-Lucinges residences, she perfected a theatrical, mediaevo-baroque ambience accented with crimson and white baldaquins and pelmets, bestrewn with an eclectic clutter of needlepoint cushions, Staffordshire spaniels, plaster busts, and glittering *objets de vertu*. On the Paris scene, where style was paramount, Baba stood out as a "personage of great influence, exuding a fantastic personal aura of fashion which in retrospect is inexplicable."

Impressed by Fulco's knowledge of the fine and decorative arts, his enthusiasm for the same then unfashionable historical periods that she favored, Baba found him a job with an antiques dealer who was in partnership with one of her cousins. It was a novel experience, and one that would have been unimaginable in Palermo, where aristocracy and trade did not mix—not even in the course of regular business transactions. Fulco's mother never actually set foot in a shop, but would have wares sent home for her inspection. In Paris, however, it was acceptable and, in certain cases, even desirable to be employed, although the old school maintained that an aristocrat might engage in artistic activity as a pastime, but not as a paid profession. There still persisted the "vague idea that a man can remain a gentleman if he paints bad pictures, but must forfeit the conventional right to his Esq. if he makes good pots or furniture." It fell to the White Russian colony to lead the vanguard of what might be called a social revolution, in favor of employment for the nobility. Most resourceful were the Youssoupovs who, leading a life of blithe desperation on the outskirts of town, supported themselves thanks to a variety of cottage industries: a beauty school, a training center for the applied arts, a couple of restaurants, a porcelain factory, and a fashion house called Irfé, combining the first two letters of their Christian names.

Short on cash, long on style and ancestry, Fulco was in a situation in some respects not unlike that of the Russian exiles. Jean-Louis

Fulco with his great friends of the 1920s and 1930s, the Faucigny-Lucinges, in fancy dress.

The Baron Nicolas de Gunzburg, photographed by Horst in 1937. Nicky, Natalie Paley, and Verdura, formed a devoted trio of friends.

observed that Fulco had the "high spirits that only those who have nothing to lose can permit themselves; poverty then becomes a heaven-sent grace." It is hardly surprising that two of his closest friends were young Slavs. Nicolas de Gunzburg belonged to a wealthy family of investors that had been ennobled by the Romanovs. Five years younger than Fulco, Nicky had actually been an expatriate from birth. With rare prescience, his father had chosen Paris (where he owned the Crillon Hotel) as a convenient base from which to manage his Swiss bank accounts; thus the Gunzburgs' opulent lifestyle remained unaffected by the Revolution. One of the wittiest and most genuinely charming men about town, Nicky also had sultry good looks: his heavy-lidded, slanting eyes, high cheekbones, and full lips gave him the prominent air of a New Kingdom pharaoh. He rebelled against his family's stifling sense of decorum and yearned for an acting career, possibly on the silver screen. His lavish allowance enabled him to make this dream come true by bankrolling the Danish director Carl Dreyer's early horror masterpiece *Vampyr*. Starring as the undead hero, Nicky was featured resting in a coffin, gracefully arranged upon a bed of tuberoses.

Princess Natasha (or Natalie) Paley also caressed the ambition of becoming an actress. A diaphanous beauty with deep-set gray eyes and pale blond hair, Natalie was often mistaken—to her delight—for Greta Garbo or Marlene Dietrich. At the end of 1927, however, she opted for the security of marriage to her employer, the couturier Lucien Lelong. Natalie's need of protection far outstripped any yearning for celebrity; hers had been a precarious existence long before the Revolution. As the offspring of Grand Duke Paul Alexandrovich's morganatic union with a divorced noblewoman, Natalie was a non-person at the Tsarist court until 1915, when Nicholas II finally granted the princely Paley title to all members of his uncle's second family. Only two years later, however, the Paleys were all placed under house arrest; after the brutal murders of Natalie's father and brother, her mother succeeded in escaping with her two daughters to Finland. She described her adolescence dramatically, as having been "bespattered with the clotted blood of the Romanovs." At one point Natalie was briefly considered as a match for Prince Albert, the second son of Britain's King George V, who after his brother's abdication reigned as George VI. When that possibility evaporated, together with her meagre funds, Natalie became a mannequin. Fulco was entranced by her fey sense of humor and strange Russian melancholy, as much as by her ethereal loveliness. Once married, Natalie gained the freedom to act in an experimental film made by the photographer Hoyningen-Huene. According to her co-star, the photographer Horst, the movie was "not merely underground; it had no title and no plot, and it was never shown." The general theme was "middle-class city life and love," grittily illustrated with street scenes and kitchen shots.

A black pearl and diamond set of cufflinks and studs made by Fulco for Nicky de Gunzburg.

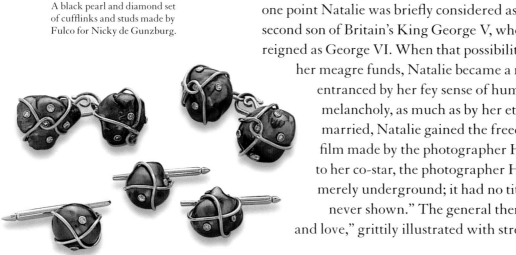

Yet another thread of Fulco's Parisian life took up where the Venice season left off—with the Porters and a crowd of 'Continental Americans', cultivated, moneyed expatriates. Linda and Cole had an extraordinary house which, though located in the center of Paris on rue Monsieur, was surrounded by an old-fashioned orchard. Within, the decor was an up-to-the-minute blend of New York glitz and Parisian elegance, featuring figured platinum wall panels, zebra carpets, red lacquered furniture, and white kid upholstery. The French, who loved the Porters' lively, gossipy soirées, punningly referred to their hosts as the Coleporteurs (from *colporteur*, meaning tattler). Sometimes, as the party drew to a close, Fulco and Linda would sing duets to Cole's piano accompaniment. There were long evenings that often ended at dawn at Bricktop's *boîte*, which served the foreign artistic community as a combined maildrop/bank/rehearsal hall/club-house. "I can't tell you how many people there were who wanted to write or paint or perform and who had the money but not the talent—and then on the other side were all those people who had the talent but no money," she recalled. "The beautiful thing was that the rich ones took care of the poor ones. F. Scott Fitzgerald later wrote that in those days in Paris it didn't matter if you were broke, because there was so much money all around you."

Fulco naturally gravitated to *le clan des italiens*, presided over by the formidable Countess Anna Letizia Pecci Blunt, a grand-niece of Pope Leo XIII. When Mimì Pecci married the American financier Cecil Blumenthal, her surname was joined to an abbreviation of his—actually his New York cable address. The Vatican made him a papal count. At the Pecci Blunt townhouse on the rue de Babylone, there was always a synergetic mix of intellectuals and moneyed socialites. An astute patroness of the arts, Mimì knew the value of the right kind of promotion for the avant-garde *créateurs* she supported. She was regarded as an unofficial cultural ambassadress between Italy and France. At her Piazza Aracoeli *palazzo* in the heart of Rome, she organized concerts to acquaint the lethargic Roman nobility with "modern international music." One series was notable for presenting new works by Hindemith, Markevitch, and Milhaud, conducted by the composers themselves.

On the outer fringes of the Pecci Blunt crowd hovered Fulco's cousin, Baron Ugo Oddo, one of many aristocrats on Gabrielle Chanel's payroll. Aware of Fulco's skill with a paintbrush, Ugo engineered a meeting with his employer. Chanel, nearing the peak of her career, had just launched the

Fulco's cousin, Baron Ugo Oddo, in hussar's uniform for a ball given by Nicky de Gunzburg in Paris in 1934.

'little black dress' that could go anywhere, any time. Paul Poiret, speaking for an earlier generation of couturiers, blamed her for fostering a "de luxe shabbiness" with the sporty *garçonne* style. He deplored the passing of women who were "architectural like the prows of ships," now replaced by "little underfed telegraphists."

Others, like Princess Marthe Bibesco, recognized the sociological implications of the change: "The Frenchwoman who first started this revolution in clothes is known to be a woman of the people. She is a genius in her way, and none of us can be grateful enough to her. Mlle Chanel has done more for aristocrats than they can ever do for her. Has she not given them the conviction that they exist independent of their fineries?... When it comes to wearing jersey, the uniform of the poor, and a necklace of glass beads, a certain manner is indispensable if [a lady] is not to be taken for a shop girl." But it was not politics that made women love Chanel; it was the understated refinement and sheer ease of her clothes.

Although their paths had crossed occasionally in Venice, it was Fulco's first close encounter with Chanel. Then 44, she already had the look she maintained to the end of her life: glossy dark hair cut in the page-boy style, powdery complexion, emphatic eyebrows, wide crimson lips. The ingratiating Cocteau called her the Black Swan; with her flaring nostrils, she reminded Colette more of a little black bullock. To Fulco, Chanel's face resembled "a wonderful Japanese mask, like a Samurai mask." The interview—for that is what it was—proved successful beyond his wildest expectations: Fulco was hired instantly as a designer in Chanel's rapidly expanding textile department. He was flabbergasted: "She was the first person ever to take me seriously."

In 1927, when Fulco entered Chanel's orbit, she was planning a major financial operation: the purchase of the Blacque-Belair textile factory in the suburb of Asnières. The introduction of social security charges in France that year had raised the cost of labor; Chanel responded by seeking control of the entire production line, from mill to *maison*. Also, from a purely creative standpoint, she was eager to experiment with supple new weaves and jerseys that would enhance her sporty designs. The firm, rebaptized Tricots and then Tissus Chanel, came equipped with an important human asset, a thirty-four-year-old Georgian painter-poet named Ilia Zdanevitch. He was a gifted draughtsman as well as a technically innovative loom builder. Before migrating to France in 1921, as Iliazd he had acquired a reputation as the most flamboyant of the Russian Futurists. He practised body painting; declared that American shoes and torn shirts were more beautiful than the Venus de Milo; composed plays in a sonorous, nonsensical tongue, the 'transmental' *Za-oom*. In his less iconoclastic moods, Iliazd was also a superb typographer and art publisher, a scholar interested in medieval grammarians, Renaissance travelers, and seventeenth-century ballet treatises.

Above The mosaic portrait of the Byzantine Empress Theodora in the Church of San Vitale in Ravenna was the inspiration for the 'Byzantine' gold and colored stone brooches (opposite) designed by Verdura, *c.*1930, for Chanel. From the collection of Diana Vreeland.

Fulco did not actually work at Asnières, but rendered his proposals after informal discussions with Chanel and Iliazd. "Why not develop this motif from the mosaics of the Cathedral at Monreale?" "What about a pattern taken from the coloured cosmatesque inlay in St Mark's Basilica in Venice?" Printed and striped materials were the basic ingredients of Chanel's versatile two-piece outfit, consisting of a coat with a lining that matched the fabric of the dress. While Fulco's compositions had jagged, angular lines in keeping with the taste of the day for "geometrical splendour", they also reflected his own interest in historical ornamentation. He favored a rich palette that contrasted with the muted gray, lavender, and fawn harmonies generally in vogue. The results were sumptuous, more appropriate for dressy damask evening suits than daywear.

Chanel had started hiring members of the nobility only a few years after she first attracted the attention of fashion reporters with what *Harper's Bazaar* termed a "charming chemise dress." At the time, she was involved with the Grand Duke Dmitri Pavlovitch (Youssoupov's co-conspirator and Natalie Paley's half-brother); thus her recruits were mainly Russian. Lady Iya Abdy made handbags for Chanel, Grand Duchess Maria designed brightly hued embroideries; a former governor of Crimea was promoted from doorman to business administrator. Their liberal 'what-is-yours-is-mine' attitude amused her, and she was captivated by the barbaric ostentation of their heritage—an exciting new source of inspiration. Successive waves of British, French and Italians operated as *agents mondains*, ensuring that her dresses got worn—and noticed—at all the right places. That pre-eminent *artiste-couturier* of the Belle Epoque, Charles Frederick Worth, was the first to recognize the value of trophy customers. Jean Patou dressed his *mannequins de ville* free of charge. It was Chanel, however, who codified the practice, establishing responsibilities on both sides: "I never paid anyone for doing nothing."

These fashion ambassadors were a public relations necessity. Dressmakers still ranked as suppliers rather than taste-makers; they did not stand on equal footing with their clients, and were not welcome as guests in their homes. Maurice de Rothschild was famous for having extended an invitation to the comely Madame Louis Cartier (née Countess Almassy) and then, when she arrived on her husband's arm, turning the couple away: "I am not in habit of entertaining tradesmen." As Princess Jane's daughter-in-law Lydia Redmond recalled, "couturiers were more modest in their ambitions; one sometimes went to their parties, but never to their houses." Lelong alone was grudgingly accepted, not as a *styliste*, but as a *grand bourgeois*; after marriage, his status improved as the consort of an ex-quasi-Imperial Highness. The cultivated Paul Poiret had a salon of sorts, but it was not one to which a gentleman might decently bring his wife, since the ladies there were all professionals: singers, actresses—or demi-mondaines.

Chanel's collection of salaried social butterflies was seen by some as a delayed reaction to the snubs she had endured as a kept woman. However, she denied employing aristocrats in order "to flatter my vanity or to humiliate them"; other, subtler forms of revenge existed, had she wished to implement them. Rather, it was their scintillating, brittle attitude which commanded her respect: "They have wit, tact, ravishing perfidiousness, classy nonchalance, and a very exact, well-honed insolence that is always on alert." Whatever her true reasons, having a battalion of glitterati in circulation meant that Chanel could sleep soundly, confident that she would be kept informed of all that had been said and done at the most select gatherings. Finally, although she would never willingly admit it, there was still much she might learn from her titled help. Chanel had made the most of liaisons with wealthy and supportive beaux such as Etienne Balsan and Boy Capel, who backed her earliest millinery venture; but she could not shrug off the memory of her wretched origins. Descended from peasant chestnut-pickers, the illegitimate daughter of itinerant village hawkers in the Cevennes, she had been educated as a charity pupil in a convent. Her brother thought himself lucky to be able to support his family by selling shoes in the marketplace at Clermont-Ferrand.

Chanel must have felt some slight twinge of satisfaction when in 1924 she enlisted Count Etienne de Beaumont to string beads for her— only four years after she had suffered the public humiliation of being excluded from one of his famous fancy dress balls. Beaumont was already a living monument to the Twenties. Eccentric, ridiculously affected, and haughty, the Count might have been a figure of fun, had he not displayed such a deep affinity for and understanding of the most avant-garde art, music and theater of his era. As a collector, Beaumont could afford to be audacious, since his eye was infallible: he was one of the first to hang Picassos alongside Old Masters. However, he demonstrated greatest flair as an amateur impresario, surpassing even Diaghilev as a talent scout. The *Soirées de Paris* which he organized in Montmartre that Spring marked a turning-point in the cultural life of the capital. The programme reflected Beaumont's conviction that contemporary theater should partake equally of aristocratic divertissement and music-hall *variétés*. Ida Rubinstein danced flamenco; Eric Satie's *Mercure* was given its first performance, with Léonide Massine's erotically charged, slow-motion choreography winding through and around huge cardboard and wire constructions by Picasso; *Les Roses*, Henri Sauguet's first ballet score, was performed against a pastel backdrop by Marie Laurencin, who lived in a pavilion in the grounds of the Beaumont townhouse on the Left Bank.

Exceedingly tall and slender, Etienne de Beaumont moved with the fastidious ungainliness of a large bird; his high-pitched voice had a sharp, yapping quality; his blue eyes seemed to protrude in perpetual amazement. Yet he was every inch the *grand seigneur*. Portrayals of the

Antonio de Ganderillas, Baba de
Faucigny-Lucinge and Fulco in
fancy dress at the 'Bal des Matières'
given by Charles and Marie-Laure
de Noailles in 1929.

Count, not always flattering, abound in the literature of the period. He
was the model for Proust's Marquis de Saint-Loup, he was satirized as the
Duc Toto d'Anche in Edouard Bourdet's play *La Fleur des Pois*. Together
with his gentle wife Edith, he was immortalized in Raymond Radiguet's
ambiguous cult novelette, *The Ball of Count d'Orgel*, in which it was
revealed that "the deepest passion of men of his class through the
centuries [was] disguise."

Etienne de Beaumont ran his private fêtes with the same ruthless
aplomb and insistence on quality that he had displayed as producer of the
Soirées. These masquerades belonged to a traditional genre of elite
entertainment, in which spectators and performers held interchangeable
roles; Louis XIV, surrounded by his courtiers, had both applauded and
danced in the ballets staged for his amusement at Versailles. Between the
two World Wars, the taste for extravagant fancy dress galas was revived
in Paris, thanks to a unique symbiosis of society, fashion, and the arts.

Competition was fierce—for invitations, for costumes, for order of precedence. Yet money never changed hands, and there were no sponsors: everyone, according to Jean-Louis de Faucigny-Lucinge, subscribed wholeheartedly to "an almost naive concept of sacrificing to beauty".

The Count drew exquisite, often sadistic, gratification from all phases of the proceedings: "I give balls for the pleasure of not inviting certain people." As punishment, latecomers were not allowed to parade in their finery, but remained sequestered in a back room until all the other guests had made their entrées. Afterwards, he commemorated each party with a fantastical collage, combining photographs of the most spectacular costumes with colorful cut-outs from seed catalogues and travel brochures. Then, with careful brushstrokes, he would ensure that, at least in retrospect on paper, his vision had been achieved in flawless detail. These dreamy party-scapes caught the attention of a young dealer interested in surrealism, who exhibited them in his gallery; his name was Christian Dior.

One of the first balls Fulco attended was the 1928 Beaumont fête: mariners and medusas were the theme, so he went as a pirate. The host, wearing a shroud-like satin sac, made an appearance as a somewhat spectral stingray, his pallid face emerging from the creature's maw. Chanel, now the Count's employer and very much *persona grata*, was a giant starfish. Dressed as a waiter, Jean Hugo staggered in under the weight of a tray bearing the Maharanee of Kapurthala disguised as caviar —and almost dropped her. The Maharajah remarked amiably: "In India, we would have put him to death on the spot."

Early the following year, three hundred of Fulco's closest friends around the world received a large card from the Duc de Verdura,

The invitation card to Verdura's '1799' ball in 1929, an event that exhausted the remains of his inheritance.

Opposite Fulco, in sailor's uniform, with Contessa di Assaro and Cav. Michele de Stefani.

embossed with the five-pronged ducal coronet, requesting—in French— the honor of their presence at a "fête at Lady Hamilton's in 1799", on the 13th of April, at Palazzo Verdura. Fulco's party, as the *pièce de résistance* of a seven-day Palermitan 'season', would consume whatever crumbs remained of his father's inheritance. In Sicily, however, the idea of dilapidating a patrimony did not carry only pejorative connotations; indifference to pecuniary matters was regarded as a sign of high breeding. In *The Leopard*, the old Prince Salina gave an historical explanation of his nephew's charm: "It is impossible to obtain the distinction, the delicacy, the fascination of a boy like Tancredi without his ancestors having romped through half-a-dozen fortunes."

With acceptances running high, and the major Parisian couturiers working day and night to complete the specially commissioned period costumes, the British, French, and American editions of *Vogue* sent a three-man team to cover what was already being referred to as The Palermo Ball. The writer was Johnnie McMullin, the magazine's Paris correspondent and constant escort of the decorator Elsie de Wolfe. Cecil Beaton, now a recognized photographer, was to shoot group and individual portraits of the smart set. There were sketches by Mark Ogilvie-Grant, the young caricaturist who was soon to illustrate Nancy Mitford's first novel, *Highland Fling*. Their arrival in Sicily after a long train journey was far from promising: "It seemed incredible looking at the ugly disorderly town from the windows of the car, that one could ever witness the wonderful series of balls that had been discussed and planned and replanned in Paris and London and Rome and Cannes. But suddenly the panorama of the country against a background of jagged mountains burst on the view and the romantic balls seemed credible. Palermo means beauty hidden behind walls of ugliness."

Fulco's ball inaugurated the round of festivities. For hours before, "the hotels were tense with excitement, everyone running from room to room, powder floating about, and with it peals of laughter. Someone needed gold powder for his hair. All the gold powder was gone. Was silver any use? *None*, with a gold costume." Finally, at midnight, the guests were ready. There was applause from the hotel staff crowding the foyer, as they made their exit to the waiting limousines. There were cheers from the populace as the motorcade negotiated the narrow streets around Palazzo Verdura, which had been cordoned off by the police. At the entrance, a resplendent majordomo brandished a gold-knobbed baton; and lining the grand staircase were footmen in perruques and sixteenth-century scarlet liveries, trimmed with gold braid and streamers. "The whole scene was in a scale of magnificence and colour exactly suited to our own dresses."

Champagne and compliments flowed freely in the salons where Lady Hamilton had once entertained Lord Nelson, until the entrées were announced in the ballroom. It was "a spectacle very like that other night,

Fulco with the Marquise de Saint-Sauveur at Nicky de Gunzburg's 'Le Bal des Entrees d'Opera' held in Paris, 1925.

when the real people of the drama were living the story for the first time." Mimì Pecci Blunt, a keen amateur cinematographer, was on hand to film the procession of "doubly historical personages." The Italian party also included the Robilants, the Morosinis, the Volpis, and the San Faustinos; even Giuseppe Tomasi di Lampedusa put in a rare appearance. Lady Erroll and Hamish St Clair Erskine were among the ranking British visitors. The Porters and the poet Louise de Vilmorin belonged to the Paris contingent, together with the Vicomte and Vicomtesse de Noailles —Charles and Marie-Laure de Noailles—who vied with the Beaumonts in their enlightened patronage of contemporary artists: "Just as sculptors and painters create art, so the Noailles create an environment in which to live the modern life."

Fulco's aunt Princess Gangi was Pauline Borghese; as Goethe's Bettina, the Duchess de Gramont wore a simple muslin corsage offset by a gaily beribboned skirt. Madame Henri Letellier, the piquant young beauty whose romance with an older man inspired Colette's *Gigi*, had a gown reproduced from a Romney canvas. Elsa Maxwell got herself up as a cross between a Bonapartist drummer and an admiral. Etienne de Beaumont made his entrance as Chateaubriand, with Lady Abdy in white and gray tulle by Alix. The South American millionaire Carlos de Beistegui, an early patron of Le Corbusier and a great collector of eighteenth-century furniture, came as Sir Reginald MacDonald: his towering blue and red feathered hat, fur-lined mantle with double pelerine was copied from Lawrence's portrait. Louise Boulanger dressed Elsie de Wolfe as Mrs. Garrick in a white gown. Chanel was well represented by Edith de Beaumont in a white velvet dress edged with sable with a feathered muff, and by Madame Henry Bernstein, the playwright's wife, also in white, with a little plumed and beaded coif.

Fulco gallantly cast Alice Wimborne as the lady of the house: her pink satin gown and green velvet cape had been copied by Worth from a Romney portrait of the Divine Emma. Fulco's was a gesture as audacious as it was gracious, tantamount to a public announcement of their liaison. Although over 40, Alice Wimborne still had the fair radiance that Fulco always found appealing in women. They shared a passion for music, and a taste for lavish entertainments. For 'Queen' Alice's famous musicales, often featuring the Quartet Society, Wimborne House in London was regularly transformed into a scented bower, with great triumphs of waxen blooms, illuminated with hundreds of candles. The overwhelming ambience was described as "Rome before the Fall."

With typically provocative bravado, Fulco welcomed his guests as Napoleon. No historical character could have been more loathsome to the predominantly French company, whose families had lost titles and properties as a result of the Revolution. The tough, sexy youth of Abel Gance's recent silent film *Napoléon* was his inspiration: he affected a hypnotic, movie-star gaze, emphasized by the use of kohl to rim his eyes,

Maria Felice with Pietro Salazan at Fulco's famous '1799' ball. Other guests, pictured below, included Elsa Maxwell, Carlos de Beistegui, and the Baroness Lo Monaco.

and his hair was combed forward in flame-like licks. A short fitted jacket with broad lapels and tight embroidered britches showed off his shapely dancer's physique to best advantage. At three in the morning, Fulco introduced his guests to an old Sicilian custom: flanked by two footmen with baskets of yellow daisies, scarlet tulips and arum lilies, he paraded through the halls of Palazzo Verdura bestowing unwieldy sheaves of blossoms upon all the ladies. Finally, supper was served on a vast terrace tented with crimson brocade; over two hundred guests sat at long draped tables lit only by rows of glittering silver candelabra.

The following day Baroness Lo Monaco gave a dinner-dance at the Villa Igiea, and the next night yet another costume ball—this time with a Second Empire theme—was held at Palazzo Mazzarino by Fulco's boyhood friend Count Fabrizio Lanza di Mazzarino and his Cuban-born wife Conchita Ramirez de Villaurriba. In a homage to the court painter Franz Winterhalter, Jola Letellier made an entrance as Empress Eugénie, in a "white satin dress with deep white lace ruffles about the shoulders and about the bottom of the skirt...and a vivid green ribbon like a slash of colour, attached at the shoulder, again at the waist, and falling away over the voluminous skirt to the floor." Also inspired by a Winterhalter portrayal was Princess Cora Caetani's Empress Elisabeth, in "yellow and red shot taffeta, with masses of ruffles and a collection of jewelled orders worn on a broad scarlet ribbon across her breast." But all eyes were on Fulco and Alice Wimborne as they made their romantic entry together, waltzing giddily to the strains of the *Blue Danube*—he in a hussar's befrogged uniform with a tall gray astrakhan hat, she in a billowing tulle confection, again by Worth, that precisely matched the cornflower circlet in her hair.

The "historic Palermo ball" was soon the "talk of all the capitals," according to *Vogue*, and "there is now a Palermo season lasting a week, following the Riviera season and preceding the London one. One had to be there." Beneath the wreathed medallion vignette of Fulco published in the magazine, the caption read: "We must put the laurels round Napoleon, the Duc de Verdura himself, who was the life and soul of all Palermo parties." As a witty, multilingual, titled single man, Fulco had always been much in demand. Almost overnight, his name—hitherto known only to a circle of intimates—began to appear in the chronicles of society columnists, not as one of Chanel's stable of designers, but as an arbiter of fashion in his own right.

By June, he had returned to Paris, to attend the Beaumont Opera Ball, where a theatrical decor was provided by Marie Laurencin's *trompe-l'oeil* panels. As Mercury from Offenbach's *Orphée aux Enfers*, Fulco wore a lamé body suit with little wings attached to his heels. He was accompanied by the Marquise Pauline de Saint Sauveur as Diana, in a matching short metallic tunic; an early fan of Chanel's millinery, she was now in charge of the designer's *parfumerie* and accessories line. Etienne

Verdura and Lady Alice Wimborne
in Second Empire costume at the
dinner-dance in Palermo given by
Lo Monaco in 1929.

Opposite A ring made with a
cabochon sapphire, amethyst, and
pavé diamonds, *c.* 1945. The second
ring consists of a black opal and
rubies, *c.* 1950.

de Beaumont was Prince Danilo, escorting the extravagant taste-maker Misia Sert as Léhar's *Merry Widow*. In the *Madame Butterfly* group, Marie-Laure de Noailles appeared as a geisha with "Yankee sailors" Carlos de Beistegui and the poet René Crevel. Proud of their gymnastic skills, Elsie de Wolfe and John McMullin executed cartwheels in an acrobatic Moulin Rouge entrance.

The Noailles' *Bal des matières* was hailed as "one of the most beautiful fêtes of modern times." A magic lantern show by Jean Hugo was projected during the performance of Auric's score, *Faust magicien*. Nijinska choreographed a ballet for a specially commissioned *Aubade* by Poulenc, played by the composer together with an ensemble of seventeen instrumentalists. The challenge for the guests was to invent costumes using bizarre or unusual materials, such as paper, cellophane, straw, glass. Marie-Laure and Charles de Noailles wore shiny plastic holly outfits. Iya Abdy was a unicorn, and Cocteau an implausible orang-outang. Valentine Hugo made the sequined heraldic masks for the Beaumonts' gothick divertissement. There were bevies of ostriches, angels and raffia lampshade chorus lines. Fulco, dressed in a coat of mail and leotard, made an entry with Baba de Faucigny-Lucinge and Antonio de Gandarillas, a handsome young Chilean who boasted a phalanx of illustrious admirers, including at one time or another Osbert Sitwell, Felix Youssoupov and John Singer Sargent. The group posed for a photograph with Max Jacob, the Chanel house poet.

That September, Venice "was never more brilliant", drawing the usual habitués: Prince Umberto of Savoy, the Sitwells, the Faucigny-Lucinges, and, of course, Alice Wimborne. So intense was the social calendar that visitors complained of needing more luggage than for the London season. "Women were covered with jewels and their only enemies were the mosquitoes." The Duke of Verdura introduced a welcome note of informality, *Vogue* reported, by launching a bold new fashion in beachwear—Chinese coolie trousers, completed with matching colored shirts and cardigans; the ladies followed suit, discarding their satin pajamas for this even more casual unisex attire. At a ball given by Elsa Maxwell and Baroness Lo Monaco at the Lido, Fulco was a winner in the dance contest.

Chanel was intrigued and impressed by Fulco's apparently effortless ascent, as well as by his sense of style—a playful blend of pageantry and nonconformity in keeping with the capricious spirit of the times. And when by chance she discovered that Etienne de Beaumont was dealing surreptitiously and very profitably in imitation Chanel jewels out of his own home, she knew instantly who would be the ideal replacement.

4 CHANEL

*A jewel is a love-token and a sign of supremacy,
a weapon for conquest and a symbol of prosperity.*
- VOGUE, 1929

One of Verdura's signature Maltese
Cross cuff bracelets.

Opposite Verdura showing his cuff
bracelet to Chanel, *c.* 1935.

CHANEL'S RESPONSE to her clients' demand for "jewelry composed especially to complete a dress" had been typically canny. Dressmaker ornaments, made of feathers, plastic, sequins, bone or fabric, were customarily used to trim couture designs. Chanel, however, intended her glamorous pieces to be worn together with, rather than instead of, fine jewels. "A woman should mix fake and real," she insisted. "I love fakes because I find such jewelry provocative, and I find it disgraceful to walk around with millions around your neck, just because you're rich. The point of jewelry isn't to make a woman look rich but to adorn her; not the same thing." Jewelry should not provoke envy, but wonder.

By the end of 1927, *Fémina* announced that "many Parisiennes [made] no distinction between wearing extremely valuable colliers and costume jewelry by Chanel." Their 'confusion' was understandable, for even the experts had difficulty in detecting the tenuous line that separated real from fake. In the heart of the *haute joaillerie* district on the Rue de la Paix, the Técla boutique sold imitation pearls mounted in platinum, as well as in white and yellow gold; reproduction sapphires, emeralds and rubies were set with real diamonds. The very terminology used to describe different categories of jewelry could be baffling. *Joaillerie* was lavishly set with precious gems as well as semi-precious and imitation stones. Metals predominated in *bijouterie*—not only gold and platinum, but also gilt, silvered and electroplated alloys, with ornamentation ranging from coral, agate and jet, to natural pearls. Gold featured prominently, though not exclusively, in *orfèvrerie*. Bibelots and clocks might sometimes qualify as *joaillerie,* while revivalist jewels in the archaeological manner were classed as *bijouterie*.

Toc was fashionable slang for *faux* jewelry. "What could be more disdainful than this little word which sounds like a fillip—*toc*! And now, today, the word is dead, killed by the *bijou de fantaisie*. The old superstitions connected to precious stones have been forgotten: a pearl is just a variety of nacre, a diamond pure crystallized carbon, ruby an aluminate of magnesium, and all the warm light of garnets is contained in the formula $3R''O,R_2'''O_3,3SiO_2$. What do you care, after all, if some variations have been made to this formula, if there is a little more manganese, or less chromium?"

Bijouterie de fantaisie, a term introduced at the 1900 International Exposition, did not apply to the cheap copies which had long been

merchandised by *bijoutiers-faussetiers*, but to original designs in a variety of materials. In conversation, costume jewels were often still referred to as *bijoux de théâtre*, because of their similarity to flashy theater accessories. Sarah Bernhardt's spectacular hoard of jewelry, which she flaunted both on and off stage, spawned countless imitations throughout her career. Of the estate sale held after Bernhardt's death in 1923, a gemologist wrote disdainfully that "a glittering curtain of gems has just fallen on the last act of the life of the famous *tragédienne*, and an idolatrous public has driven bids up at an auction where rings, earrings, necklaces, queens' crowns and empresses' diadems cast their last hypocritical flares." Many pieces, notably those invented by the Art Nouveau designer Lalique, would not be regarded today as costume jewelry. They were "the refulgent gems of Cleopatra, of the Distant Princess, of Theodora, of Tosca, the Aiglon's Austrian decorations, Fedora's tiara encrusted with turquoises and various stones."

When Chanel moved from the provinces to Paris just before the First World War, she was refreshingly ignorant about jewelry. Mistaking a pearl frontlet presented to her by an admirer for an ill-fitting choker, she asked him indignantly where on earth he had bought it. She misunderstood his answer, and assumed he had purchased the offending trinket at some shop in the neighborhood, the *quartier*: she had never heard of Cartier. Later Chanel learned to recognize, and to scoff at Cartier's delicate, airy designs: "A jewel should not be meager."

Grand Duke Dmitri furthered her education, smothering her with what remained to him of the heavy chains, bejeweled crucifixes, and emerald parures that had been fashionable at the Romanov court. His successor in her affections, the fabulously wealthy Duke of Westminster (in Sacheverell Sitwell's opinion, the "nearest one will ever get to Henry VIII"), could afford to be even more generous. Chanel's own jewels soon formed a startlingly opulent contrast to the streamlined, sporty style she pioneered. Sharing a train compartment with her, Bettina Ballard was staggered and thrilled by the bounty that tumbled out of the "sausage bag" in which the *couturière* stowed her jewelry: "a great jumble of strings and strings of real pearls, necklaces of mixed rubies, emeralds, diamonds and pearls. There was every type and color of earring. There were wonderful strings of ruby beads, a fifteen-strand necklace of small rubies that was twisted like a rope, precious diamond and ruby and emerald bracelets. I don't remember any straight diamond pieces—color pervaded everything, except the strings and strings of pearls which came in every length and every size."

The financial worth of her jewels was a matter of indifference to Chanel, who refused to insure them, sometimes lost them, even tossed them into the sea out of pique. The only piece she was sentimental about was a topaz and gold pinkie ring, a souvenir of her liaison with Balsan that she wore at all times. "There is nothing prettier than the gilded waters of a topaz," she would repeat, and often highlighted her fashions with a topaz clip or buckle.

Etienne de Beaumont's line of costume jewelry, which Fulco was to develop, mirrored the diversity of Chanel's personal collection. There were triple strands of red, green, and yellow beads; necklaces of variegated Murano glass, of coral, of turquoise, and wood; paste diamond dog-collars and *lavallières*; ropes of rock crystal disks and rhinestone balls interspersed with *faux* engraved emeralds, rubies and turquoises; grooved melon-shaped beads alternating with irregular variegated baubles; and cascades of *perlouse*—imitation pearls—garnished with ruby and emerald clusters. This kaleidoscopic medley gave Chanel's *bijouterie* a jaunty, yet extravagant character. Finish and setting were equally important. Stones were mounted without backing to achieve maximum translucency; and thanks to a special patina, golden chains, though "ancient in design,[were] modern in appearance." Most items were produced by the Gripoix firm, which had been active for several decades, progressing from the manufacture of buttons to the concoction of secret recipes for pearlizing *pâte de verre*.

Beaumont was not alone in composing jewels for Chanel; he was occasionally assisted by two internationally renowned arbiters of taste, Sybil Colefax and Elsie de Wolfe. Although ridiculed for her frilly, historically incorrect 'Old French Look', the American decorator had developed a sophisticated eye for exquisite *objets de vertu* which influenced her taste in jewelry. For a brief spell, the artistically inclined Countess d'Harcourt also belonged to the Beaumont jewelry circle, but she soon wearied of the routine. "It's always beads on a piece of string," she would sigh. "So boring."

Misia Sert was Beaumont's closest associate: "the queen of modern baroque, who based her whole life on the bizarre." Born in Saint Petersburg in 1872 of a Polish father and a Russo-Belgian mother, Misia Sophia Olga Zenaida Godebska had been married to Thadée Natanson, the publisher of *La Revue blanche*, then to the magnate Alfred Edwards, before winning—temporarily—the heart and hand of the voluble Catalan muralist, José Maria Sert. The quintessential *Belle Epoque* muse, Misia's portrait was painted by Bonnard, Lautrec, Vuillard, Vallotton, and Renoir, who pleaded in vain for her to unveil her ample charms. A gifted pianist, she had played for Liszt, Fauré, Grieg, Debussy, and Ravel. Misia was recognized to be the model not only for the socially ambitious Madame Verdurin, but also for the open-handed Princess Yourbeletieff in Proust's *Remembrance of Things Past*; Diaghilev and Stravinsky, among others, depended on her financial and emotional support. When Chanel was ignored by the *beau monde*, Misia won her lifelong friendship (not untinged with resentment) by staunchly facing down those who excluded her from their guest lists. "For me," Misia maintained, "there have always been kings, artists and then those who were neither one nor the other."

A pair of golden sapphire and diamond cluster earclips brilliantly illustrates Verdura's passion for using colored stones.

Endowed with "magically lucid hands," Misia had a flair for camp decor. In the sombre hispano-italo-Napoleonic ambience of her Left Bank flat glinted mother-of-pearl shells, hardstone flowers, and the miniature oriental trees that were her speciality. Carved out of quartz, jade and coral, the branches were embellished with feathery fronds and pearly berries. Misia was incomparable in so many ways that it seemed to her contemporaries she could only have come into existence through spontaneous generation.

Chanel also enjoyed creating real jewelry for herself. In particular, she loved the challenge of remounting gems pried loose from pieces of which she had tired. "She would use either genuine or imitation stones, taking into account only their overall effect in the design. She possessed magnificent emeralds and the loveliest and the rarest rubies, but she was just as fond of pink Siamese rubies and pale sapphires from Ceylon, which were of no great value." Surrounded by rows of little bowls and boxes brimming with brightly hued chips, Chanel taught Fulco to mould mounts in soft putty, and to play with the stones, until the right balance of form and color was attained.

Jewelry design was in transition in the late Twenties. At the 1925 Exhibition of Decorative Arts in Paris, large flat pieces had been all the rage, particularly brooches and pendants that served as focal elements of costume. Only a few years later, however, the hard-edged elegance of Art Déco was already on the wane. During the summer of 1929, the Palais Galliéra costume museum held a show devoted to *Le bijou et la joaillerie moderne*. Curated by Georges Fouquet, who was also an exhibitor, it featured creations by leading Parisian firms—Ostertag, Lacloche, Mauboussin, Boucheron, Van Cleef & Arpels, Chaumet. Although some designs still reflected the frigid "beauty of a geometrical theorem," a subtle change could be discerned. The "great white silence" of diamonds, pearls, and platinum was shattered by touches of color—not only that of emeralds, sapphires and rubies, but of the semi-precious stones that had been gaining in favor. "The character of contemporary life is speed," Fouquet pronounced. "It is necessary that the composition of a jewel be grasped instantly, and therefore it must be conceived along simple lines, without any finicky, superfluous detail." Sharper relief was also desirable, to avoid the undifferentiated uniformity reminiscent of a "company badge."

Fulco's first works for Chanel were broad, colorful and curvaceous, but without the full-blown sculptural quality of his later designs. The petals of a stylized yellow gold blossom brooch were encrusted with a rectangular-cut blue sapphire, circular and oval-cut green tourmalines, blue sapphires, citrines, garnets, aquamarines, yellow orthoclase feldspar, rock crystal, pink tourmalines, and pink sapphires. The seemingly random placement of the stones and the suggestion of depth through shading were to remain constants in Verdura's oeuvre.

Opposite A 540-carat golden sapphire 'bib' necklace with diamonds.

Many of the jewels he made for Chanel were copied in semi- and non-precious materials for her boutique—after she had been widely photographed in the fashion press wearing the originals. "Father would become distraught whenever Chanel left her jewelry with him," according to Josette Gripoix. "He'd have to store it in the safe." One of Chanel's most effective marketing strategies—which proved highly successful in launching her scents—consisted in feigning that certain creations were intended to remain her exclusive property, and then allowing herself to be persuaded to share them with a privileged few. Fulco's rainbow-hued pieces were a phenomenal success, embodying the voluptuous aura of luxury that was synonymous with the name of Chanel. "The little, narrow rue Cambon is a glittering river of discreetly expensive cars," a British journalist gushed. "One hundred yards from the door you are greeted by a wave of sweet, exotic perfume, which accompanies you through the forest of showcases in the entrance hall dripping with necklaces, bracelets, jewels of every colour, up the glass-walled staircase into the great salons."

Decoration-style pins were one of his earliest signature designs, "wonderful medals that looked like *croix-de-guerre* in gold, studded with semi-precious stones that were on all the Chanel suits." Since the war, fascination with awards and insignia had been on the increase. In 1919, *bijoutiers* were crafting brooches modeled after the Order of the Holy Spirit, as well as hefty silver and gold pendants "of a primitive effect" that were more attractive than "delicate jewels" on serge suits and dresses. A history enthusiast, Fulco had become well-acquainted with the holdings of the Musée de la Légion d'Honneur et des Ordres de Chevalerie since its inauguration in 1925. The sparkling arrays of heraldic decorations and military honors from every nation and epoch impressed him more than the bloodless refinement of *haute joaillerie*. Another event that fired his imagination was the 1929 Bibliothèque Nationale show of memorabilia relating to the Sovereign and Military Order of the Knights Hospitaller of St John of Jerusalem. The aristocratic Catholic confraternity was founded in the eleventh century to succor pilgrims in the Holy Land; its members became known as the Knights of Malta after establishing headquarters on the island several centuries later and adopting the distinctive crimson Maltese cross as their symbol. Fulco transformed the cross into an emphatic, eye-catching motif by accentuating its contours and scattering cabochons over its flared, arrowhead extremities. Soon gilt Maltese crosses shone on Chanel belts, lapels, jabots and hat-bands; over the decades, they came to be recognized as a Verdura trademark.

News of the Wall Street Crash on 29 October 1929 produced panic reactions in Paris. "Farewell then. That is what I must say to luxury, to the superfluous, and to myself," was the bleak reaction of one of Chanel's entourage. Although the luxury trades had in fact been losing money steadily over recent years, the most devastating effects of the

A portrait by Horst of Verdura in his
Paris apartment, 1930.

Depression were not felt immediately. By 1932, however, the lucrative
American garment market had been wiped out, due to a 90 per cent duty
levied on finished imports. French silk exports dropped by three-
quarters, woollens by two-thirds; scents and jewelry registered a 50 per
cent decrease. If in the aftermath of Black Tuesday prospects appeared
uncertain in Paris, they were dire in Palermo. The fortune of the Florios,
Sicily's passport into the twentieth century, had collapsed. Ironically,
proof of the family's destitution now hung for all to view in the Paris
residence of Maurice de Rothschild: in 1928 he had acquired Boldini's
portrait of Donna Franca, draped in imitation pearls, from her debt-
ridden husband.

     As for Fulco, he was comfortably ensconced in a flat in the rue de
Berri off the Champs-Elysées, not far from the residence of another
Italian designer, Elsa Schiaparelli. In a photograph by Horst, Fulco is
portrayed—suavely wreathed in cigarette smoke—in his booklined
sitting-room. Bibliophilia was one of the passions he shared with Chanel.
"I learned life from books," she would say. "If I had had daughters, I
would have given them novels for their entire education." Fulco enrolled
in drawing classes with Princess Marina of Greece, and went antiquing
with Nicky de Gunzburg, Elsie de Wolfe, and Syrie Maugham. There

Opposite A sautoir of seed pearls and diamonds.

were skiing holidays in Sestriere, the Alpine resort constructed by the industrialist Senator Edoardo Agnelli to compete with Saint Moritz and Cortina. There was a winter cruise to South Africa in the company of the Prince of Wales, who mercilessly forced everyone on board to sing and dance along to his favorite hit, Vivian Ellis's "The Sun Has Put His Hat On." Long afterwards, Fulco dined out on imitations of the little royal jig that accompanied the ditty.

Amazingly, 1930 was destined to be remembered "as the greatest fancy-dress ball season of all years. Masquerades were given which in other centuries might have made their way into memoirs but which will now probably only land in light literature," according to *The New Yorker*'s Paris correspondent Janet Flanner. For a 'Celebrities Ball' given by Elsa Maxwell and Daisy Fellowes, Chanel mischievously disguised a bevy of svelte dandies as famous Parisian beauties. Another Maxwell party, with a 'Come as You Are' theme, predictably attracted guests in various risqué or comical stages of undress. Four Rothschild dances were given within a single week that was referred to as *la Semaine Sainte*.

The giddy social whirl continued through the following year, although a studied lack of ceremony was now the keynote. Buffets, cocktails and 'conversation parties' replaced formal banquets and dances; afternoon dresses were worn more often than evening gowns. Fulco continued to be seen lunching at the Ritz, dining at the most exclusive Russian bistrots and Harlem *boîtes*. He was an habitué of Bricktop's new cabaret, where Hoyningen-Huene installed revolutionary lighting that "after midnight will be becoming to middle-aged people who are slightly under the influence of liquor."

London remained a frequent destination for Fulco, as he had been given his own apartment in a lodge on the grounds of Wimborne House. He was starting to tire of the pompous grandeur of Alice's life style, and after dark would clamber discreetly out of a ground-floor window to meet up with a lively young band that included Evelyn Waugh and Diana and Duff Cooper, or to crawl Soho pubs with Tallulah Bankhead. Fulco's irrepressible, brittle wit also contributed to the cooling of his romance. When a country house fire in Hampshire claimed the life of the young Duc de la Trémoille, as well as that of Alice's nephew, Fulco recalled Joan of Arc's prediction at the stake that the last descendant of her Trémoille persecutor would perish by fire, and triumphantly concluded: "So she *was* a witch after all!"

A snapshot of Tallulah Bankhead, right, partying with Fulco at El Morocco.

There were relaxed beach holidays with the 'Côte Crowd'—Sitwells, Guinnesses, Boothbys, Mosleys, and Trefussises—with countless children's games. A photographer caught Fulco, Louis Mountbatten, Cecil Beaton, and Elsie de Wolfe tumbling to the ground after a dizzy bout of ring-a-ring-o'roses by the pool at Edward Molyneux's Cap d'Ail villa, La Capponcina. Fulco was a regular guest at La Pausa, the monastic retreat situated high above Cap Martin amidst gnarled olive trees, orange groves and drifts of lavender, for which Chanel had paid an exorbitant price. At her request, he would do the honors of the house, always marveling pointedly: "What genius to have spent all that money without its showing!" Intentionally backhanded or not, it was the compliment Chanel preferred.

Etienne de Beaumont's Colonial Ball, with sultry entertainment by Josephine Baker, was the peak of the 1931 season. Chanel attended in the garb of Cocteau's unlucky mariner, Pas de Chance; Iya Abdy was disguised as a Siamese goddess, Princess Colonna as a grass-skirted Hawaiian. Fulco, Baba, and Natalie performed a "Cambodian dance in all points worthy of professionals" expressly choreographed for the trio by Lifar. The exotic attire was inspired by the Colonial Exhibition, a Disneylandish celebration of European overseas possessions—from Danish Greenland to Italian Somaliland. In the suburban Bois de Vincennes fairgrounds, the temples of Angkor Wat and Septimius Severus at Leptis Magna stood side by side, and Algerian mosques towered over Tahitian huts. Despite the inexplicable disapproval of Surrealist agitators, who distributed pamphlets entitled *Don't Visit the Colonial Exhibition*, over a six-month period the gaudy theme park drew thirty million visitors—including the cream of Parisian *bijoutiers* and *joailliers*. The displays of Oriental and tribal artefacts inspired the novel *style sauvage*, based on the stylized shapes of non-Western adornment and body sculpture.

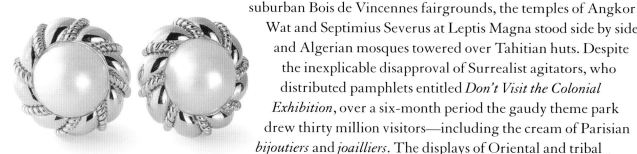

Two pairs of mabé pearl and diamond earclips.

Opposite Chanel, photographed by Cecil Beaton in 1937, at her most enigmatic. She is seen here sporting two of Verdura's Maltese cross cuff bracelets.

Unlike his confrères, Fulco was absorbed by a show of Byzantine art that ran for just five weeks at the Musée des Arts Décoratifs, with over seven hundred pieces on loan from major international museums and private collectors, such as Joseph Duveen, Otto Kahn and R.W. Bliss. Ranging from the fourth through the twelfth centuries, the magnificent exhibits included Late Antique diadems, earrings and bangles, Merovingian fibulae, Carolingian liturgical vessels, reliquaries and book covers enriched with semi-precious cabochons, painted ivories, gold and silver pectoral crosses. Openwork mounts, patterned after Byzantine *opus interrasile* (pierced work), start to appear in Fulco's jewelry at this time. Long barpins are embellished with elaborate formations of open-set oval cabochons and cushion- and emerald-cut stones. Irregular designs become increasingly frequent: in a curved lozenge-shaped brooch, a row of three simulated emeralds—oval, cushion-cut and *pendeloque*—is

framed by five smaller rectangular and oval green glass stones. Massive quadrilobate pins and brooches with pendant pearls are reminiscent of the clasps and pectoral ornaments in the sixth-century mosaics of the Church of San Vitale in Ravenna, which represent the Emperor Justinian and his consort Theodora in full regalia.

Abruptly, with the instinctive perversity that was an essential ingredient of the *couturière*'s personality, enabling her to keep one step ahead of fashion, Chanel changed course. In 1932, the champion of *faux* surprised the world by accepting the invitation of the International Guild of Diamond Merchants to create a collection of diamond jewelry. At the height of the spendthrift *années folles*, Chanel had promoted costume jewelry because it was "bereft of arrogance in an age of facile splendour." Now, in response to Depression-era conservatism, she endorsed brilliants as having "the greatest value in the smallest volume." In any case, she noted ambiguously, "nothing so much resembles a fake jewel as a very fine real jewel."

Chanel's creations were sensationally presented on lifelike painted wax busts surmounting black marble columns that were draped in furs. The principal motifs were old-fashioned bowknots, feathers, and stars. "I wanted to cover women with constellations, with stars! Stars of all shapes and sizes to sparkle in their hair, tassels and crescent moons," she exclaimed. "See these comets, their heads resting on a woman's shoulder, their shimmering tails slipping behind the shoulders to fall in a shower of stars on the breast." Because of their unusually flexible construction, Chanel's jewels felt "like ribbons on women's fingers." Another trait was versatility, since most pieces could be dismantled and re-combined in various ways—necklaces might be broken down into bracelets and clips, earrings linked to form impressive brooches.

Chanel's chief navigator in this firmament of brilliants was her lover, Paul Iribarnegaray, called Iribe, an exceptionally gifted designer of Basque origin. He burst onto the Paris scene in 1901, a precocious seventeen-year-old armed only with pen, ink, and cheek—and proceeded to leave his mark on almost every aspect of French style. He was a ruthless political caricaturist, as well as a fashion illustrator whose fluid draughtsmanship recalled that of Beardsley and Erté. The stark originality of Iribe's furniture and interior decors captivated Jacques Doucet, the most discriminating of connoisseurs. His publicity campaigns for Nicolas wines, Wagons Lits, Citroën, Peugeot, and Ford made advertizing history. In a 1931 photography contest, Iribe was ranked above Man Ray, the Baron de Meyer, and Hoyningen-Huene. As early as 1912, Iribe was hailed as a "Lord of the Thousand and One Nights, with the power to make everything he touches original and seductive." By the Twenties, he had emigrated to New York, where he easily determined that "the worst enemy of the United States is bad taste." He was scouted by Jesse Lasky for Paramount, and spirited off to Hollywood where he created sets for *The Ten Commandments* and *King of Kings*. Although the grandeur of his vision rivaled that of Cecil B. De Mille, Iribe's insistence on complete historical accuracy drove the director to distraction. He was soon back in Paris, accompanied by a rich but cumbersome American wife.

Iribe's defence of the French luxury trades was fierce, sometimes to the point of absurdity: "Luxury is a need that starts when necessity ends." He called for the Elite and Labor to unite against the three scourges of modernity: Machinism, Internationalism, and Standardism. The inventor of the famous Iribe Rose (successively adapted for the perfumer Lubin, the jewelers Cartier and Linzeler, the designer Poiret and the Bianchini-Férier silk manufactory) would thunder rhetorically: "Are we going to sacrifice the flower on the altar of the cube?"

Two pairs of 'Byzantine' earclips, set with pink tourmalines and amethysts.

The impact of Iribe's "modern baroque" was nowhere more evident than in jewelry design. In a review of the watershed 1925 Decorative Arts exhibition, *Vogue* perceived his influence—generally unacknowledged—in the widespread use of large gems and the painterly juxtaposition of translucent and opaque stones. The embossed plates of his album *Choix* showed huge stone pendants in slender gold tendrils, together with the shooting star motif that he was to adapt for Chanel. At the diamond show, there was a single splash of color to suggest the chromatic fancy that had until then been Chanel's hallmark: a decoration-style brooch in the form of a radiant sun, with rare canary diamonds mounted in yellow gold. Yet this one piece—rather than the chill Hollywood glamor of Iribe's white jewels—set the tone for what was to come. By 1933, a veritable gold rush was on, coupled with a fresh appreciation of bright-hued precious gems, as well as semi-precious stones "whose cost was inferior to their beauty": aquamarines, tourmalines, amethysts, jade, and topazes. Jewelry of "weighty sumptuousness, Byzantine opulence and erudite barbarism" had returned to favor. The consensus was that a jewel should be valued not as an investment but above all as a work of art.

Fulco's designs of this period display higher and more intricate relief, thanks to raised collet settings reminiscent of the polychrome inlay of early Germanic jewelry. On their travels, Fulco and Chanel visited the cathedral treasury at Aix-la-Chapelle; they examined royal jewels and trophies, and late medieval church ornaments preserved at the Munich Schatzkammer. The massive mounts and simple yet arresting color contrasts of other pieces betray the influence of Mannerist gems *en trompe l'oeil* bordering the pages of rare illuminated manuscripts preserved at Palazzo Verdura: red cabochons in blue and gold settings, and green and blue lozenges in gold and pearl frames. Fulco's designs are also indebted to the revivalist manner of Louis Wièse, a jeweler of German origin who was active in Paris until his death in 1923.

"The modern idea in jewelry" was summarized in *Vogue:* "We are now witnessing a revival of 'real' jewels in contrast with the fashion for synthetic stones of a few years ago. Much of the new jewelry is reminiscent in its large solidity of the ornaments of our grandmothers, and many of the semi-precious stones popular in the late Victorian period have also reappeared. But the designs into which they are set are distinctly of our age and reflect the current liking for simple austere shapes which depend for interest on colour contrast and the juxtaposition of unusual textures. The fashion of setting sparkling jewels of real value, such as diamonds, sapphires and aquamarines into a solid bed of such semi-precious stones as chalcedony, lapis lazuli and crystal, is one which has led to unusual results and a number of colour harmonies hitherto unknown to jewelry. Many of the whims of the day, shells straight from the paintings of Pierre Roy, stars dropped from a ballet backcloth, tiny gold wings from an imaginary Mercury, find themselves rendered in pearls, diamonds and a dozen other gems, and transformed into clips, ear-rings (which are also clips and do not pierce the lobe of the ear) and clasps. The brooch is rivaled, though by no means replaced, by clips of every variety, the bracelet of solid structure is gradually becoming a serious rival to the hinged and supple band of individual stones which for years has been the only ornament for the arm, and necklaces, so long neglected, are back once more."

Illustrating the article is a shield-shaped gold clip by Fulco, belonging to Elsie de Wolfe, that is described as "a jewel for wearing with sports clothes." Partially open-worked, it displays an important emerald-cut central gem surrounded by several rows of smaller square, rectangular and oval stones. Similar pieces were lasting favorites with Chanel, who wore them in pairs at her neckline. A set for Maria Felice, consisting of fan-shaped earclips and an oval brooch with a cruciform motif, has variously cut emeralds, citrines, diamonds, and sapphires mounted in gold pierced work. Inexpensive versions of such creations appeared in Chanel's Spring 1934 collection, "bracelets and earrings of barbarian inspiration, treated with a gold base and colored stones."

Fulco was now publicly recognized as Chanel's principal jewelry designer. "At the annual opening of the Ambassadeurs restaurant, a gala occasion also, the Princess Jean-Louis de Faucigny Lucinge wore gold sandals matching her gold sequined Lelong dress. She wears some of Chanel's already famous jewelry, designed by the Duke de la Verdura [*sic*]. The bracelets of heavy gold are sunk with brilliant stones, reminding one of the Byzantine or Merovingian barbaric splendours."

Designers were only just beginning to discover the monetary worth of a name. Chanel was locked in battle with the Wertheimer family who had acquired control of her company ten years earlier. A careless business deal depriving Paul Poiret of the right to his own name had reduced him to penury: one morning during the summer of 1934, he strolled into the 9th *arrondissement* town hall and registered for unemployment. The cautionary lesson of the great couturier's debacle was not lost on anyone in the fashion industry.

The time was clearly ripe for Fulco to move out of Chanel's shadow. Although her commitment to the arts was unstinting, many like Jean-Louis de Faucigny-Lucinge had observed that she could be "hard, demanding and not so generous with those who worked for her"—no matter how cozy their personal relations. While Fulco was fond of repeating that Chanel was "so ill-natured that no man would ever have her," it was now rumored that she and Iribe were to marry; if so, the scope of Fulco's activity would be severely limited. A firm of his own was out of the question, since he did not have the means to staff a competitive atelier, or to assemble a stock of top quality gemstones. Paris was full of talented jewelers with conspicuous financial backing, of whom the most prestigious was Jeanne Toussaint, known as *La Panthère* since she introduced the big cat motif to Cartier's *haute joaillerie*.

A total change of scenery, even of profession, seemed to be in order; a career in the movies could not be dismissed as an unlikely or unrealistic choice. "The making of private films has become one of the popular pastimes of French society," according to *Vogue*. The Noailles had financed Buñuel's *L'Age D'or* and Cocteau's *Le Sang d'un Poète*, albeit at the cost of some social ostracism. Chanel herself had recently spent several unhappy though extremely profitable months designing costumes for MGM productions. Nicky de Gunzburg and Natalie Paley were both contemplating acting careers in Hollywood. Although Nicky's employability in the American film industry was a matter of pure conjecture, Natalie's chances of success were strong. After appearing with Charles Boyer in *L'Epervier*, directed by Marcel L'Herbier, she had landed the lead in Jean de Marguenat's *Le Prince Jean*, and now had an offer to star with Maurice Chevalier in Marcel Achard's American production of *L'Homme des Folies-Bergère*. In moving to California, she also hoped to escape the attentions of Cocteau, whose infatuation with her had reached epic proportions. Assuming for himself the advantageous role of Tristan, he compared her to Yseult the Blond—and cast her husband Lelong as the inconvenient King Mark.

Hollywood seemed to beckon Fulco as well. His detailed knowledge of the fine and decorative arts, of fashion and costume, his familiarity with etiquette, diplomatic protocol and aristocratic genealogies, ideally qualified him for the job of technical advisor on the period dramas that were then a studio staple. His love-life was no longer a consideration: Alice Wimborne had just embarked on a serious affair with the composer William Walton. Fulco's final Paris fête was *Nuit à Schönbrunn*, a Waltz Ball evocative of the Habsburg court in Vienna.

A pair of gold brooches, inset with an earlier pair of art déco colored stone clips.

Fulco and Chanel at Nicky de Gunzburg's 'Nuit à Schönbrunn' ball in 1934.

A drawing by Verdura for two ray brooches. Opposite: a jewel of similar design.

Burning the last of his father's inheritance, Nicky de Gunzburg, as the unfortunate Archduke Rudolph, co-hosted the party with the Faucigny-Lucinges who obligingly impersonated his imperial parents, Franz Josef and Elisabeth. The ball was held on the island in the Bois de Boulogne lake, which for the occasion was carpeted down to the water's edge in white velvet, creating the effect of a snowy landscape that magically offset the gorgeous costumes by Bérard, Mainbocher, Lanvin, and Valentine Hugo. Carlos de Beistegui was perfect in pale blue and white ermine as the demented royal aesthete, Ludwig of Bavaria. Elsa Maxwell came as Napoleon III. Fulco, as an officer of the Austro-Hungarian guard, escorted Chanel dressed as the ill-fated Empress Carlotta of Mexico in layers of rustling black taffeta ruffles. Princess Marina of Greece was there, too; and upon learning that a fellow guest hailed from the United States, she enquired simply: "I wonder if you could get me a film test in Hollywood? I'm so tired of being poor." A reporter reacted to the parade of doomed personages: "They are almost all weighed down by a fatal future, these beings with tragic destinies, but never have they been so gay as this evening."

A few days later, Nicky, Fulco, and Natalie left for America.

America is a state of mind, a passion. And any
European may, from one moment to the next,
be stricken by America.
- M. SOLDATI

A 30-carat aquamarine and diamond ray brooch designed by Verdura for Mrs. Henry Fonda, Christmas 1940.

Opposite Nicky de Gunzburg, Mrs. Alistair Mackintosh, Nin Ryan, and Fulco (with arm outstretched) at Palm Beach in 1935.

"THERE WAS NO PAST FOR ME HERE," was Fulco's first, euphoric reaction to the New World when he arrived there in the autumn of 1934: "I didn't have to say 'My God, Venice isn't what it used to be!'" Yet Hollywood proved little more than a dream factory for most of the gorgeous young hopefuls attempting to break into the burgeoning film industry. As the French writer Blaise Cendrars observed at the time, "there's not one in a thousand who will make a name for himself on the screen." A mock price list drawn up by Nunnally Johnson gave a daunting idea of the interest newcomers might hope to elicit. The scriptwriter's "fees" ranged from $20,000 for attending amateur shows of unpublished material, to $100 for meeting "new faces (male)." The charge for "new faces (female)" was a token $1—waived in the event of an encounter behind closed doors.

Natalie Paley's career, though short-lived, held the most promise of stardom. Her performance in *Folies Bergère* led to a role in *Sylvia Scarlett*, alongside Katharine Hepburn and Cary Grant. But after one more film with L'Herbier, she drifted out of the camera's range, returning to the set only in 1948 to advise Alexander Korda on tsarist manners and mores in *Anna Karenina*. Never professionally driven or desperate to impress, Nicky de Gunzburg was even less fortunate. On a brief visit, Horst found him "just being his elegant, ironical, imperturbable, sympathetic self, vaguely pursuing the success that many of his friends believed should have been his, but never really came his way in the New World." One of his most memorable stage appearances was in a drawing-room comedy; acting with his back to the audience, his interpretation was so understated as to be utterly inaudible.

Fulco was discovering that, while the White Russian aristocracy enjoyed some cinematic prestige, the studios attached no value—financial or otherwise—to a Sicilian, albeit of noble birth. At the time, prejudice against immigrants from Italy in general, and Southern Italy in particular, was running high. An honorary Frenchman by virtue of his Paris connections, Fulco—as the Duc de Verdura—joined the expatriate *bohème* at the Garden of Allah on Sunset Boulevard, formerly the home of the actress Alla Nazimova. Converted into a hotel, it represented "a small corner of France" for residents such as Marcel Achard and Annabella. Although Fulco did not lack for American friends—notably Tallulah Bankhead and Anita Loos—California began to seem desperately remote from his former existence: no theaters, no cafés, no

teeming street life. After months of waiting, Fulco's expectation of designing "clothes and things" for the movies evaporated: "Nothing happened, absolutely nothing." Verdura's fame as a jeweler had not yet reached the West Coast, where socially insecure actors and impresarios preferred the reassurance of an instantly recognizable Cartier or Van Cleef hallmark.

There was no option but retreat to New York, where Fulco's international fashion experience counted as a marketable commodity. Diana Vreeland, who was one of Chanel's most stylish clients, introduced him to Paul Flato. A personable Texan just a year younger than Fulco, Flato had dropped out of Columbia University to go into the jewelry business in 1928; he was already famous for ice-cube solitaires and 'letter' jewels that spelled out a name, date, or droll message. Flato's flair for self-promotion was sensational, even for the United States. He had debutantes model his collections in exclusive shows held at the Ritz-Carlton, he invited customers to bring in their pets to be portrayed in jewelry, he wrote his own flamboyant advertising copy. One typically compelling vignette read: "It is indeed gratifying to have your dearest friend *or* fondest enemy rush up, exclaiming, 'Darling! Where did you get that *perfectly marvelous, amazing* new clip?' And it is even more gratifying to be able to answer, 'Oh, my dear, it's one of Paul Flato's new designs!'" The only thing Flato did not do was render his own pieces. "I don't know how to draw a line," he explained with aplomb. "I am a creator of jewels and guide my designers."

The team working under Flato's supervision at 1 East 57th Street was second to none. Chief designer Adolph Kleaty's forte was 'drippy' jewelry, shop talk for elaborate diamond and platinum pieces. George

Jean Howard, Paul Flato, and Fulco at the opening of Flato's Hollywood salon on Sunset Boulevard, 1937.

Headley, who had trained at the New York Art Students League as well as the Ecole des Beaux-arts in Paris, specialized in gold jewels and *objets*. He later married Barbara Whitney, whose mother Gertrude had founded the Whitney Museum of American Art in New York. In 1968 the couple established their own Headley-Whitney Museum in Lexington, Kentucky, as a showcase for their art and jewelry collections. A couple of celebrity designers were responsible for the fanciful trinkets Flato called 'whimsies'. 'Fat' or 'puffy' hearts set with colored stones were the signature of the Standard Oil heiress Millicent Rogers, who worked closely with Headley before she developed into an accomplished jeweler in her own right. Her pieces, reflecting the opulence of pre-Columbian artefacts, are now on display in the Millicent Rogers Museum in Taos, New Mexico. Josephine Forrestal, the wife of FDR's future Secretary of the Navy, was known for 'wiggly clips', *tremblant* floral sprays. She also had a hand in

A sapphire and diamond Maltese cross brooch, designed *c.* 1950.

introducing the curb chain to Flato's repertory: he copied in gold a flat-linked silver bracelet she had picked up as a souvenir during a trip to Europe.

It was Kleaty who gave Fulco his first real instruction in rendering, and soon his vaporous draughtsmanship *à la française* acquired a keener edge. A number of his sketches, some initialed F.V., have survived among the drawings in Flato's albums. Fulco's ideas appeared "very modern" to Flato, who admired above all his cigarette and vanity cases; both men shared a penchant for highly defined, sculptural forms and a willingness to seek inspiration in unexpected quarters.

At the end of 1935, despite the congeniality of Flato's entourage, Fulco was contemplating a return to rue Cambon. After Iribe's sudden death that September, Chanel appealed to Fulco to help continue her jewelry line. By the following Spring, back in Paris, he had obliged her with one of his most durably popular designs: a pair of *bombé* enamel bracelets decorated with gold Maltese crosses set with bright cabochons. Bettina Ballard remembered being bedazzled by these novel creations during an Easter trip south with the *couturière*. Predictably, just a year later, the boutique version was being billed on both sides of the Atlantic as the accessory of choice for every outfit—from rough woolen cardigans and flannel trousers to crimson silk dinner suits to black lace evening gowns. Touting the "massive white lacquer bracelets studded with colored stones" in September 1937, *Harper's Bazaar* wrote approvingly of a look in which "not a stone, not a setting, not a color match. So the effect is that of a gypsies' tinsels, wild, profligate, unrestrained. No combination is too fantastic."

Verdura's sources were eclectic. Paired bracelets had been fashionable at various times; during the last quarter of the nineteenth century, the effect of scalloped gold cuffs was achieved with tapering *manchettes.* Inspiration also came from the Twenties fad for wide ivory

hoops worn several to each arm, launched by the social eccentric Nancy
Cunard. Gold-studded ivory pennanular bangles by Boivin were all the
rage at the time of the 1931 Colonial Exhibition. Verdura's hinged
originals featured a translucent white enamel over a warm gold base.
This subtle effect was borrowed from the work of the goldsmith Johann
Melchior Dinglinger (1664–1731), which he had admired at the Dresden
Grüne Gewölbe (Green Vaults). In subsequent variants of the cufflets,
stones were collet-set in straight rows or arranged in floral and star
patterns on a dark ground. Less expensive boutique reproductions were
crafted in tinted bakelite with simulated rubies, emeralds, and diamonds
in gilt or gray metal settings.

Chanel loved her bracelets—they turn up in sketches by Bérard
and Cocteau, in portrait photographs by Beaton, Horst, and Man Ray,
and in countless candid snapshots for years thereafter. Despite this coup,
Fulco was not tempted to linger in France. In May 1936, a coalition of
Radicals, Socialists and Communists had come to power, and the political
climate was deteriorating: there was unrest not only among automotive
and construction workers, but also employees in the luxury industries.
That summer Abbé Mugnier, the astute confessor to the *beau monde*,
recorded worriedly in his diary: "Continuation of the strikes, some dying
down, others starting up. Anxiety. The red flag is shown here and there.
The new legislators are making haste. All this does not smell good."

Prospects were rosier in the United States. Fulco saw that there
might be an opportunity to build up a transatlantic business, as Arnold
Ostertag had done, by catering to the seasonal clientele in Florida,
Cannes, Deauville and Biarritz, while keeping footholds in Paris, Los
Angeles and New York. Verdura's name and talent had begun to
circulate not merely in a circle of intimates, but in the fashion world at
large. Although he was freelancing, the magazines were quick to credit
"a new clip with a sense of humor, a rearing sea-horse studded with
topazes, nice for the red-headed" as "Verdura for Flato." Reminiscent of
the hybrid hippocamp depicted in Renaissance jewels, it is one of the
many marine motifs that were to constitute a dominant theme in
Verdura's art.

Verdura's next piece—his first major American commission—
was to become "the most talked-of bauble" in New York, according to
Vogue. On 29 October 1936, Cole Porter's musical *Red, Hot and Blue*
opened at the Alvin Theater, with Ethel Merman belting out "It's De-
Lovely," and Bob Hope in his Broadway debut. It was Linda's custom to
mark a première by giving Cole an inscribed cigarette case; in this
instance, it was a gold box by Cartier. But Cole trumped her with a
masterpiece by Verdura: a square platinum case with a detachable round
and baguette diamond starburst that could be worn separately as a
brooch. Pavéd with faceted rubies and sapphires, the ground is scattered
with small diamond stars; inlaid gold stars adorn the sides and bottom. Its

Opposite A pair of cocholong cuff
bracelets inset with gold, colored
stone and diamond Maltese crosses.

Verdura's design for a cigarette case that was presented at the première of Cole Porter's 1936 show, *Red Hot and Blue*. (The diamond ray motif in the center detaches to be worn as a brooch.)

general design and color scheme are reminiscent of a Chanel box of the same period, probably also by Verdura, set with rubies and white and blue sapphires. However, the starburst in high relief on the Porter case is an imaginative improvement over the flat, rectilinear motif on the French piece. Flato considered the box to be Verdura's best ever, and priced it at $10,000, with half the profit going to Fulco. This spectacular object, always on show in the Porter flat at the Waldorf-Astoria, embodied emphatically, yet effortlessly, the big-time glamor and romance of the era.

In jewelry, big was becoming increasingly synonymous with beautiful. Although a few critics like *The New Yorker*'s complained about brooches "as wide as two axe handles" and pieces that Mae West would find "downright vulgar," most fashion journalists were adamant: "We've said it before, but we say it again (it's one of those great verities that bear repeating), nothing strikes such a false note in this day and age as dinky, small-fry jewels. A wan string of molecule pearls, insignificant clips and bracelets—they count for precious little now. The Real Thing is enormous, entertaining ornamental, personal and witty—flora and fauna immortalized, sea-lions, nails, thistles, toadstools, grapes, roses, chrysanthemums. The road to glitter in 1937 is paved with huge and humorous jewels." A diamond and sapphire bracelet in the shape of a sailor's bowknot, by the Duc de Verdura at Paul Flato's for Mrs. William Ladd, was designated by *Vogue* as just such a fabulous Real Thing.

Flato's jewelry was irresistibly attractive to show people: not only did it look rich, it photographed magnificently, even from a distance. No wonder Flato achieved more screen credits than any other jeweler before the demise of his firm in 1942 when, despite protestations of innocence, he was sentenced to two years in Sing Sing for pawning customers' gems. By 1938 Flato's movie clientele claimed so much of his attention that he opened a shop in Los Angeles. Located on Sunset Boulevard, this architectural marvel was a blend of "Egyptian monumentality, Babylonian splendor and Greek subtlety of balance." The *vernissage* was hosted by Constance Collier, Flato's august Hollywood 'sponsor', whose first film had been D. W. Griffith's *Intolerance* (1916) and who had recently appeared in *Stage Door* with Katharine Hepburn and Ginger Rogers. Fulco was on hand to greet guests from the Old World—including *l'Italienne*, Chanel's hated rival Schiaparelli. Flato jewels, with their madcap brand of sophistication, complemented her bizarre, Surrealist fashions. Among Schiap's purchases was a cactus brooch by Verdura—his flippant response to the cloying Flower Style in favor during the late Thirties.

Opposite A *Vogue* advertisement for a Verdura dolphin clip, and a clip of similar design made with pink tourmalines, diamonds and a baroque pearl. Bottom: a black opal, pearl and diamond Naiad clip.

DOLPHIN CLIP
*Chased gold with pink
rubies and diamonds.*

VERDURA
incorporated
SEVEN TWELVE FIFTH AVENUE
NEW YORK

NAIAD CLIP
*Jewelled with opal, pearls
and diamonds. $2500.*
Federal tax included

VERDURA
incorporated
SEVEN TWELVE FIFTH AVENUE
NEW YORK

Nature was an endless source of inspiration for Verdura. These drawings depict a pomegranate brooch of rubies and peridots, and an eggplant brooch comprising a large cabochon amethyst with small faceted rubies and diamonds.

Above Verdura's drawing for a blue chalcedony, diamond and ruby bleeding heart brooch designed for Joan Crawford in 1940.

Right Joan Crawford wearing Verdura's ruby and diamond three part cornice brooch.

Opposite Greta Garbo wearing her Verdura watch bracelet, 1941.

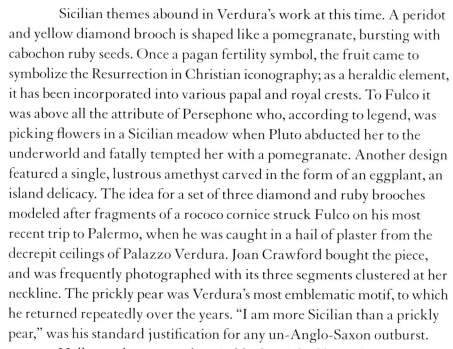

Sicilian themes abound in Verdura's work at this time. A peridot and yellow diamond brooch is shaped like a pomegranate, bursting with cabochon ruby seeds. Once a pagan fertility symbol, the fruit came to symbolize the Resurrection in Christian iconography; as a heraldic element, it has been incorporated into various papal and royal crests. To Fulco it was above all the attribute of Persephone who, according to legend, was picking flowers in a Sicilian meadow when Pluto abducted her to the underworld and fatally tempted her with a pomegranate. Another design featured a single, lustrous amethyst carved in the form of an eggplant, an island delicacy. The idea for a set of three diamond and ruby brooches modeled after fragments of a rococo cornice struck Fulco on his most recent trip to Palermo, when he was caught in a hail of plaster from the decrepit ceilings of Palazzo Verdura. Joan Crawford bought the piece, and was frequently photographed with its three segments clustered at her neckline. The prickly pear was Verdura's most emblematic motif, to which he returned repeatedly over the years. "I am more Sicilian than a prickly pear," was his standard justification for any un-Anglo-Saxon outburst.

Hollywood was more hospitable than it had been three years earlier, and a bi-coastal career began to look feasible. On extended visits to California, Fulco would stay with Cole, who was often in residence while composing film scores, or with the actor Richard Cromwell. Best known for his roles in *Four Feathers* and *Gunga Din*, Cromwell was a kindred spirit with an artistic bent who executed murals for Colleen Moore and sculpted decorative masks for Joan Crawford and Greta Garbo. Still, Los Angeles could not compare with New York, a city in the thrall of "a new, colorful, prodigal, social army, the ranks of which are made up of rich, carefree and quite often idle people. Apparently the votaries of the new cult prefer to go to bed at dawn, to dance—with the endurance of dervishes—at night clubs; to dine well and drink late in cafés. They have been heralded as restless and haunted spirits who, three times a day, wave at one another in an ecstasy of amazed recognition, first at the Colony, then at 21 and finally, after midnight, at El Morocco."

Café Society's swelling European contingent now included many of Fulco's friends, to whom the world of fashion offered a living, or at the very least, an excuse to travel. The resourceful Grand Duchess Marie was active as a milliner and a magazine writer. Nicky found his calling as an

editor with *Harper's Bazaar*. Shed at last of Lelong, Natalie settled in Connecticut with a new husband, John C. Wilson, who was Noël Coward's producer. She made frequent trips into Manhattan to assist a fellow exile from Paris, the American dressmaker Mainbocher. Another welcome visitor was Gabriella di Robilant, now a sportswear stylist in Rome, who convinced Fulco to accompany her on a literary pilgrimage through the Old South. "We had just read the American bestseller *Gone with the Wind* and we wanted to travel through Scarlett O'Hara territory. We were like kids on holiday and pretended to be the characters in the novel in our old car which was constantly breaking down." Their final destination, Palm Beach, was a letdown, with its mature moneyed élite basking in a *papier-mâché* decor.

American society regarded Fulco with puzzled fascination: one doyenne characterized him as a "sparkling monkey." He did not fit the average profile of the extra man about town. His mordant wit and bookishness were as unsettling as his bouts of gloom and childish delight in rude jokes. Yet he was a superb raconteur, and played his Sicilian origin for all its exotic worth. In a long article for *Harper's Bazaar*—part nostalgic memoir, part erudite travelogue—he brought to life "the strange people of many lands in strange crafts attracted alike to this fatal Calypso, Phoenicians, Greeks, proud Romans in their galleys, Arabs with their canny sciences, blond Norsemen with their new courage, French, Spanish, all came this way, some seeking fortune or a crown, some with full, some with empty hands, some by force, some by right—they all came to conquer, but were conquered in the end by the power of this red soil." Myth faded into history in Fulco's evocation of Ulysses slaying the Cyclops, Dionysius the Tyrant, Archimedes, and his hero Frederick II, the German Emperor who "in his heart [remained] always King of Sicily." Plunging headlong from the sublime to the ridiculous, Fulco would denounce the plight of a tubercular cousin whose family—too miserly to book him into a sanatorium in the Swiss Alps—sent him to recover his health on the top floor of their *palazzo*. Or he would poke fun at the obscure but emblematic Palermitan social climber nicknamed *Toujours*—an abbreviation of his mother's dismissive phrase: "*Toujours présent, rarement présentable, jamais présenté.*"

Fulco happened to be in Hollywood on 13 March 1938, when news of the Austrian *Anschluss* was broadcast. A young English friend of Cole's, Michael Pearman (who much later opened a popular restaurant-bar in New York called Michael's Pub), quizzed him about his plans. "But darling, I'm an officer!" Fulco exclaimed brightly. He had demonstrated his patriotism in combat, and his faith in the monarchy was bolstered by fondness for the Crown Prince, Umberto. Like many Italians of his class, he was confident the House of Savoy would neutralize Mussolini's worst excesses, and hoped that Fascism might provide some defence against Communism. But ambivalence soon gave

way to disillusion: Fulco elected to stay on, and to consolidate his professional status in the United States.

Pearman, who had a contact at Lord & Taylor in New York, convinced the store to commission a new logo from Verdura. Fulco's proposal, involving a ducal coronet hovering over a pair of scissors, needle and thread, was rejected as irreverent. Helena Rubinstein was approached unsuccessfully to engage Fulco to produce prototypes for compacts, vanities and lipstick cases; ironically, a decade later, she was manufacturing flagrant copies of Verdura originals.

When Cole, together with other investors, offered to back Fulco in his own jewelry business to the tune of $20,000, he was eager to accept. Although he had been designing jewelry for some ten years, going into trade remained a momentous decision. Perhaps his only predecessor as an aristocratic 'art craftsman' was Bijou d'art, the Serbian Prince Bojidar Karageorgevic, who made a name for himself at the turn of the century in the employ of the Art Nouveau master jeweler Lalique. But, as Verdura would have been quick to point out, their backgrounds were hardly comparable: a century earlier, the founding fathers of the Southern Slav dynasty had been herding pigs in the Balkans.

Fulco found a peerless business partner in the person of Joseph Byrd Mann, who had acquired as Flato's head salesman all the management skills that Fulco lacked. It was Joe Mann who discovered an unbeatable location for Verdura—the premises Cartier had occupied thirty years earlier at 712 Fifth Avenue, its façade a copy of the French Naval Ministry in the Place de la Concorde. It was Mann who recruited the craftsmen who realized Verdura's designs. The Valiant and Dauvergne atelier was entrusted with the execution of gold and colored gem jewelry. Diamond and gold earclips and rings were assigned to Hugo Huber. Naturalistic floral and foliate designs were the speciality of the Schuler workshop, with its secret methods for casting leaf-shaped jewels from impressions of real plants.

Another top member of Flato's sales staff, Joseph Alfano, was lured away a few months later. Of Sicilian ancestry, Alfano venerated 'The Duke' and was responsible over the years for preserving a vast quantity of Fulco's sketches that would otherwise have been destroyed— relentlessly ripping pages from his sketchbooks, sweeping scraps off the floor, retrieving crumpled sheets from wastepaper baskets.

Top A maple leaf brooch in yellow diamonds and multi-colored enamel.
Center A maple leaf brooch in tourmalines and zircons.
Bottom Leaf brooch and matching earclips in multi-colored zircons.

Verdura's drawing for a bow brooch, and the brooch in gold and diamonds.

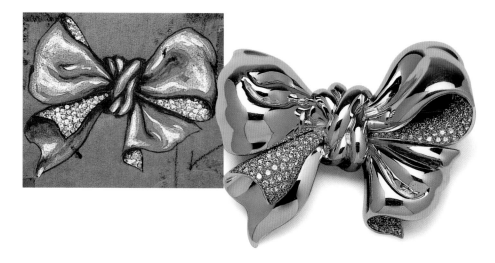

A pair of emerald and diamond bowknot earclips.

Opposite The entrance to Verdura's first New York salon at 712 Fifth Avenue.

The Verdura showroom was inaugurated on 1 September 1939—ironically only a few weeks before Chanel was forced to close her *maison*. The atmosphere was that of an old-fashioned European jeweler's salon—luxurious, but discreet. The spacious seven-room office was furnished with Louis XVI antiques; tall arched mirrors punctuated the oak-paneled walls; heavy red velvet draperies hung at the windows. Although the ambience was traditional, Verdura's style was revolutionary. Most jewelers were attempting to craft elegant 'white jewelry', substituting palladium for platinum, already in short supply due to the war in Europe. Unfortunately, 'the youngest of the precious metals' was labor-intensive, requiring plating to mask its grayish tinge. Verdura chose instead to enhance the versatility of gold, devising finishes and settings that made it suitable for both day and evening wear. He combined diamonds and gold, preferring the soft radiance of old rose-cut stones to the sparkle of the newer sharp cuts—kite, hexagon, square, lozenge and bullet. One reporter observed: "Verdura is mad about the idea of putting gold on diamonds instead of diamonds on gold, and also uses a great deal of hammered gold dipped in oxide to give an antique look."

From the start, Verdura's range was impressive. There were multi-purpose pieces, of which the most stunning was a diamond-encrusted bracelet with a detachable bowknot that could serve as a brooch. His lavish bow jewels hark back to the curvaceous baroque ornaments known as *sévignés*. However, his fluid, asymmetrical designs display an unmistakable couture quality; from Chanel he had learned that what can't be seen matters just as much as what can. Verdura bowknots are finished to an extravagant degree of perfection: precious stones are not only scattered over the surface of the ribbon, but also hidden deep within its folds, where they remain invisible to wearer and viewer alike. Verdura never tired of bowknots: they embellish earrings, brooches, necklace clasps and finger rings. A diminutive version captured the fancy of *The Junior League Magazine*: "dull satin gold bowknots lined with glimpses of tiny diamonds, that look new pinned to the cuffs of your gloves."

L. ALAVOINE
& CO.
FURNITURE
TAPESTRIES
L. ALAVOINE
& CO.
FURNITURE
TAPESTRIES
VERDURA

One of the truly remarkable pieces in Verdura's inaugural collection was a necklace "of breathtaking grandeur," formed of outstretched diamond eagle wings encircling the throat. Many wing jewels, referred to as Mercury or Valkyrie wings, derive from representations of the messenger of the gods, or from Wagnerian theater costume. An earlier source is the Egyptian winged globe, which in the late 1800s had inspired designs by the London firms of Carlo and Arthur Giuliano and Child & Child, both associated with the Pre-Raphaelite Brotherhood. In Paris, wing tiaras were produced by Fouquet and Debut & Coulon just before the turn of the century, and until 1935 by Cartier. As the number of occasions to wear important parures dwindled, the wing motif migrated to smaller, less formal pieces—hatpins, brooches and earrings. Interestingly, the Chanel Spring 1934 jewelry collection—one of Fulco's last—had included a suite of gold wing earclips and paired wing brooches to be placed at the center of the neckline, creating the impression of a jeweled collar.

In a second Verdura wing jewel, a substantial pear-shaped aquamarine is caught between two diamond-edged gold wings. The brooch differs from the usual pattern in that the wings do not spread, but lie close to the stone—not unlike the coats-of-arms framed by fluffy white wings painted on the ceilings at Villa Niscemi. Another brooch had a topaz wreathed in dull gold leaves glistening with round solitaires. Oriental rubies, emeralds, and sapphires were already becoming scarce, but Verdura mounted semi-precious stones with the same care and refinement he devoted to precious gems. His American clientele responded enthusiastically. In the United States, jewelry never had the same investment value it had acquired over the ages in Europe, where easily transportable wealth was essential in times of strife or revolution. Furthermore, pioneering designs by Tiffany had contributed to making native sapphires, garnets and moonstones acceptable in fine jewelry. Awareness of the aura and peculiar beauty of semi-precious stones was on the rise, thanks also to such publications as *Magical Jewels of the Middle Ages and the Renaissance* by Joan Evans, and to the conspicuous example of Edith Sitwell. This improbable, anachronistic fashion icon was widely photographed, bristling with gigantic aquamarine rings—at least two to a finger—and plastered with vast brooches of semi-precious stones. In her 1939 article "On precious stones and metals," she recommended mixing precious and semi-precious stones to revive the rich, variegated palette of ancient jewelry. Verdura massed cabochon amethysts and emeralds to form plump violet posies. Inspired as much by the bunch of silk violets that Granmamà used to tuck into her waistband as by the Parma violets that were a Napoleonic talisman, these gold-stemmed nosegays were soon recognized as one of Verdura's signature designs. Later variants of this old-fashioned *boutonnière* were delicately highlighted with yellow diamond hearts, or white diamond dew.

A pink topaz and diamond-wing brooch, *c.* 1940, designed for Mrs. Henry Fonda.

Opposite A pair of pink topaz, aquamarine, and diamond wing brooches designed for Lady (Slim) Keith, *c.* 1968, and an aquamarine and diamond-wing heart brooch.

Verdura's 'intoxicated' snowman
brooch was executed in sapphire,
gold, and enamel, 1941.

The lapel pin was the ideal accent for the strict suits and tailored
dresses then in vogue. According to *Harper's Bazaar*, "every woman's
fancy pops out in gold or enamel or precious stones upon the lapel of her
suit. Humour, history, sentiment are flaunted in the buttonhole like a
heart on a sleeve." Brooches, always the jeweler's greatest challenge, were
a Verdura forte. His "nonsense trinkets and magnificences" captivated
the fashion experts. There were dressy versions of the Maltese cross,
pavéd with sapphires, rubies and diamonds; romantic trophies in the
Victorian manner, such as a quiverful of arrows with a dangling red
tourmaline heart. A jolly snowman pin came equipped with two tiny
interchangeable hats—one pristine, the other squashed. A six-inch-long
flexible gold kite, studded with cabochons and trailing seed pearl tassels,
qualified as the ultimate 'conversation piece'. Sometimes Verdura
introduced a deft topical touch, such as a red-striped parasol clip with ruby
tassels, copied after the canopy of the Ethiopian Negus, Haile Selassie.

A certain interest in Renaissance-style baroque pearl jewelry was
emerging. It was revealed in *Harper's Bazaar* that "jewelers [were]
scouring the rivers of China and Australia and the upper waters of the
Mississippi for these pearls, and collectors [were] buying up all the old
pieces." The article was illustrated with pictures of two pieces Fulco
knew well: the sixteenth-century mermaid pendant belonging to Mimì
Pecci Blunt and Baba de Faucigny-Lucinge's jeweled knight in gold
armor. The American public was uncomfortable with such ornate,
foreign-looking confections: most of Verdura's early pieces featuring
baroque pearls did not attract buyers or press coverage until the late
1940s. Even in Europe, baroque pearls had always been something of an
acquired taste. At a time when they were highly prized, Benvenuto
Cellini still warned his Medici patrons against purchasing any such
misshapen "fish bones," for "they are not round, neither are they all of a
size, and some of them are old." However, Josephine Forrestal, Fulco's
former Flato colleague, was enchanted with Verdura's "wonderful
Renaissance baroque pearl surrounded with jewels" that represented a
putto astride a sea-monster. And newlywed Minnie Astor, one of the three
Cushing sisters from Boston who were to become Fulco's dearest
American friends, chose a crowned dolphin brooch, its body sheathed in
diamond scales.

Verdura's jaunty pebble jewels, launched in the Autumn of 1940,
were exactly in tune with the times, resembling "beautiful polished
pebbles, fished from the bottom of the sea and caught in a net of gold." He
transformed a hoard of antique Chinese buttons, made of polished sea-
green aquamarines, bubbly pink tourmalines, and other colorful stones,
into pins, cufflinks and earclips, all wrapped in gold wire, singly or in
bunches. He also used them as lids for minuscule, irregularly shaped gold
pillboxes. "Flawed but perfect," *Vogue* pronounced; "Any jewel that
Verdura touches becomes a more interesting jewel."

A *Harper's Bazaar* cover (January 1944) featuring brooches and bracelets by Verdura.

Verdura's design for a lightning bolt brooch to make use of a broken amethyst, *c.* 1940s.

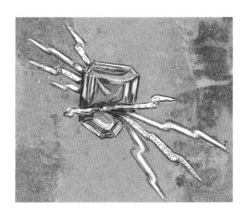

Verdura offered a remount service, almost unheard-of in America, but widespread in Europe, where the practice of resetting outmoded family jewels was commonplace. One magazine urged readers with "a few old rings and some rose diamonds hanging around" to have Verdura make them into "something lovely and dramatic" that would not be duplicated. The lightning style, one of Verdura's most imaginative inventions, originated as a remount. The image of a jagged diamond thunderbolt sundering an amethyst was devised for a client who insisted on finding some way of saving a broken stone to which she attached enormous sentimental value.

The blaze of publicity around *Red, Hot and Blue* made Verdura cigarette cases instant collectors' items. Fulco never carried one himself, insisting that "there's nothing better than a pack of Camels, with no weight." A particularly desirable model was an immaculate, totally

Above A black and gold cigarette case made for William S. Paley and bearing his monogram, *c.* 1955.

Opposite A woven gold and leather cigarette case, and a case with a map of South America, engraved in two-color gold, commemorating a journey taken by Mr. and Mrs. William S. Paley (later Dorothy Hirshon) in 1940.

Below Verdura's popular shell gold cigarette case; it was also made as a compact.

impractical box of bleached white pigskin covered in gold mesh. Personalized cases ranked as the supreme status symbol. The outline of the doors of the Abbey of St Alban's was engraved on the lid of a box for an Anglophile history buff. William S. Paley, the buccaneering president of CBS, commissioned a case decorated with a map of South America to commemorate his 1940 whirlwind tour of eighteen countries, during which he established the *Cadena de las Americas* broadcasting network. Souvenir boxes celebrating significant trips had been made popular by the Windsors during their courtship. In the mid-Thirties, Wallis Simpson and Prince Edward exchanged gem-set gold cases marked with the enameled routes of their scandalous pre-nuptial Mediterranean cruise. There were also earlier examples, such as the yellow, white, and red gold cigarette case by Fabergé bearing a map of the Nile Valley, with sites picked out in diamonds, rubies, emeralds, and sapphires.

Fulco designed five Porter boxes in quick succession. On 16 October 1939, the opening night of *The Man Who Came to Dinner*, Cole received his first Verdura cigarette case, in recognition of the song he contributed to the George S. Kaufman and Moss Hart play. The slim rectangular silver box is decorated with black enamel caricatures of the authors and the two leads, Monty Woolley and John Hoyt. The inscription reads: "For Cole Porter, because we think you're wonderful. Moss and George." On 6 December, it was Linda's turn to give Cole a Verdura box, in honor of the première of *Du Barry Was a Lady*, another vehicle for Ethel Merman. Cole was never disappointed by Linda's presentation cases, because in the planning stages she would confer at length with his mother and friends, before submitting her final selection for his approval: "Coley passes upon the design, but the finish is always a surprise to him." Fulco described the two-tone yellow and pink gold Du Barry case: "On one side I had the fleur-de-lys very stately, then on the other side I had a lady's hat with little ribbons flying, and all the fleurs-de-lys sort of bee-bopping all over the place." The next box, marking the February release of the movie *Broadway Melody of 1940*, with a cast headed by Fred Astaire and Eleanor Powell, and a score by Porter, had a scrolly calligraphic inscription—*Cole Porter Composer*—enameled on the lid; the movie's title was similarly inscribed on the bottom. For the *Panama Hattie* case (commemorating another Ethel Merman show), presented to Cole on 30 October, Fulco reproduced the fine weave of his own Panama hat. The elegant box he created a year later for Columbia Pictures' *You'll Never Get Rich*, starring Fred Astaire and Rita Hayworth, was to become a Verdura classic; though rectangular, it was always called the Shell Case because its wavy ridges suggested the surface striations of a clamshell.

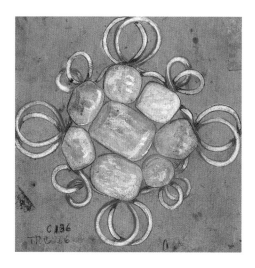

Mrs. Fairfax Potter (later Pauline de Rothschild) examining a collection of loose stones at the Verdura salon. Below: Verdura's sketch for the pink quartz and aquamarine brooch worn by Mrs. Potter in the photograph.

With the exception of Ronald, the albino rabbit who posed for a 1940 fashion shoot with a smoky Madeira topaz bracelet on his head and a gold leaf between his paws, Verdura jewels were now being modeled by celebrities of the first magnitude. Mrs. Harrison Williams (later Mona Bismarck), described by Beaton as a "rock crystal goddess" with eyes like "pools of magic" had a passion for his aquamarine gems. Mrs. Fairfax Potter, a blue-blooded taste-maker descended from Thomas Jefferson and Francis Scott Key, was photographed lost in admiration before Verdura's unpolished stones. The roster of his Hollywood clients included Vivien Leigh, Norma Shearer, Irene Selznick, Marlene Dietrich, Samuel Goldwyn and Orson Welles. Verdura created the jewels Katharine Hepburn wore in *The Philadelphia Story* (1940). Yet he was never tempted to open a boutique on the West Coast. He had learned his lesson: "The movie people like to wear things that come from New York."

Fulco had become a Manhattanite. When in 1941 he finally moved into a brownstone walk-up at 421 Park Avenue, over the Rosary Flower Shop on the corner of East 53rd Street, the event was considered newsworthy by The *New York Times*. Monroe Wheeler, in charge of publications at the Museum of Modern Art, was a fellow tenant, and the Cushing girls kept a pied-à-terre nearby. To the interior decorator Billy Baldwin, Fulco's flat appeared "very European, wonderfully comfortable and obviously the residence of a person of intelligence and wide interests. He used books everywhere—books on architecture and decoration, history, music, anything he liked—they were the heart of the place." Fulco would generally lunch at the Vesuvio on 48th Street, where they knew how to cook Mediterranean dishes like *calamari*. In the evenings, he organized small dinner parties with the help of Lillian, a "handsome and elegant black lady with a wide range of famous acquaintances, a rare fund of entertaining gossip and an air of almost formidable personal distinction." She was on first-name terms with all Fulco's friends; when she announced "Barbara called," she didn't need to add Hutton.

On 29 October 1941, it was with a *frisson* of gratification not unmingled with disgust that Fulco heard his name sung at the Imperial Theater by an all-star cast—Danny Kaye, Eve Arden, Nanette Fabray and Vivian Vance. The occasion was the opening night of Cole's *Let's Face It*, and the *pièce de résistance* of the twenty-one songs was "Farming," about celebrities returning to the land. For two decades, Cole had delighted in teasing Fulco: "It's really too bad, there just doesn't seem to be anything that rhymes with your name." In "Farming," however, Cole had at last lined up the elusive syllables:

> *Liz Whitney has, on her bin of manure, a*
> *Clip designed by the Duke of Verdura.*
> *Farming is so charming, they all say.*

Some time after this, Cole and Linda went for a holiday in Mexico, and from there Cole, with his usual comic flair, sent a telegram which read: "Acapulco rhymes with Nicky."

Early in 1941, Fulco was waylaid by a revenant from pre-war Paris, Caresse Crosby, founder—with her husband Harry—of the avant-garde Black Sun Press in Paris. Caresse had published Hemingway, Lawrence, MacLeish and Crane; she was also (or so she claimed) the inventor of the backless brassiere. A blend of *fin-de-siècle* decadence, erudition and breezy New World naiveté, Caresse had succeeded in impressing even the fastidious Beaumonts when she first slinked into their salon in a short Vionnet cloth-of-gold evening suit with her black whippet Narcisse Noir "dressed in his best gold necklace and his toenails lacquered gold."

Caresse, now widowed, was living near Fredericksburg, Virginia, in a plantation house designed by Thomas Jefferson. Like all her past houses in and around Paris—particularly the celebrated mill at Armenonville—Hampton Manor had become a haven for displaced artists and writers. Among these were Gala and Salvador Dalí, who elected it as their headquarters upon their arrival in the USA several months earlier. Dalí divided his time between working on his autobiography and practising headline-worthy "enchantments" about the estate that involved tree-borne pianos, floating manikins, rainbow-tinted rabbits and spiders with girls' faces. In a series of *tableaux vivants* enacted for the benefit of a Pathé cameraman and a *Life* photographer, Caresse, Gala and Dalí mimed the rigors and delights of Surrealist rustication. One picture portrays the group huddling around the fireplace in a gracious sitting-room, together with a "purebred Hereford bull which Dalí invited in for after-dinner coffee." In another shot, the master himself arranges a politically incorrect black-and-white composition in a wintry landscape, titled *Effet de Sept Nègres, un Piano Noir et Deux Cochons Noirs sur la Neige.*

A suite of pink tourmaline and golden sapphire brooch and earrings designed by Verdura in 1942 and featured in a Salvador Dalí surrealist landscape.

Opposite The front and back of the articulated amoeba brooch with 57 carats of rubies.

With the instinctive opportunism of the best cultural impresarios, Caresse wanted to enlist Verdura in one of her "let's-get-together-and-everyone-make-a-combination-chic-party-and-business-venture-in-honor-of-the-arts" events. Her plan was for Verdura and Dalí to design a new jewelry collection together, to be unveiled at Dalí's upcoming exhibition. Although at first glance it might have seemed somewhat farfetched to pair Verdura the society jeweler with Dalí, famous for excremental themes and obscene religious icons, it was not a totally outlandish proposition. After all, as former habitués of the Beaumont and de Noailles salons, the two men were hardly strangers. Dalí's supporters included Chanel, who had installed an atelier for the painter on her premises, as well as the Faucigny-Lucinges. As charter members of the Zodiac syndicate, they had been faithfully contributing to Dalí's upkeep since 1933.

Social connections aside, from an artistic viewpoint Verdura and Dalí now stood as close as they ever would. After his recent travels in Italy, Dalí was in the throes of a conversion to classicism, while Fulco's work had acquired an unmistakably Surrealist flavor. Ring designs often feature the characteristic parted-lips or open-eye bezels. Huge stones are ensnared in wavy tentacular settings resembling sea-anemones' feelers— or they may cast stylized flares. Schiaparelli modeled one such *soleil* brooch for *Vogue* in January 1940, and Mrs. Henry Fonda acquired a spectacular suite consisting of earclips and a brooch set with a rectangular-cut 30 ct aquamarine, surrounded with circular-cut diamond and platinum rays. Verdura's most exciting and bizarre creation of this period clearly mirrors the 'soft constructions' Dalí advocated: the fan-shaped Amoeba brooch, with a large central ruby cabochon and three superimposed mobile sections reminiscent of splayed digits, diamond-encrusted and ruby-tipped. Last but not least, being "one hundred percent Sicilian of Spanish descent," Fulco was culturally attuned to the more macabre aspects of the painter's Iberian genius. Caresse's idea

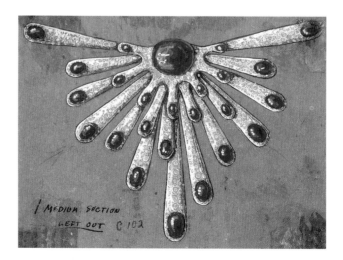

A drawing for the amoeba brooch in rubies and diamonds, 1940.

intrigued Fulco, and she pressed him to come and discuss the project further with Dalí.

Fulco's own report in the guise of a telegraphic missive to Diana Vreeland was printed in *Harper's Bazaar,* together with Dalí's garish impression of Oak Grove: a yolky sun dropping to the horizon, little dark stickmen staggering under the weight of the visitor's luggage, a lustrous mound of skulls beneath a gnarled tree. Dalí was penning a chapter about his prenatal experiences in the womb when Fulco entered ("nice and warm, thought I"). On a tour of the property, the artist "raved against the lurid sunset: '*Merveilleuse—truculent—inspiration Frankenstein. La chute de la maison Usher.*" Unmoved by enthusiastic comparisons to the atelier of Picasso, Fulco remained haughtily diffident: "This I have never seen, but I am told it is of the same squalor, with no ash tray emptied since the Blue Period."

The moment of truth came when dinner *al fresco* was announced. "'Yes, we have a pavilion in the cemetery. It will be wonderful, and after dinner we are going to pick the graves. You will find the most lovely shiny little bones, you could make jewels of them. We must be there in time for the moon.' As one in a dream, I began struggling with my overcoat. I have had few principles, God knows, but one I have had and I stick to, is *not* picking the bones of the dead. I started for the door, and almost stumbled over a radio trailing a long electric cord. With a wild surmise, I turned to Dalí. 'How do you use this in a house with no electricity?' Dalí was in paradise."

Executed almost overnight, the Verdura-Dalí collection was displayed from 22 April to 15 May at the Julien Levy Gallery in midtown Manhattan which, since its inauguration eight years earlier, had established itself as the premiere American showcase for Surrealist art. Levy's 1941 exhibition programme also promoted such eclectic personalities as Tamara de Lempicka, Joseph Cornell and Eugene Berman.

Described as "Freudian jewels" by *The New Yorker*, the pieces actually reflect a certain number of Dalí's pet conceits. The hammered gold case, with a pearl and opal beetle entranced by the inlaid miniature of a gorgon-headed spider, is related to the composition of *Araignée du soir, espoir*. The painted statuette of Saint Sebastian affixed to a column of petrified wood is an obvious reference to the famous 1927 poem *St Sebastian, or Holy Objectivity,* in which Dalí defined his "aesthetic of putrefaction"; jagged golden rays rim the figure bristling with arrows, and cabochon ruby blood-drops stud the agate base.

In other pieces, Dalí's paintings are visible through faceted semi-precious stones, in the manner of Renaissance relics set under crystal. This unusual device served to enhance the multiple image effect that was a Dalí trademark. There was the visage of a Fallen Angel; a Medusa under morganite wreathed with coiling ruby-eyed serpents; an Apollo and Daphne brooch with the god's effigy under pink tourmaline and the

A hammered gold and colored stone cigarette case with an applied painting by Dalí, *Daddy Long Legs of the Evening—Hope!*, on the lid, 1940.

Overleaf Three Verdura sketches: a St. Sebastian *objet*; a Medusa brooch in pink tourmalines; and a classical mirror brooch with a surreal face in the pediment, all 1941.

A fashion shot from *Town & Country* (February 1943) portraying Mrs. Desmond FitzGerald wearing an urn brooch containing a miniature painting by Verdura.

nymph's head surmounting the portal-shaped mount—perhaps a reference to Apollo as the deity of the Seventh Door.

Caresse's venture was destined to remain a one-off media triumph: Verdura did not intend to specialize in precious foils for Dalí's "handpainted dream photographs." He did, however, begin to try his hand at miniature painting, applying the meticulous techniques of jewelry rendering to landscapes, interiors and still-lifes on tiny ivory plaques. Although he did not attempt portraiture, he emulated the brilliant brushwork of his step-grandmother's father-in-law, Jean-Baptiste Isabey. Eventually, the thumbnail *capricci* began to show up in his jewelry: in one brooch, a pearl-framed medallion is held aloft by a golden angel.

When Dalí's visits tapered off, Verdura's staff missed his wildly fluctuating linguistic skills as much as his camp histrionics. Despite a chronic inability to master even conversational English, the artist known as Avida Dollars always managed to clearly enunciate the words: "I have come for my money."

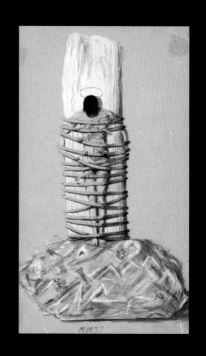

6 WAR

A woman can be loved or smiled at because of her clothes. If she lets these clothes create a misunderstanding between herself and the world, she is guilty; guilty also if she lets them remain anonymous. Miracles have been worked by women who have understood this. These women make the anatomy of everything they wear fit the anatomy of their minds.

- PAULINE POTTER

An antique Indian carved ivory chessman brooch, with a maharajah on his elephant, *c.* 1940.

Opposite, top and bottom Ten drawings by Verdura of Rajput warriors, as studies for brooches. In the center are three brooches based on the drawings: a dyed ivory Rajput with a lemur on a leash; an ivory Rajput gentleman holding a flower; and a dyed ivory warrior with diamonds and pearls on a camel.

"THE CHESSMEN, that's what really started us." Joe Alfano could trace Verdura's success to the day a woman came into the showroom, hoping to interest him in buying a set of eighteenth-century painted ivory chessmen from India. There were twenty-seven pieces, and Fulco took them all: the Mughal figurines had the potential for a more stylish allure than the scantily clad Mayan Ape Man he had just completed. Since the Colonial Exhibition, Indian-style jewelry and *objets* had been all the rage in Paris. Fulco had admired a green-coated knight astride a crimson steed on show in Elsie de Wolfe's sitting-room. By 1939, that brilliant connoisseur of brooches, Baba de Faucigny-Lucinge, was sporting ebony chessmen mounted as clips—probably by Boivin—on both lapels. But rather than merely equipping the colorful, chunky figures with a pin, Fulco transformed them into Verdura originals. His main inspiration was the Dinglingers' early eighteenth-century masterwork at the Dresden Schatzkammer (Green Vaults), *The Delhi Court on the Birthday of Grand Mogol Aureng-Zeb*. In this miniature scenographic extravaganza, encrusted with 5,000 rose diamonds and hundreds of emeralds, rubies, sapphires, and pearls, over a hundred enameled statuettes—courtiers, white elephants, griffons, and camels—are arrayed upon a gold and silver stage inlaid with agate and lapis lazuli panels.

Verdura's chessmen were tricked out with jeweled turban ornaments and fans, pendant pearl earrings and medallion necklaces, gold belts, precious and semi-precious cabochon buttons, and trim. The two most elaborate figurines were an elephant with a howdah, and a king and queen seated side-by-side on a twin throne. Others were given graceful pets on leads: leopards, gazelles, and lemurs. Stands on which the chessmen could be displayed when not being worn were planted with golden bushes and gemstone cacti. "We sold every last one of them," Alfano recollected, to society leaders such as Mrs. Joshua Logan, Mrs. William Woodward, Irene Selznick, Mrs. William H. Harkness and Mrs. Jules Stein. "People would come in for years afterward" to place orders for chessmen, and it became firm policy to buy back any originals that reappeared on the market.

"In times of stress, sentiment comes quickly to the surface and seeks expression in gifts that have lasting beauty and value," was the opinion of one jeweler interviewed by the *New York World-Telegram* in December 1942. Jewelry sales remained strong during the early Forties,

A Verdura sketch for a shell brooch.

Opposite A brooch of gold and scallop shell, encrusted with diamonds and faceted citrines.

despite the introduction of a 10 percent luxury tax, the dearth of skilled labor, the lowering of the gold quota and the lack of platinum. Even Verdura found himself obliged to use palladium, albeit sparingly, between 1943 and 1945. But restrictions had no noticeable impact on the variety of his designs. Verdura's wartime jewels are among his most individualistic creations, whether full-blown romantic love tokens or simple mementos.

Verdura's natural shell jewelry became an instant collector's item—a souvenir of carefree times when beaches were for bathing and partying, rather than amphibious landings. It exuded fresh appeal, although the history of natural shell ornaments reaches back to palaeolithic times. In Middle Kingdom Egypt, metal cowrie shells were carried as talismans, and shell-shaped gold baubles appeared *c.* 1500 BC in various Greek sites. Frequently depicted in antiquity, the scallop shell was adopted during the Middle Ages as the emblem of St James's shrine at Compostella. Benvenuto Cellini wrote of unearthing antique urns filled with ashes, among which he discovered iron and gold rings set with tiny shells. He crafted his own version of these amulets "in fine tempered steel, chased and inlaid with gold."

The re-emergence of shells as a decorative motif in mid-nineteenth-century jewelry was symptomatic of a widespread fascination with all aspects of marine and maritime life. On both sides of the English Channel, shell forms invested all categories of jewelry, from cheap trinkets to *haute joaillerie*. Shell-like whorls enlivened Art Nouveau jewels. Diamond-encrusted ear-clips, brooches, and necklace clasps in the shape of whelk and ammonite shells became indispensable elements of Art Déco style. According to the September 1933 issue of French *Vogue*, "the shell is a new jewel because it is eternal." However, the special beauty of shell-shaped jewels is that they are the product not of nature, but of human ingenuity. Whatever his sources, Fulco was genealogically predisposed to design shell jewels: the Verdura crest consists of three golden shells on an azure field.

While continuing to invent shell shapes in the sleek Thirties manner, Verdura realized that a natural shell in a precious mount was the ultimate inimitable jewel. No one piece would ever exactly resemble another, and the result was impossible to classify exclusively as either formal or informal. To prove this last point, Horst photographed Paulette Goddard for the 15 January 1941 issue of *Vogue* with an orange shell brooch pinned to her "dinner-in-cabaña" outfit by Hattie Carnegie, an embroidered silk crêpe jacket and shorts. Verdura shell brooches had startling hues so pristine—russet, rose, lavender—that they looked as if they had just been plucked from the sea. The most sought-after design featured an orangey lion's-paw awash in a sea of diamonds bubbling with blue sapphires or turquoises; the most delicate was a pale powder-blue shell with "trickles of sapphires and diamonds licking the edges like

foamy waves." A white nacre shell brooch was rimmed with a gold running-wave border. Turban shell earclips were wrapped in spiraling gold wire and tipped with coral or turquoise cabochons. Brazilian tree snail shells studded with diamonds and tourmalines were fitted with button or cufflink mounts. Speckled brown shells were embedded in chased gold brooches shaped like tortoises.

Fulco beachcombed at Fire Island or Newport whenever gas shortages did not confine him to Manhattan on weekends; he also patronized the Museum of Natural History shop. "What I get a kick out of is to buy a shell for five dollars, use half of it and sell it for twenty-five hundred," Fulco informed *The New Yorker*. He built jeweled compacts around natural bivalves, reviving the notion Schiaparelli had toyed with in 1937. The use of shells as cosmetic holders has its origins in antiquity: examples exist in civilizations from Mesopotamia to Magna Graecia. During the eighteenth century, elongated conus shells fitted with silver or gold lids served as snuffboxes and *bonbonnières*. Verdura also included shells in purely decorative pieces that were evocative of sixteenth-century *objets de vertù* or ceremonial vessels featuring large polished nautiluses. A tilted shell containing several freshwater pearls rests on the outstretched arms of a nude male figure sculpted in crystal and mounted in gold. "It can't possibly be used as an ashtray," he explained. "It's nice but utterly useless."

A suite of coral and shell brooch and earrings, *c.* 1940.

Opposite Paulette Goddard, photographed by Horst in 1941, wearing a diamond encrusted lion's paw shell brooch by Verdura.

Right One of Verdura's many shell brooches, encrusted with sapphires and diamonds, 1950. Below: a drawing for a table *objet* in smoky quartz depicting Atlas supporting a large shell on a gold scrolled base.

A gold and diamond double crescent bracelet designed for Mrs. Merriweather Post, *c.* 1945. Opposite: a fashion shot featuring this bracelet.

In times of uncertainty and leave-taking, when personalized keepsakes acquire special significance, monogramming is invariably rediscovered as the easiest, most effective way to render a jewel unique. The decorative and symbolic aspects of lettering had always intrigued Fulco. As a boy in Palermo, he wondered at Princess Torremuzza's tentacular sofa, in the form of four Ts joined together at their bases, signifying the ancestral connections between the Tarente, Thouar, Trémoille, and Torremuzza families. He enjoyed pondering alternative ramifications, such as if the old lady had been related to Wellington, Walpole, Wallenstein, and Washington. While Flato had used letters to spell out messages, Fulco preferred to emphasize the ornamental aspect of initials—an interest he shared with Chanel; the *couturière*'s trademark interlaced Cs derived from the double Cs carved into the wooden benches of her great-grandfather's tavern.

Although Fulco did not copy specific historic items, he was acquainted with the sumptuous initial jewels associated with Renaissance rulers, such as Henry VIII's *H* ornaments and the celebrated *AA* pendant in the Green Vaults, probably a betrothal gift from Augustus I of Saxony to Anne of Denmark. He was familiar with modern royal badges, such as the *E* brooches Queen Elena of Savoy bestowed upon her ladies-in-waiting (including Granmamà), and the *U* rings handed out by Prince Umberto to beauties who caught his eye. His library included sources ranging from medieval alphabet handbooks to E.G. Lutz's *Practical Art of Lettering* (1930). Months after her triumphant marriage to Vincent Astor in 1940, Minnie Cushing had Fulco design foliate gold *K* and *C* pins set with diamonds as a Christmas gift for her mother, the formidable matchmaker Katherine. Lieutenant Tyrone Power commissioned for his new, but soon to be ex-wife Annabella, a pair of star-shaped gold earrings that combined the suggestion of military valor and big-screen glamor with a personal touch: one was embossed with an A, the other with a T. Verdura was one of the first designers to succeed in persuading customers to wear his logo; during the war years, formations of gold *V* clips—for Victory as well as Verdura—clustered on patriotic lapels.

A drawing for a wrapped heart jewel as well as two brooches: one an amethyst studded with small round diamonds; the other a pink tourmaline studded with small round diamonds and surmounted by a pavé diamond and gold *putto*.

Opposite A ruby and diamond wrapped heart brooch, 1949.

Tyrone Power was also among the first to acquire a Verdura heart, a brooch of cabochon rubies tied with a softly knotted gold sash. Fulco had been right to allow Hollywood to 'discover' him on his own turf, in New York. When in December 1940 Joan Crawford was seen wearing a ruby-set platinum brooch in the form of an arrow-pierced heart, she launched a fashion: bejeweled hearts epitomized the romance and drama that propelled the not-so-private lives of the West Coast élite. Gene Tierney, then married to the designer Oleg Cassini, bought a Drape and Spear Heart; its mass of pink tourmalines, shaded with rubies and glistening with diamonds, was surmounted by a gold swag caught up by crossed spears. Mrs. Mervyn LeRoy ordered a precious pink topaz heart bound in gold rope. Another variant was the pink tourmaline Ardent Heart, crested with diamond flames and bound with a diamond-linked gold chain. Verdura also made small gold flaming hearts, for everyday wear, in twos or threes, as well as suites of winged aquamarine hearts.

Heart brooches had been in evidence since 1937, when *Vogue* remarked upon a lady who exhibited a "great blazing ruby heart on or above her heart on every occasion." Verdura hearts avoid the distended, buxom contours of the "puffy hearts" Millicent Rogers made for Flato; nor are they morbidly wounded, like the stabbed hearts, taken from Spanish religious iconography, that accessorized Schiaparelli's 1939 collection. Although Verdura was influenced by baroque Sacred Heart imagery, his designs are closer to the courtly heart jewels that were highly prized in Elizabethan England. In Shakespeare's *Henry VI*, the king's bride Margaret of Anjou seeks to calm the tempest by casting to the waves one such "costly jewel from my neck, a heart it was, bound in with diamonds." The best known surviving example is the enameled locket that belonged to the Countess of Lennox, Mary Queen of Scots's mother-in-law; beneath its crowned and winged sapphire heart cover lie two more hearts, shot with arrows and tied with lovers' knots.

During the Renaissance, the winged heart could "betoken those desires/By which the reasonable soule aspired/To mysteries and knowledge more sublime." Later, it was viewed as a symbol of amorous attraction—though not necessarily of fidelity: a fluttering heart on an ivory box carved at Dieppe during the eighteenth century is accompanied by the flirtatious motto *Sa beauté m'attire*. The chained heart device is uncommon, yet there exists a prototype for Verdura's design: Sir Edward Burne-Jones's published rendering of a pendant which Fulco, a voracious reader, might have come across. In several of the Pre-Raphaelite artist's compositions, winged and flaming hearts denote spiritual elevation as well as carnal passion.

Other jewels, influenced by the extravagant historical modes revived in Paris during the Twenties and Thirties, proved too quirky for Verdura's new mainstream American clientele. In one earclip design, a row of six tiny gold hoops seems to perforate the lobe, thanks to a

concealed clasp—an imitation of the multi-pierced style originating in the Bronze Age which has today returned to favor. "Polished gold earmuffs," adapted from a Louis XIV sunray motif, were worn looped over the ears. In some earrings, patterned after late nineteenth-century Italian and German models, an arrow or a cloth of gold appears to be drawn through the lobe.

Knotting emerged as one of the most distinctive motifs in Verdura's jewelry at this time. He studied the ornamental designs of Dürer and Holbein, Verrocchio's bronze grille in the Church of San Lorenzo in Florence, and above all the complex knotted patterns with which Leonardo da Vinci bedecked his *trompe-l'oeil* frescoed bower in the Castello Sforzesco in Milan. Verdura's knots, however, were based more often on utilitarian than decorative examples. Ropework had intrigued him since boyhood, when a stroll along the Palermo harbor afforded opportunities to observe fishermen repair their nets and to learn new nautical knots. Reference books on all forms of weaving, from Navajo baskets to Chinese macramé, crowded Verdura's office shelves. The volume he consulted most frequently was the exhaustive *Encyclopedia of Knots and Fancy Rope Work* by R. Graumont and J. Hensel (1939) which, according to one reviewer, "roped and hog-tied everything that was ever known about tying knots, on land and sea."

Verdura used knotting to enrich his standard designs. Sapphire and ruby Maltese crosses were bound with gold knots of heraldic origin. The polished yellow gold feelers of ray-style brooches were ensnared in the triple loops of diamond-encrusted platinum Bugler's Braids. Salmon-pink shells were caught in gold nets. Gold lattice was wrapped around cases covered in delicate white or crimson kidskin. Other items were entirely crafted in gold rope. The gold cord versions of Verdura's curb-link chain bracelets were often embellished with diamond clusters, watches or dangling charms; worn in pairs, they could also be joined to form a necklace. Broad mesh collars, sometimes strewn with topazes, were intended for stylish daywear, offsetting the upward sweep of a turban or chignon. Compacts were molded to resemble miniature lidded work-baskets, or rustic wicker trays brimming with tourmalines and turquoises. Knotted gold cufflinks were copied after the silk *passementerie* cufflinks produced by the Parisian *chemisier* Charvet in 1904. Knotted triple-strand brooches followed specifications from Virgil's *Eclogues*: to please the gods, love knots must be uneven in number.

Three gold and diamond ladies watches by Verdura.

Opposite A fashion shot featuring two rope knot bracelets by Verdura, as well as a ring and earrings.

A gold rope bracelet and a victory knot brooch *en suite,* set with diamonds and sapphires, made for the White House wedding of Harry Hopkins and Louise Gill Macy in 1942.

The Victory Knot brooch, actually a triple carrick bend, became Verdura's most widely sold jewel ever—thanks to unofficial White House endorsement. Fulco had been on the presidential guest list ever since the eldest Cushing sister, Betsey, married to Franklin D. Roosevelt's son James, had started to relieve the First Lady of tiresome hostessing duties. Even after Betsey's divorce in 1940, Fulco's wit guaranteed him continued attendance at White House events: FDR craved amusement. Another *habituée* was Louise Gill Macy, a former Paris editor of *Harper's Bazaar* now working for the Red Cross, who was involved with Harry L. Hopkins, the President's closest confidant. When the Victory Knot brooch was launched in the Spring of 1942, it was priced at $45, with part of the proceeds going to Navy Relief. The demand soared for entire parures when it was disclosed that Macy, "the country's most famous Nurse's Aide," was engaged to marry Hopkins in an East Room wedding —and that she would be wearing "a complete matching 'jewel trousseau' designed on the theme of the victory knot." The 28 July edition of the *New York World-Telegram*, printed on the day of the ceremony, explained that "the several pieces of the set—some of which are wedding presents— are made of precious stones and triple strands of gold rope adapted by the jeweler Verdura from a manual of sailor knots. Even the buttons on the wedding gown will be mounted with dainty gold ropes. Among the items of the 'jewel trousseau' are Mrs. Macy's engagement ring—a lariat of gold rope around a dome of diamonds—and 'victory knot' earclips, a large butterfly with flexible wings of gold rope and a body of diamonds, and two bracelets. The wedding ring will be a single twist of gold rope." All the magazines carried spreads of Mrs. Hopkins modeling the Victory Knots, which proved as becoming on tailored suits as on her blue wedding gown.

The gold twine butterfly was a particularly ingenious invention: the instinctive gesture of pinching, then releasing the two wings activated its hidden catch. Filigree was widely used during the war years, to stretch available gold as far as possible. Fulco coiled smooth tendrils of gold wire around two cabochons to form a wide-eyed owl brooch for Minnie Astor. As the companion of the goddess of wisdom, the owl was an appropriate badge for the book-loving woman whom Verdura nicknamed Minerva. He also made skeleton leaves, gold veins gleaming with diamond dew or ruby sap.

In Verdura jewelry, North American flora acquire a distinctly Old World gloss. Brushed gold crossover bangles with tourmaline acorn terminals set in pavé diamond caps hark back to penannular Greek bracelets of the classical era. Golden bough brooches with pendant sapphire acorns are in the tradition of the *tremblant* oak sprays that were as popular in Victorian England as they had been in rococo France. Verdura paid homage to native species such as the tobacco plant, devising a gentleman's gold cigarette holder shaped like a loosely furled leaf. He was especially entranced by the fiery palette of the New England autumn, so unlike the colors of the Mediterranean. One day an Indian dealer came to the showroom and emptied a sack filled with variegated zircons onto Alfano's desk: "There were hundreds of stones, wrapped in tissue paper like candies." Verdura used them to make huge oak and maple leaf brooches, measuring up to six inches in length. He massed red, green and amber jargoons amidst the gold tracery of the mounts, highlighted with yellow sapphires and cinnamon-colored hessonites, to achieve the translucent effect of stained glass.

Many of Verdura's elongated frondy designs are almost indistinguishable from his feather jewels. For the soprano Lily Pons, he crafted a claspless diamond and platinum necklace in the form of a single flexible ostrich plume that curled loosely around the neck. This elegant *sautoir*, deriving from the question-mark necklaces introduced by Boucheron and Debut in the 1880s, also reflects the glamor of Kleaty's 'drippy' style. A pair of gold brooches—one with two, the other with three plumes, tied with diamond bows—seem to wave gaily in the breeze. Verdura revived the single wing brooch, an adaptation of the insignia of the Order of St Michael which had been modish in Paris during the early Thirties. A diamond and platinum winged brooch with a pear-shaped pearl pendant has two pinions raised heavenward, as if beating in flight.

Overleaf Left: An oak leaf brooch of multi-colored zircons, 1940s. Right: Verdura's drawing of a bangle, terminating in two gold pavé diamond-capped acorns, and the finished piece.

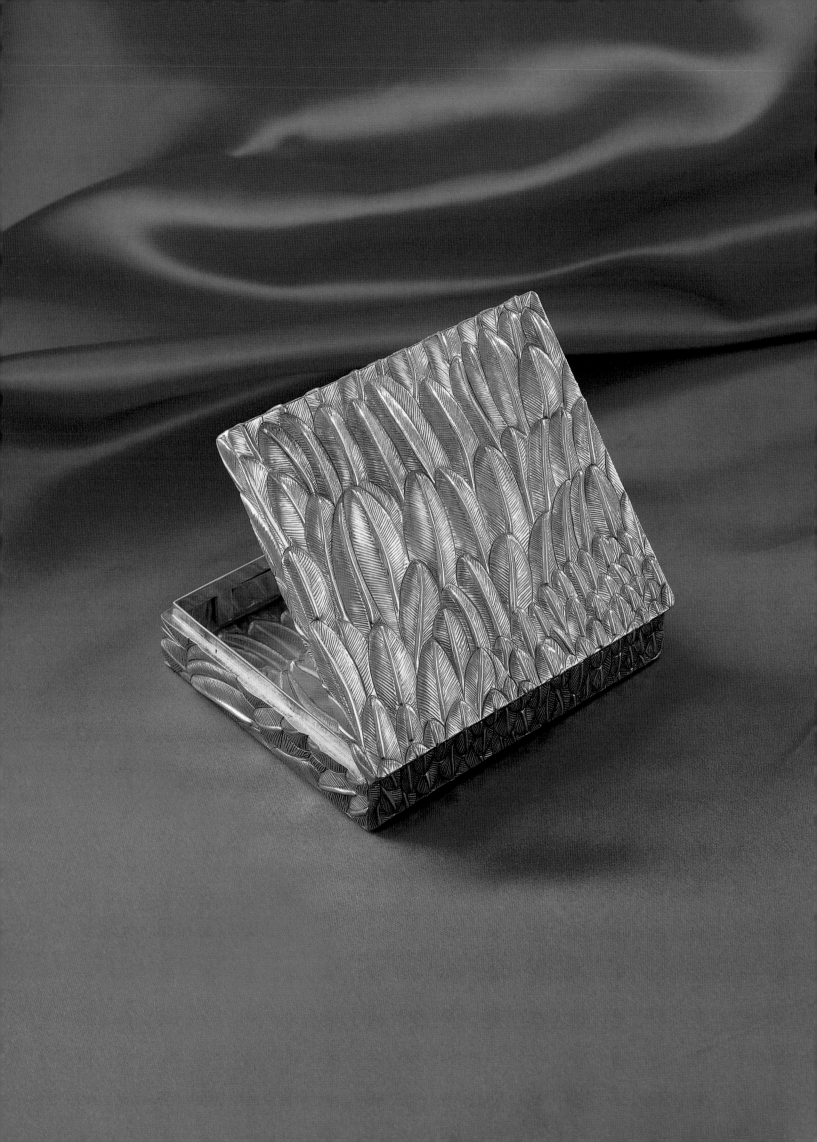

Opposite The feathered gold
cigarette case made for Cole Porter
to celebrate his score for the 1942
movie *Something to Shout About*.

A lapel watch in a winged frame is a punning reminder that *Time Flies*.
Engraved plumage covers the entire surface of the extraordinary 18-carat
gold case Fulco made to celebrate the release of Cole Porter's movie
Something to Shout About in February 1942. The exquisite texture rivals
that of feather-patterned *objets* by eighteenth-century goldsmiths as well
as by Fabergé.

Verdura's next Porter box was for the first night of Billy Rose's
The Seven Lively Arts in December 1944, a revue starring Beatrice Lillie,
Bert Lahr, and Alicia Markova. Its design is inspired by the religious
iconography Fulco knew so well: the flame-shaped surrounds of the
seven gems—diamond, ruby, emerald, sapphire, topaz, aquamarine,
amethyst—are a reference to the sevenfold gifts of the Holy Spirit. The
wittiest of Verdura's Porter creations was the 'Night and Day' set of
unmatching spherical cufflinks, inspired by the lyrics of the famous song
introduced by Fred Astaire in *The Gay Divorcee* (1934):

> *Night and day you are the one,*
> *Only you beneath the moon and under the sun.*

A gold-and-azure-enameled globe depicts the world, while a
dark blue ball twinkling with diamond studs represents the starry
firmament. Presented to Cole in 1941, within a year 'Night and Day'
were available to Verdura's clientele singly as 'Heaven and Earth' dress
buttons.

Fulco was increasingly drawn to constellations, although he
continued to elaborate on the starburst brooches of his Chanel years. Star
clusters had been part of his youth, from the Stellario, the starry crown of
Palermo's most venerated Madonna, to a couple of minuscule planets
supposedly discovered by a great-great-uncle. Prince Giulio Fabrizio
Tomasi di Lampedusa (1815–85), a reputed astronomer, was believed to
have named his celestial finds Palma and Lampedusa, after
two estates belonging to the family.

Verdura's 'Night and Day' cufflinks,
designed for Cole Porter in 1941.

Above and opposite The Pleiades brooch that Verdura first sketched in 1940. The jewel consisted of seven cabochon sapphires weighing 54 carats and diamonds, 1945.

The double image may well have been in Fulco's mind when he made buttons and earclips in the form of a gold star casting a shadow over its dark onyx twin. His star-shaped jeweled button clips have big round centers of rose quartz, surrounded by small garnet and gold points. *Harper's Bazaar* advised that one could "use them in endless ways, to clip on your collar, on the side of a skull cap, on your belt or, if you have a dress with a high plain round neck, pin them one below the other like a row of buttons. We think they're bewitching. If pink is not your colour, you can get them in blue quartz, which is heaven on earth."

The most magnificent of Verdura's constellations is the Pleiades brooch, a group of seven diamond-encrusted sapphire-centered stars. In Greek mythology, the Seven Sisters, daughters of Atlas and Pleione, were changed first into doves, then into stars to escape the pursuit of the hunter Orion. The Pleiades were known as the 'sailing stars', because their rising in May signaled fair weather to mariners. The design is clearly connected to Flato's Hand of God brooch with seven astrological 'stars' scattered across an open hand: the image, taken from a palmistry manual, has its source in the Book of Revelation, where the Lord is described as holding "in his right hand seven stars." Verdura made several two-brooch variants of the Pleiades—versatile clusters of three and four, or two and five stars, enabling each wearer to assemble her own individual constellations. The asymmetrical composition is close in spirit to the lavish ornaments of the late Romantic period: the randomly positioned star hairpins worn by Empress Elisabeth of Austria in Winterhalter's portrait, and the whirling galaxies of Julienne's Milky Way parure. Though the Pleiades brooch was conceived in 1940, it was not until the end of the war that American taste warmed to its unconventional extravagance.

Brooches pinned in groups of three to a scarf, a jacket pocket or epaulette, a waistband or a hat brim, proved lasting favorites. Verdura's jeweled head clips were a novel variation on the old-fashioned scarab and ladybird pins. There were suites of crowned heads, and musketeers with plumed caps tipped over heart-shaped citrine faces in the manner of eighteenth-century French hat-shaped jewels. However, the unmarked visages also reflect contemporary fashion illustrators' quirk of drawing mannequins with blank faces. A notorious offender was Christian Bérard, one of Chanel's intimates, referred to by his exasperated publisher Condé Nast as 'Featureless Freddie'.

The stern and mirthful profiles of tragedy and comedy were the focus of the double mask brooch commissioned in 1941 for Clare Boothe Luce by Jock Whitney, one of Mrs. Luce's many admirers. The pearl-tasseled gold clip, topped with emerald and sapphire cabochons, was intended as a souvenir of a theatrical award she won for her play *The Women*. The two-faced motif was also a fitting emblem of the female duplicity that was the play's theme; Luce always took credit for being its "leading bitchy character."

Overleaf The 'Tragedy and Comedy' brooch with cabochon emeralds and sapphires, designed in 1941 to celebrate Clare Boothe Luce's Tony award for her play, *The Women*.

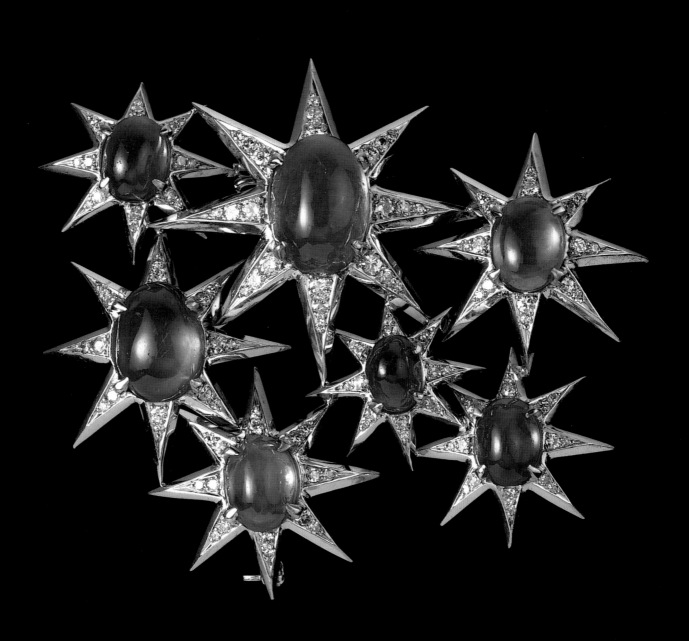

A pavé diamond antique coin brooch surmounted with gold and ruby plumage; and a Greek coin sunburst brooch with blue and yellow enamel.

From the start of the war, numismata were an increasingly recurrent motif in Verdura's work: the medal-like seal of Texas is engraved on the lid of the box Fulco made for Porter in December 1942, to celebrate the opening of *Something for the Boys*, his last Ethel Merman vehicle. Fulco had a preference for coinage, the universal lucky charm: it had been worn as jewelry throughout the Roman Empire, in Europe from the Middle Ages into the modern era, in India, China, and Japan as well as various Islamic nations. A client's assorted antique specie—from Hungary, Macedonia, Florence, and Venice—was mounted in radiant gold frames, to shine on a lapel like a "constellation of suns." Gold dollars adorn curb link bracelets. The case Linda Porter commissioned in 1943 for the première of *Mexican Hayride* has a couple of eighteenth-century Spanish pieces-of-eight scattered across the top; the gold 8-escudos were ingeniously set so that their obverse is visible on the inside of the lid.

Designs resembling decorations were similarly popular. *Vogue* decreed that "if you could have only one jewel, it might be a decoration, an order, or a jewel that is a modern translation of one." Verdura created a spectacular ribbon-weave Maltese Cross for Pola Negri, with baguette- and round-cut diamonds set in widely spaced platinum strips around two half-moon diamonds. Clare Boothe Luce also purchased a Maltese Cross brooch, with emerald-cut, round and old-mine diamonds pavé set in platinum and surrounded by diamond and gold rays. Some years later, she brought in a diamond and emerald bracelet to be remounted in platinum as a Maltese Cross: she had just been received into the Catholic Church, and wore her new faith "like a badge of pride." "Pinned to a ribbon like an old swimming team medal," a diamond sunburst by Verdura—reminiscent of his creations for Chanel—was the only adornment *Vogue* recommended for the 'Spectacularly Simple Look', exemplified by Valentina's black dress and brown jerkin. The Russian-born *couturière*, Garbo's favorite, was an eccentric given to portentous non-sequiturs like "Children are for suburbs, mink is for football."

Mainbocher was another stylist whose gowns were often enhanced by Verdura jewelry, in fashion shoots as well as in real life. Born in Chicago, Main Rousseau Bocher had studied fine arts and music in the United States before joining French *Vogue* as an illustrator and editor. Launched by a syndicate of Parisian socialites in 1929, he was credited with the invention of the strapless evening dress. His classy minimalism appealed to actresses like Irene Dunne, Constance Bennett and Loretta Young; Mrs. Simpson chose him to design her famous Wallis blue wedding outfit. Mainbocher believed that "even the simplest dress must not look timid."

The understatement of Valentina and Mainbocher provided the ideal canvas for Verdura's chromatic fancies: draped bibs of pearls, amethyst or emerald beads hitched up at one side with a thick gold cable; 'effective' brooches with huge pink tourmalines nestling among cabochon emeralds, or yellow and blue sapphires; big, bold, feminine rings with tender green peridots framing a pink sapphire; emeralds and pink tourmalines floating in pink gold; aquamarines and sapphires like changeful blue seas.

One chronicler summed up the situation: "From where I sit, it would seem that the smartest women buy their bombazines from

The cigarette case made for Cole Porter's 1943 Broadway musical, *Mexican Hayride.*

Overleaf A large diamond Maltese cross brooch made for Clare Boothe Luce. A second Maltese cross brooch set with diamonds and emeralds, also made for Mrs. Boothe Luce, both 1942. Right: a ribbon weave brooch, consisting of six interwoven pavé diamond ribbons with two half-moon diamonds in the center, made for Pola Negri, *c.* 1947.

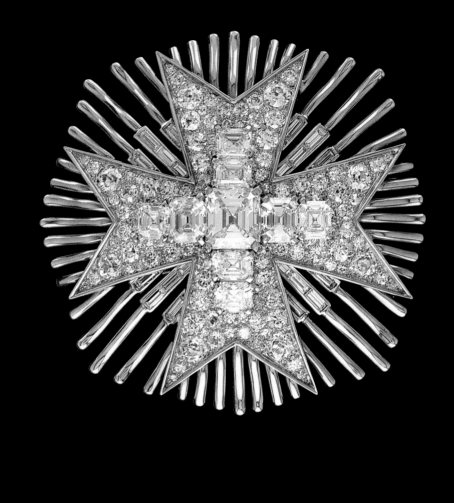

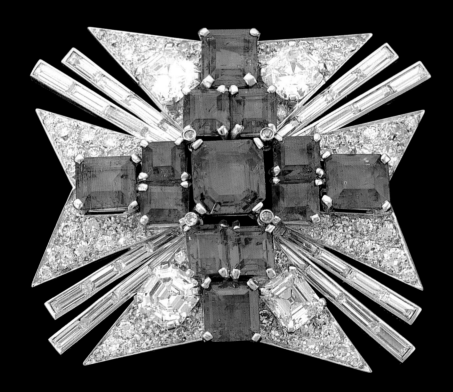

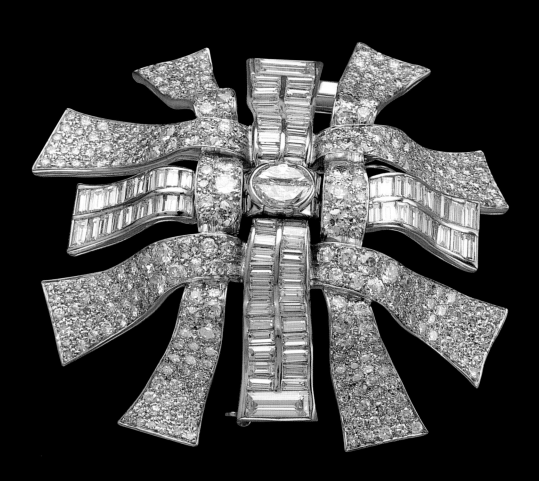

Mainbocher, their sparklers from Verdura. Jessica at Bergdorf's is their oracle for bonnets and Syrie Maugham is called in to decorate their flats." Despite the personal acceptance, financial stability, and professional recognition that finally came Fulco's way, the war years were somber. He was engulfed by what one friend diagnosed as "the black nexus of Sicilian gloom," for what little news reached him from home was not reassuring. Maria Felice's husband, Tom Lequio, was leading the Italian troops in North Africa. His mother Carolina's safety was also at risk, since Palermo's Fascist Party had established headquarters next door, making Via Montevergine a prime target for both partisans and the Allies. Fulco had troubles of his own in the United States: after Italy followed Germany into war, American firms owned by Axis nationals were being shut down. FBI agents came to inspect Verdura's premises and confiscated his radio, fearful that he might be receiving coded messages over the airwaves. Alfano commiserated: "The Duke wasn't able to work without his little radio next to him, with classical music playing all the time." To avoid further government attention, Mann was promoted to President and Verdura demoted to Vice-President.

Fulco made light of his status as an alien under surveillance, and was cheered by visits from old British friends such as Diana and Duff Cooper on a lecture tour of the United States. Major Peter Coats, who after the war became a renowned gardener and published books on gardening, praised him as "an ally, and one of the most brilliant, if acerbic talkers I know." He was a regular at the outdoor concerts held to benefit the USO by the composer Prince George Chavchavadze and his wife, the former Elizabeth Ridgeway, at their New Jersey estate; as a souvenir, Fulco gave the Princess a little box decorated with a miniature of their columned music kiosk. Not entirely in jest, Winston Churchill proposed parachuting him into Sicily behind enemy lines as an *agent provocateur*, to prepare the way for Operation Husky. Fulco developed a repertoire of absurd accounts of being tailed in broad daylight. Once while strolling down Fifth Avenue, he realized with a sense of panic that in order to allay his minders' suspicions, he must instantly "do something pure." As St Patrick's loomed providentially into sight, the appropriate gesture of piety suggested itself. Fulco entered the church, approached the font, dipped his hand in the holy water—then proceeded absentmindedly to splash it behind his ear.

A necklace of cabochon sapphires and diamonds, suspending a large baroque pearl.

7 Postwar

*New York offers the spectacle of a variety of objets d'art – women,
women upon whom men display their fortunes, idol-women,
covered with the fine, rich spoils of vanquished enemies.*
- Jean Cocteau

Verdura's target brooch in
platinum, yellow gold, diamonds,
and sapphires, 1941.

Opposite Drawings from the
Verdura design archives, illustrating
his rich and varied imagination.

BY THE END OF 1944, jewelry had "entered on a new phase calling for a standard of artistry, workmanship and creative invention comparable to that which distinguished the great designer craftsmen of the past," according to the *Art News Annual*. Verdura was singled out as "the most truly creative of modern designers and the one most closely related to the Renaissance." The Verdura style appealed to cultivated patrons with the knowledge to appreciate his sly historical references, and the self-assurance to enjoy his lack of pomposity. One of these was John Nicholas Brown, scion of the wealthy Rhode Island dynasty that founded the university of that name in Providence. A connoisseur of Italian Old Master drawings, Brown also championed modernism in the arts: he was, for instance, one of the first American clients of Viennese-born architect Richard Neutra. Brown recognized in Verdura not only an inheritor of the Renaissance tradition of sculptural jewelry, but a significant contemporary stylist. Verdura approved of Brown's refusal to treat jewelry as a financial investment; he would often opt for semi-precious stones enabling him to stretch his dollars in the design department. Brown was a great favorite with the Verdura staff: "the richest baby in the world," as Alfano called him, quoting newspaper headlines on the day he was born.

Since it was Brown's custom to celebrate Christmases and anniversaries with gifts of jewelry, over the years his entire family acquired a highly representative collection of Verdura gems. The birthdays of his wife Anne Kinsolving were often marked with heart-shaped jewels, of which the most romantic was a brooch featuring a beautifully proportioned 142-carat deep pink tourmaline of rare clarity, bound with a double string of diamond-set gold stars. Pink stones had never been popular in *haute joaillerie*, but Fulco loved the sweet nuances of rosy kunzite, sapphires, rubies, and tourmalines. When it was rumored that the world's largest hoard of precious pink topaz had come onto the London market, Fulco lost no time in despatching Joe Mann to locate and acquire the entire lot of forty gems.

Another important client was Mrs. Albert Lasker, the philanthropist whose well-publicized love of beauty took many forms—from a superb collection of canvases by Picasso, Van Gogh, Monet, and Renoir, to a donation of 150,000 tulips to be planted along Park Avenue so the city wouldn't look like "a woman without lipstick." Between July and November 1945 alone, she made six major purchases of the morganite

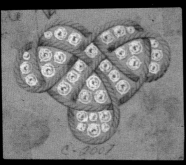

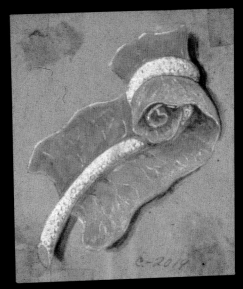

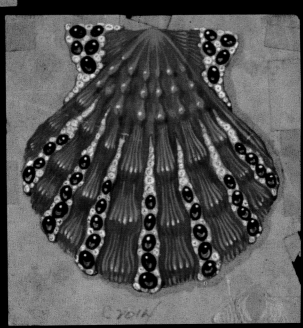

and tourmaline jewels for which Verdura was becoming famous. The actress Ruth Gordon was also a fan of his "beautiful, original, wildly expensive jewelry." In her autobiography, she outlines an imaginary comedy entitled *23 Beekman Place*, to star Katharine Cornell and Clifton Webb, with costumes by Mainbocher and jewels by Verdura. She supposed that the show could not fail to be "the chic-est thing in town, everyone would come to see it, they'd have to, it would be a must."

When Gordon's husband, Garson Kanin, gave her a 75-carat emerald cabochon, she insisted on having it mounted by Verdura. By chance, she found herself in the elevator at 712 Fifth Avenue with Marie Harriman, who was bringing in a pink diamond, a present from her husband Averell, then Roosevelt's envoy to the Soviet Union. When Gordon went in to pick up her ring some weeks later, she was thrilled with the gold rope setting that was so unmistakably Verdura. And what had Fulco done, she enquired, with the Harriman stone? "I didn't," he replied significantly. Gordon gloated: "How about the Kanins get emeralds and the Harrimans get pink glass for their money?"

Fulco was his own worst salesman, disconcertingly honest when not feigning indifference to hide his discomfort at selling. He implemented a liberal policy regarding exchanges and upgrades, obliging even when one young magazine editor asked him to take back a bracelet so she could afford a Louise Nevelson sculpture, of which he heartily disapproved. When an important customer entered the shop, Alfano would tap softly at Fulco's door: "Mrs. So-and-So's here, do you want to see her?" The lapidary response never varied: "Tell her I died." He subscribed to Chanel's perversely effective sales philosophy, according to which "every client met is a client lost."

American women of style—and personality—made up the majority of Verdura's clientele; it included women such as Anita Loos, Diana Vreeland, Mrs. Paul Mellon. In one of his first post-war catalogues, he wrote: "We are endeavouring to offer jewels that are truly artistic and unusual—jewels with an old-world touch yet with a smart distinction that makes them right for the modern woman." Not a new, but a rare breed, these tastemakers displayed an "inordinate aesthetic sensitivity," and were often inspired to reach "beyond the fashions of their times, as well as into other periods and places, to develop a style that is essentially American in spirit and completely a projection of themselves." Truman Capote compared these beauties to carefully wrought icons: their appearance was the result of an "adherence to some aesthetic system of thought, a code transposed into a self-portrait; what we see is the imaginary portrait precisely projected." The most exquisite of these creatures he called "swans," and indeed many of them—the three Cushing sisters, for example—wore Verdura swan brooches like the badge of an exclusive sorority. It was an appropriate emblem, associated in antiquity with the goddess of love Aphrodite and Artemis the virgin

One of Verdura's swan brooches; this example is made of a baroque pearl with diamond coronet and wings. Opposite: the rhinoceros and 'Asta' terrier brooches also feature baroque pearls and diamonds.

Overleaf Platinum, diamond, cultured baroque pearl, and enamel swan brooch, 1955. On the right, Verdura's design for a large baroque pearl and diamond swan brooch, with Indian briolette diamond drop, made for Babe Paley in 1948.

huntress. Later, immaculate swan maidens and the Swan Knight, Lohengrin, appeared in Northern mythology. According to one seventeenth-century treatise, the swan embodied "the whiteness of peace." Like the Tudor jeweled swan pendants that inspired Fabergé at the turn of the century, Verdura brooches feature huge baroque pearls for the body; the head and wings are of chased gold, highlighted with diamonds; sharp accents are provided by ruby eyes and black enamel webbed feet. Some swans bear pear-shaped diamonds in their beaks, or clutch old-fashioned briolettes. Others preen, glide or soar in flight.

Baroque pearls, with their unique imperfections, sparked Verdura's imagination in a way no flawless gemstone ever could. The result was reminiscent of Renaissance *grotteschi*, hybrid creatures first inspired by the decor of Nero's Golden House. Michelangelo defended these protean inventions, maintaining that an artist was justified in "changing some limb or part if, in starting with a griffin or a stag, he modifies its posterior to that of a dolphin, or if he puts wings in the place of legs, if wings go better, whether it be a lion, a horse or a bird." The most outrageous juxtapositions were admissible, in the interest of "better decoration," or just "for the pleasure of mortal eyes, which often desire to see that which they have never seen." The fashion spread quickly: soon Netherlandish jewelers were universally recognized as specialists in baroque pearl gems, supplying the courts of Europe with pendants in the form of whimsical sea-sprites and mythological beasts. There were also other less remote origins. Dalí had introduced Fulco to the Surrealist

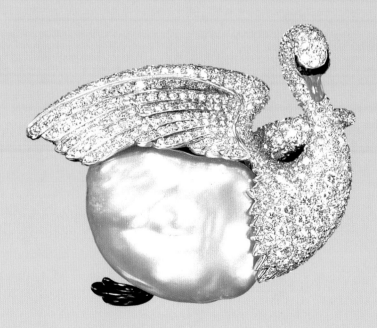

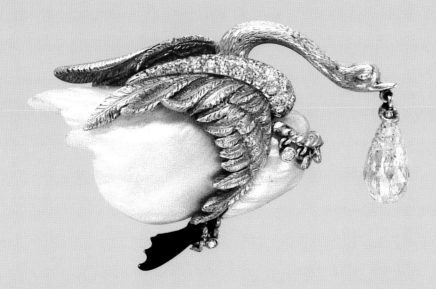

A drawing for a baroque pearl and gold hedgehog.

Opposite and below Verdura produced several unicorn designs in the 1940s. The finished pieces were usually made of ivory and set with diamonds, turquoises, and rubies.

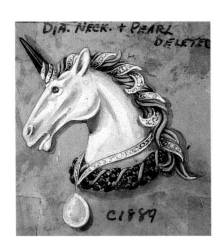

cadavres exquis, combining outlandish fragmentary figures sketched by different hands. The sculptures at Villa Palagonia were another source: Fulco had always been entranced by the freakish array of "bodies of winged women with elephant's feet and hog's heads, camels that end in eagles, Chinamen that begin as fish…"

Nin Ryan's daughter Ginn, who had special permission to visit Fulco on her way home after school, was one of the few people allowed to watch him at work. "He'd put a baroque pearl onto a sheet of heavy tracing paper, and draw around it very quickly—a head, then a tail. It would become a camel, then he'd move the pearl and do a triton, followed by a swan and finally, something completely different, like a mermaid. Then he'd set little stones all around." Fulco designed turbaned Arab warriors, winged dragons, and a tricky porcupine whose gold quills had to be affixed in dentist's cement. He enjoyed reinventing designs from the past. His Chinese junks are an exotic variant of boat-shaped nef pendants produced in Genoa, Venice, Sicily, and Spain as seafarers' ex-votos. His unicorns only faintly resemble the beasts of medieval heraldry or the *Dame à la Licorne* tapestries; in fact, they are patterned after the robust folk carvings on early American carousels. He gave the most extravagantly Old-World creations a topical twist, like the merman bearing two conical sapphire torches pictured in a Pearl Harbor Day ad with the patriotic caption: "Light the Path to Freedom."

Fulco participated in the full spectrum of New York social life, from charity benefits for Sister Kenny, the Australian nurse who advocated physical therapy against polio paralysis, to coming-out parties in honor of Christine Jurgensen, the first known transsexual. The American fashion world was in a state of effervescence: a major revolution was in progress, launched in Paris on 12 February 1947 by Christian Dior. From the sidelines, Chanel poured scorn upon his New Look, dismissing the narrow-waisted, wide-skirted silhouette as mere "upholstery." But the very *créateurs* who had rallied around her in her heyday—Bérard, Cocteau, Poulenc, the de Noailles—realized that Dior had revitalized the true spirit of French couture, which somehow contrived to be both frivolous and rigorous. Even Etienne de Beaumont allowed himself to be coaxed out of retirement to craft jewelry for the new *maison*. And when Dior established headquarters in Manhattan the following year, Nicky de Gunzburg was recruited to give the Fifth Avenue premises a Gallic gloss: the result was a sprightly mélange of Provençal, Louis XVI and 1910 styles.

Fulco's glamorous designs perfectly accented the New Look. *Vogue* recommended "one bold jewel" by Verdura, "a great deep blue Ceylon sapphire wreathed in diamonds…as a favour for your suit." As if the end of the war had released new energy, his creations become more vibrant, more flexible—'crushable' in the language of fashion—than ever before. Bracelets and necklaces seem to bounce with life, embellished

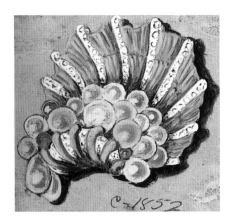

Drawing of a shell brooch with pearls. Opposite: the finished jewel.

Below Design for an elaborate diamond 'white lilac' brooch.

Right A nosegay of violets: a brooch set with amethysts, emeralds and faceted diamonds, *c.* 1945.

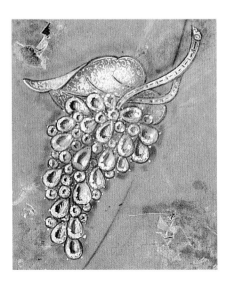

with golden tassels and 'cages' in which captive pearls dance. One extravagant brooch features a golden Naiad clasping billows of loosely strung fancy colored pearls to its lustrous opal bosom. A gold shell brooch overflowing with pearls of all sizes and colors combines *rocaille* elegance with *belle époque* opulence. Gold wheat stalks bend under the weight of marquis diamond grains. In a palm-sized lilac brooch, a mass of heart-shaped amethyst florets glistening with diamonds lies across a leaf in pavé emeralds and peridots; each heart-shaped blossom is articulated such that the cluster bends as naturally as fresh lilac. The lilac, symbolizing young love, was associated in the second half of the nineteenth century with Empress Eugénie: in Winterhalter's portrait of her among the ladies of the court, her dusky beauty requires no other ornament than the blossoms in her hair. During the Second Empire, lilac jewels were composed by all the major Parisian *joailliers*; Verdura's piece is closest to the stylized diamond spray Rouvenat made as an Imperial commission in 1867.

The return to prosperity sparked Verdura's interest in the delicate garland style which had been popular for court jewelry – tiaras, bowknot brooches, entire parures – from the eighteenth century through the Edwardian era. However, he was also responsible for reviving a variety of less formal historical modes. Pins decorated with rows of sapphire bluebirds on golden boughs exude Victorian sentimentality. Of Verdura's many floral brooches, the most coveted remained the violet posy. When the heiress Brenda Frazier was forced to return some $300,000 worth of jewelry to a delinquent suitor, the only item she genuinely regretted losing was the bouquet. Unaware that the original brooch came from Verdura (costing $4,500 in 1948), she ordered a similar one from Harry Winston.

The indispensable accessory of the man-about-town was still the gold cigarette case. There was no better endorsement than the 1946 film *Night and Day*, in which a sequence showed Cole Porter (portrayed by Cary Grant) receiving Linda's traditional first-night gift, those unmatching spherical cufflinks mentioned earlier. That year Verdura designed a three-colored gold box to celebrate the premiere of the Orson Welles version of *Around the World in 80 Days*, for which Porter provided the songs; its engraved lid reproduces the frontispiece of the first edition of Jules Verne's book. In 1948, two more cases marked the opening nights of the movie *The Pirate*, starring Judy Garland and Gene Kelly, and of Porter's greatest hit, *Kiss Me Kate*. Two years later, a basket-weave case lined in black Morocco leather was produced to commemorate the far less successful *Out of This World*.

Cole's only rival in such matters of taste was the Duke of Windsor, whose approach was mercifully straightforward. The scenario never varied: the Duke would ask Fulco to show him all his sketches, and bring out all the stock, which generally consisted of several trays of brooches, a dozen substantial rings, seven to ten gold, diamond, and gemstone parures, an assortment of bracelets and earrings. After a brief pause, he would point with one finger, and utter the magic words: "That one." Two days later, the check would be delivered. The Duchess was another matter entirely. Although her exacting manner and penchant for wisecracks barred her from unconditional swan status, she was indisputably a woman "whose sole creation was her perishable self," as Capote put it. Fulco did not find dealing with the Duchess easy, and not just because, as a monarchist, he could not but secretly resent her role in the abdication. Her perfectionism, verging on indecisiveness, drove him to exasperation: she would happily spend two or three hours deliberating on a single choice, fondling the jewels like a child at play. But the Duchess shared Fulco's pleasure in unusual color combinations, such as the rich mix of amethysts and rubies used in the first piece the Windsors commissioned, a heart brooch. The Duchess collected hearts as souvenirs of joyous events, just as she did crosses to symbolize the troubles that beset her.

Horst, who photographed the Duchess on countless occasions, noted that although she bought from several jewelers, it was Verdura who succeeded in transforming her: "he alone understood how to make her a duchess." Not long after the Duchess topped the Best Dressed List, a number of her jewels disappeared in a mysterious heist; it was not surprising that she turned to Verdura for suitable replacements. As a substitute for an aquamarine and diamond brooch, he suggested a spectacular platinum clip with one large aquamarine ringed by sapphire cabochons and diamonds. She also selected two pairs of mabé pearl earclips, one with a diamond-set wire border, the others crisscrossed with four strands of gold rope—elegant jewels appropriate for all occasions,

Opposite Platinum and diamond butterflies on a large heart-shaped 61-carat aquamarine brooch, 1969.

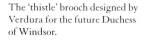

Top Pair of mabé pearl and diamond earclips designed for Wallis Simpson. The second pair, below, is based on a similar motif.

The 'thistle' brooch designed by Verdura for the future Duchess of Windsor.

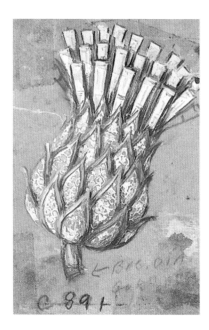

whether formal or informal. Verdura earrings were prized for what he called their "facelift effect": even button and pendant earclips were designed to cling to the lobe with a flattering, upward slant. To celebrate the publication of his autobiography *A King's Story* in March 1951, the Duke gave Wallis several pairs of earclips in styles synonymous with Verdura—snail shells set with turquoise cabochons, mabé pearls with woven style mounts, plus a heart-shaped gold vanity topped with an aquamarine cabochon. At Sotheby's 1987 auction of the Windsor "love tokens," the case fetched the equivalent of $146,667—over 56 times its estimate and almost a hundredfold its original price.

Relations between Fulco and the Windsors, whom he referred to in private as the "Two Old Boobs," became slightly strained once he learned that the Duchess was passing off his pieces as her own inventions. She had no reason to expect a refusal when she came into the shop to exchange a diamond brooch in the form of a thistle which the Duke had given her several years before. A fashionable motif in jewelry well before the turn of the century, the thistle was also one of the historic emblems of British royalty. She wanted to trade it in for a delectable rosebud pin in pink topaz, emeralds, and diamonds, with gold-fringed emerald leaves, which Richard Avedon had just photographed for *Harper's Bazaar*. Fulco looked embarrassed. "I'd love to exchange it for you, but, alas, I cannot," he explained apologetically. "You see, everything here is designed by me, and I understand that this thistle is *your* design."

After the war, word of Verdura's success reached Europe before he did. Lady Abdy glided into Gabriella di Robilant's high fashion atelier in Rome, soon after the Liberation of Italy in 1945. As she tried one gown after another, she brought her old friend up to date, informing her that she had finally decided to embrace Communism. "So what about *this?*" Gabriella asked indignantly, gesturing towards a lavish cigarette case topped with a pink tourmaline wrapped in gold net that had slipped from her open handbag. It turned out to be a creation of Verdura's.

Fulco's long-awaited return to Italy the following year was heart-breaking. He disembarked as the country was preparing to vote in the referendum that was to abolish the monarchy. A group of Sicilian diehard royalists had hoped to interest the House of Savoy in founding an independent Kingdom of Sicily; predictably, their efforts failed. Fulco sat up with his old friend Umberto, who had become King after his father's abdication, on his last night on Italian soil. After 13 June 1946, the day Umberto II went into exile, Fulco never wore any tie but a black one in mourning for the monarchy.

Upon his arrival in Palermo, he discovered that Palazzo Verdura had taken two severe hits when 400 US flying fortresses bombarded the city in May 1943. Lampedusa's home had also been devastated, and he would mourn the extent and irreversibility of the losses in *The Leopard*: "From the ceiling of the ballroom the Gods, reclining on gilded couches, gazed down smiling and inexorable as a summer sky. They thought themselves eternal; but a bomb manufactured in Pittsburgh, Penn., was to prove the contrary." As no money was available to restore Casa Verdura to anything approaching its original splendor, Mamà's existence continued as usual in the wings that remained intact. Even the magnificent Florios had lost all their wealth, except for the handful of jewels Donna Franca had succeeded in hiding from the Nazis and for which Fulco helped her find a rich American buyer. There was an oppressive sense that nothing would ever be the same again. Adapting Talleyrand's nostalgic quote about *la douceur de la vie* in pre-Revolutionary France, Fulco insisted that only those who had known pre-war Sicily had truly experienced the pleasure of life. Still, he delighted in introducing foreigners as well as mainland Italians to the island. His standard airport greeting was: "I want your first impact with Sicily to be a shock."

The jewels of this period reflect Verdura's renewed fascination with his heritage. For a few close friends, including Cécile de Rothschild, he devised *pupo* brooches, inspired by the traditional wooden marionettes that still today enact the adventures of the Crusaders on Palermo's street corners. *Pupi* were popular children's gifts on the Feast of All Souls, when an annual outdoor toy fair was held. Fulco remembered the air filled with vendors' cries. "Did the dead bring you any gifts?" would elicit the stock response: "A *pupo* with twisted hips!" Verdura's figures reproduce every last structural detail of the puppets: jointed limbs, retractable visors, and swords that can be drawn from their sheaths. Emerald plumes bob above

A brooch, in the shape of a charging warrior in armor, made by Verdura for Mrs. Edward R. Murrow.

pink tourmaline faces, nacre breastplates bear coats-of-arms picked out in olivine and gold. Gradasso, the "bravest of the Pagan knights" to challenge Charlemagne, wears armor encrusted with rubies, sapphires, diamonds and pearls; billowy pantaloons cut from paper-fine green silk add a distinctive dressmaker touch.

The mood in Paris soared before long to pre-war levels of gaiety. Baba and Jean-Louis de Faucigny-Lucinge held open house every evening, an informal gathering of friends that was part cocktail, part salon. Duff Cooper had been appointed British Ambassador, and Diana's *petite bande* congregated at their Faubourg St Honoré residence. When Fulco was not staying with the Noailles, he could be found at the Hôtel Lotti on the Rue de Castiglione, where his favorite room was hung with Italianate crimson damask. Eventually he found a flat of his own near St-Germain des Prés, at 5 rue Casimir Périer, overlooking a small leafy square. He took his meals at fashionable Left Bank restaurants, such as the Mont Blanc in rue Las Cases, and the Méditerranée opposite the Odéon. Normality was deemed to have returned definitively when Bricktop's nightclub reopened in May 1950. Janet Flanner and Art Buchwald reported that "the elegant international set" packed into the red, gold, and white damasked premises included Dalí, Barbara Hutton Troubetzkoy, Schiaparelli, Marcel Achard, Simone Simon, Nicky de Gunzburg, and Verdura.

Fulco (seated) with friends at the Villa Marlia, the Pecci Blunt estate near Lucca, 1956.

Fulco with Count de Beistegui, Mrs.
Paul Rogers, Stavros Niarchos, and
Ann Marie Aldobrandini at de
Beistegui's Palazzo Labia in Venice.

Overleaf An assortment of
Verdura's distinctive cocktail rings:
a large star sapphire set in a pavé
diamond mount; an emerald cut
diamond in a wrapped enamel
mount with pavé diamonds; a
golden sapphire and pavé diamonds;
a large yellow diamond in a pavé
diamond turban mount; a spinel
and pavé diamonds, all *c.* 1955–1965.

Summer invitations to the Pecci Blunt estate in Tuscany were
highly coveted. French *Vogue* even advised on the proper dress for those
so fortunate as to be invited to the Villa Marlia. No matter that the food
was known to be bad, the drink scarce, and the fun strictly regimented by
Mimì herself: the principle of exclusivity worked wonders. A huge
collage at the pool house of portraits of guests were numbered according
to the date of their visit, and great snobbish significance was attached to
the low figures. At 62, Fulco was almost family. Each season a fancy dress
dance was held at Marlia. Mimì would announce the theme at a weekend
lunch, commanding silence by rapping imperiously on her wineglass
with a knife: "The theme for the ball is"—suspenseful pause—"Mad
People" or Stars, Kings and Queens, Operas, Current Events, Drinks, the
Olympic Games. Plays were performed in the topiary open-air theater;
Fulco would invariably write his own piece, a monologue in which he
shared center stage with a telephone. The opening line was always a
querulous "Pronto, PRONTO!"

In Venice the shutters of the great *palazzi* along the Grand Canal
slowly began to creak open. The most desirable invitations were to
Palazzo Labia, the home of Carlos de Beistegui, a mysterious figure
whose wealth was attributed to bottomless South American tin mines. A
discriminating art collector, he was also an unsurpassable snob, reputed to
be so fastidious that he had never courted a woman below the rank of
duchess. The ball he held on 3 September 1951 was universally
recognized as a landmark in social history. "As you know," the aged Aga
Khan repeated to all who would listen, "I have been to many parties
starting in Queen Victoria's days, but I am certain that this was the best
one of them all." The event was conceived as a living continuation of
Giambattista Tiepolo's magnificent frescoes (1745–50) of the loves of
Antony and Cleopatra decorating the halls of Palazzo Labia. The

settecento was all the rage in Venice, thanks to the premiere of Stravinsky's opera *The Rake's Progress* at the Fenice—not to mention a major retrospective exhibition of Tiepolo's work. To famous Hollywood actors pleading abjectly for invitations, Charlie Beistegui's response—except to Gene Tierney—was a petulant: *"La réponse est non, non et non."* One day shortly before the ball, as Fulco sat at a café in Piazza San Marco, he espied Artemus, a friend of his housekeeper Lillian, who occasionally waited on him in New York. Artemus explained that he was spending the summer in the employ of an odious American couple. Fulco exulted as he recognized a marvellous opportunity to subvert Beistegui's intentions and crush the ambitions of two social climbers, while emancipating Artemus. He enquired solicitously: "Would *you* like to attend the ball?" It turned out that Artemus would, and so it was arranged that he would swell the numbers of the African entrée. The day of the ball, his employers chose to leave town rather than reveal they had been excluded from the fête of the century. Artemus settled them into their train compartment, then announced that he had an invitation to Palazzo Labia, seized his suitcase and disappeared into the crowd milling alongside the tracks.

The evening proved memorable. In a fine bit of typecasting Beistegui impersonated Count Alessandro Cagliostro, the society alchemist who had boasted of transmuting base metals into pure gold. Diana Cooper as Cleopatra was costumed by Schiaparelli, Mary de Rothschild attended as "Dior's idea of a Tiepolo peasant girl," Daisy Fellowes provided a rococo interpretation of America, Marie-Laure de Noailles was particularly "monstrous as the Lion of Saint Mark," Dalí and his wife Gala portrayed the "ghosts of Venice," Horst tottered about in cothurnes as a bewigged procurator of the Venetian republic. Arturo Lopez-Willshaw, the Chilean tin magnate, led an Imperial Chinese entrée, with a cast of fifty clad in eighteenth-century embroidered silk robes. Scantily disguised as Old Father Time, Fulco chaperoned the Four Seasons, delectably embodied by Princess Milagros Colonna as Summer, Princess Domitilla Ruspoli as Autumn, the American-born Countess Consuelo Crespi as Spring, and 17-year-old Princess Laudomia del Drago as Winter. Domietta, as she is always known, had not yet made her society debut, and Fulco, who was struck by her beauty, had to use all his powers of persuasion with her mother for permission for her to appear. In what was hailed as the most sensational entrée of all, Fulco had introduced an entirely fresh cast of international trend-setters.

Opposite left: a faceted amethyst ring with red enamel and diamonds; right: gold and platinum ram's horn mount set with white and yellow diamonds centering a large square-cut peridot.

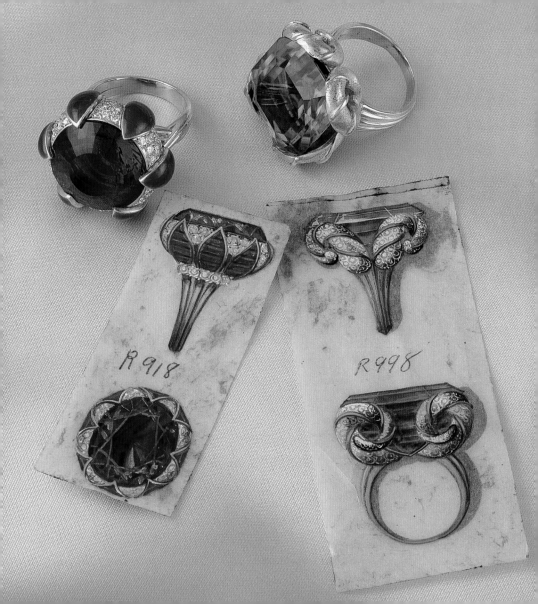

R 918

R 998

8 Prosperity

Working as it does quite outside the black side of life,
the ills, suspicions, sorrows and dark depths of human
nature, the purpose of goldsmithery has always been
and is to keep happiness and goodwill alive.
- H. C. Bainbridge

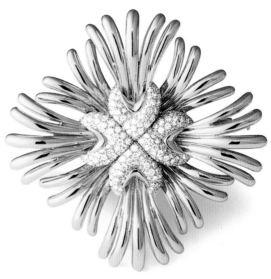

A ray brooch of gold and
diamonds, 1940s.

Opposite A fashion photograph
(*Town & Country*, October 1948)
featuring Verdura jewels.

THE FIFTIES—the age of affluence—were the Verdura decade. Fulco's
dream of establishing a Paris branch of Verdura was brought within the
bounds of possibility when the French luxury tax dropped from 33 to 13
per cent. It was not just the prospect of returning to old haunts that
attracted him, but the opportunity of working with skillful master
craftsmen like Drouet and Verger in the world capital of *haute joaillerie*.
In terms of quality of execution as well as cost reduction, invisible-set
jewels could now be made in two stages. In Paris, the basic design could
be entrusted to specialists in *serti mystérieux*, the technique of aligning
stones so as to conceal the metal mount; then jewelers in New York
would add the final touches. It was Charles de Noailles who came to the
rescue in 1953, offering Verdura the use of a small office suite in an inner
courtyard at 9, rue Boissy d'Anglas, ideally located for the carriage trade,
a few blocks from Place Vendôme, between the Hôtel Crillon and the
American Embassy. The four rooms were handsomely furnished with
wood panels from an eighteenth-century provincial apothecary, and the
forest green wall-hangings that were Fulco's own decorator signature.
The fact that there were no streetside vitrines was considered an
advantage: Verdura's European clientele still preferred discretion to
ostentatious consumption.

   The new generation was epitomized by Giovanni Agnelli, the
handsome, high-living heir apparent to Italy's foremost automobile firm.
By virtue of his long-time friendship with Gianni's American
grandmother, the formidable Princess Jane di San Faustino, Fulco had
always occupied a vaguely avuncular role in the extended family circle.
The ties had become closer when Gianni served as a cavalry officer under
Tom Lequio during the war. Agnelli's patronage was instrumental in
launching and sustaining Verdura's French operation. Able to recognize
and afford excellence, he displayed in all his dealings a seductive form of
elegance that bordered on nonchalance. When Fulco misplaced a rare
pink diamond intended for delivery to Gianni, instead of throwing a
tantrum he shrugged amiably at the mishap.

   During the Fifties 'break-the-bank' presents and 'scene-stealing
jewels' were no longer considered vulgar, but exuberant expressions of
self-confidence and prosperity. It was the heyday of the *celébarite*—Elsa
Maxwell's combination of the words celebrity and sybarite. In her gossip
columns and how-to-entertain books, Maxwell, the famous international

hostess, never failed to heap fulsome praise upon Fulco, whom she selected as one of the eleven international personalities whose presence around her dinner table would guarantee the "most perfect party imaginable." The others were the Duchess of Devonshire, Maria Callas, Evangeline Bruce, Mrs. Fell, Clare Boothe Luce, Prince Aly Khan, Somerset Maugham, Lord Astor, Noël Coward, and Cole Porter—all signally endowed with at least one of the "big six in the catalogue of personal allure: beauty, glamour, intelligence, charm, wit, gaiety." She commended the Duke of Verdura in particular for his flawless manners and his erudition: "all history both of Europe and of America, all poets from Dante to Auden, are open books to him, as well as every artist from Botticelli to Picasso and Peter Arno." Fulco, however, would probably have preferred to attend Elsa's "nightmare party" that included Elvis Presley. "He looks just like a Roman emperor," he explained nonchalantly to friends startled to discover *Hound Dog* and *Blue Suede Shoes* on a shelf alongside Puccini's *La Rondine* in his new New York apartment.

His sense of humor and his infectious love of laughter were remarked upon by all his acquaintances and friends. His passions were drawing, reading, and listening to music. He carried a book with him wherever he went. History was his favorite subject, in the form of memoirs, letters, and biographies. He also adored nineteenth-century novels and could have won first prize in any competition of knowledge on the works of Wilkie Collins. This reading of books in three languages was topped by regular doses of *History Today* and *Historia*, depending on the country he was in. It is no wonder that he amassed a fund of knowledge, and this led him to refer to himself as '*Le petit Larousse roulant.*'

A summons from Fulco to "come wallow in the green room" at 107 East 60th Street was regarded more or less as an invitation to join an exclusive club. At his after-theater gatherings, fare was basic (Fulco liked to cook a large bowl of spaghetti for his friends), but the conversation sparkled, thanks to his "heart of gold and tongue of quicksilver." The expression was Cecil Beaton's, by then a close friend and frequent house guest. Purists might dismiss the eclectic clutter of Fulco's apartment as "poor man's Charlie Beistegui," but Beaton enjoyed the "avalanches of good art, books and long-playing records of the classics; a mixture of Mannerist paintings, seventeenth- and eighteenth-century engravings and sketches by Bérard; nice bits of china, palm-trees and dark green walls, an effective if slightly sketchy attempt at interior decoration." London decorator Nicky Haslam still treasures one of Fulco's tips: "Always remember, chairs walk in the night," the point being that furniture should not be placed, but allowed to "migrate."

Fulco's personal and public lives meshed seamlessly, at least in the public eye. He would entertain Umberto of Savoy with the Duke and

Duchess of Windsor, delighting in the inevitable diplomatic skirmishes. At one memorable soirée, to which the former "King of May" arrived almost an hour late without apologizing to the other ex-royal, the Duchess was heard to observe that "at least, *my* King went of his own accord, while *you* were kicked out." Fulco was at Tallulah Bankhead's side when she celebrated her television debut at an all-night champagne bash; pinned to her gown was his glittering lion's paw brooch from her famous 'tragedy fund' of jewels. He was not above gloating at having retained his position as jeweler 'by appointment' to Brooke Marshall even after she married Minnie Cushing's ex-husband Vincent Astor. Fulco was thrilled when Gianni Agnelli became an even more frequent buyer: he instantly guessed the lucky woman's identity when the Fiat heir insisted that the pendant earrings—black and white drop pearls suspended from diamond bows—had to be "*lunghi, lunghi, lunghi.*" It could only be "European swan *numero uno,*" as Capote referred to the long-necked Princess Marella Caracciolo di Castagneto. The half-American aristocrat had, at the age of 24, just embarked on what was to be a very short New York career as model and assistant to the photographer Erwin Blumenfeld.

Another of Fulco's young expatriate protégées was Countess Afdera Franchetti, involved in a secret liaison with Henry Fonda, whom she eventually married. Verdura miniatures were the love tokens of this tempestuous May-December romance. The actor commissioned a view of the Piazza San Marco complete with tiny pigeons for his homesick fiancée; she gave him a painting of a view of Toledo as a reminder of a happy Spanish holiday. Other gifts were less successful. One Christmas, when Fonda surprised his young bride with a Tiepolo *veduta*, she instantly dissolved into floods of tears as she realized there would be no white mink coat under the tree for her. As one whose forebears had often negotiated dire financial straits by selling off ancestral treasures, Fulco tried to cheer Afdera with the assurance that "one day, that canvas will be far more valuable to you than a fur." After Verdura's death, Afdera expressed the wish to visit the undertaker's chapel where his body was resting. She claimed that whenever she had wanted to say anything to him, he would interrupt her; now she had the opportunity to tell him all the things she had wanted him to know.

Enthusiasm for Verdura's paintings began to spread beyond his immediate coterie, and in December 1953 the Hugo Gallery on East 55th Street offered him his first exhibition. Cole Porter was quoted on the invitation, praising "these small tranquil timeless pieces of beauty... [which] only a great jeweler's hand could have created. In fact their jewel-like size is one reason for their exquisite taste: Fulco di Verdura has used his paints in the manner that diamonds should always be worn: preciously." Admiring reviews appeared in all the major art periodicals, citing Verdura's "magic realism

A pineapple watch charm bracelet.

The Friars, one of Verdura's humorous miniature paintings.

and...dreamlike evocation of time and space." Some motifs—shells, insects, blossoms, and carved masks— were borrowed from his jewelry. Other subjects, in particular the distant Italianate vistas, were unique. All were executed in the same meticulous technique: Fulco applied tempera to parchment with the aid of a powerful hand-held magnifying glass, adding a light coat of transparent nail varnish to fix and brighten the soft hues. *Art Digest* remarked that "choosing his elements with great care and classic disdain for the superfluous, the artist endows his landscapes with a silvery serenity and enigmatic silence that borders on surrealism." Fulco, who took to signing his letters 'Father Moses', began to make invidious comparisons with another public figure with a known penchant for art: "As a *painter*, Winston Churchill is much less good than I am."

A few years later, the Iolas Gallery held another show, where Verdura's *capricci,* Botticelli-inspired allegories and composite architectural views were compared by the painter and critic Michael Ayrton to "the miniature paintings Edwardian ladies propped up on their drawing-room tables amid the clutter of carved ivory paper knives and *repoussé* snuff boxes, souvenirs of grand tours past." In 1956, the first European presentation of his pictures was held in Rome's Sagittarius Gallery, run by Princess Stefanella Barberini Colonna di Sciarra. The compositions had become more extravagant. Belying a serene palette, one small tondo depicted a modern disaster in the making: two locomotives steaming towards each other on the top level of a three-tiered bridge, high above a river in a verdant landscape. In his introduction to the catalogue, the distinguished journalist Luigi Barzini compared the concision of Fulco's miniatures to that of poetry.

In contrast to these meticulously composed images for public consumption, Fulco continued in private to caricature friends, clients, and the odd passerby, with pen strokes that were as sharp as his tongue. The bandeau-coiffed pianist is instantly identifiable as the patroness of the arts Marie-Laure de Noailles. The "Eleventh Best-Dressed Woman" is an expensive, yet anonymous amalgam of big jewels, blond chignon, brown mink coat, and lapdog. The lank-haired young woman in sandals, with a portfolio tucked under her arm, can only be "Faintly Connected with the Arts." "Artistic Ecstasy" is an equally universal figure, lost in open-mouthed contemplation of some unfathomably avant-garde work.

Despite Fulco's attempts to downplay what he insisted on referring to as his 'craft' (or sometimes even 'hobby'), the press recognized Verdura *invenzioni* as twentieth-century classics: the medals and decorations, the polished pebbles in nets, the lightning style, the use of pink gems, the romantic profusion of hearts and feathers, and especially the fantastical baroque pearl jewels. A whimsical bestiary was born of these irregular, oversize pearls: a sapphire-horned rhinoceros bearing a ruby obelisk, a camel in circus garb resembling the beloved Moffo, a dodo brooch patterned after a famous sixteenth-century Netherlandish pendant belonging to Fulco's friend Arturo Lopez.

There were surprising Sicilian sources for several designs. The crowned eagle brooch with baroque pearl breast and outstretched wings, clutching a round pearl in each talon, is reminiscent of such imperial insignia as the Austro-Hungarian single-headed eagle. However, there are greater similarities to a popular motif in Sicilian *settecento* decorative art: the crowned eagle of the Senate of Palermo, with a white breastplate and a pair of roundels in its claws. Verdura's elephant brooch, with its diamond-set baroque pearl body, counts among its obvious sources the Royal Danish Order of the Elephant and the jeweled elephant at the Schatzkammer Residenz in Munich, as well as the pallid 'space elephants' that stalk Dalí's later surrealist landscapes. But there were also Sicilian antecedents: Fulco had been fascinated since childhood by the elephant in the coat-of-arms of his Leofante relatives and the elephant device emblazoned on the Florios' porcelain. And the Liotru fountain in Catania, with its rough-hewn elephant centerpiece, is one of Sicily's best-loved monuments, inspired by Bernini's elephant in Piazza Santa Maria sopra Minerva in Rome. Verdura elephant pins and charms were collected by such taste makers as the Duchess of Windsor (who insisted upon raised trunks for good fortune) and Baba Metcalfe, the daughter of the Viceroy of India, Lord Curzon, whom her staff referred to as 'Lady Babar'.

Verdura's heraldic eagle brooch of sapphires, diamonds, rubies, baroque and cultured pearls, 1956.

Overleaf Elephant brooch made with a baroque pearl and diamonds, designed for Lady Metcalf. The inspiration for the rhinoceros brooch of baroque pearl with a sapphire horn came from the Bernini elephant in Piazza Santa Maria sopra Minerva in Rome.

c.1335

The Gladiator Blackamoor, with
large baroque pearl, diamonds,
and a ruby, c. 1960. Below: double
Blackamoor brooch made for
Babe Paley.

Opposite Kissing Blackamoor
brooch consisting of a gold mount set
with two large baroque pearls and
numerous small round diamonds,
rubies, emeralds, and pearls,
suspending a large drop emerald.

The blackamoor brooch, Verdura's most glamorous baroque pearl jewel, portrayed a turbaned Moorish warrior of antiquity with a pearly cuirass. Like many distinctive pieces in his repertory, the blackamoor associated Thirties-style elements with references to historical pieces. Sculpted busts worn as gems as early as the fourth century BC influenced the ebony and sardonyx statuettes crafted by European goldsmiths during the nineteenth century. Venetian *camée habillée* or *tête de noir* brooches representing Othello—the Moor of Venice—or Hannibal were highly prized as tourist trinkets. By 1933, this "absurd, delightful creature, [whose] costume is generally that of the East of Persia or Byzantium," was swarming over the most sophisticated Parisian salons—from Chanel's suite at the Ritz to Misia Sert's bohemian Rive Gauche flat. Predictably Baba de Faucigny-Lucinge had been the first to flaunt a Cartier blackamoor brooch in black and cream lacquer, spurring Diana Vreeland to display her own vast collection across her chest, in "rows and rows." Verdura's most idiomatic pieces were generally also discreetly evocative of some aspect of the designer's personal experience, and the blackamoor was no exception. The exotic personage was a tribute to his handsome childhood playmate, Abu-ba-Ker. Fulco considered the double blackamoor pin William Paley bought sight unseen for his second wife, the former Barbara Cushing Mortimer, to be his supreme achievement in the genre. One day Jo Mann literally bumped into Paley on Madison Avenue, on his way to the workshop on 53rd Street. He apologized, explaining that he was rushing two exceptionally large American baroque pearls to be mounted—as a single piece. Paley's inquisitive, acquisitive instincts were instantly aroused when he learned that the unprecedented design would feature two embracing figures.

"Fine, send it to me when it's finished," he said. Attired in motley costumes of ruby, emerald and canary diamonds, each bust was fitted with a sculpted onyx head adorned with a plumed gemstone headdress and a diamond parure consisting of eardrops and choker with detachable pendant.

Babe Paley, elected to the Best Dressed List in 1953 and elevated to Fashion's Hall of Fame five years later, was the quintessential trophy client: not so much for the money her socially ambitious husband invested each year in her appearance, as for her exquisite taste and manner. "Aura," "beacon of perfection" and "nobility" were the words most often used to describe the impeccable impression she conveyed. In fact, as Capote put it, "Mrs. P. had only one fault, she was perfect; otherwise, she was perfect." Babe put together each one of her outfits "as if making a painting of herself." She was faithful to those stylists —first Mainbocher and Givenchy, later Halston and Valentino—capable of enhancing her ladylike femininity. Verdura's opulent creations added a luscious note to

her studied elegance: a 21.25-carat canary diamond ring with a special
gold and diamond crown setting, 44.48-carat pear-shaped emerald
earrings set with thirty-four round diamonds, a fabulous 700-carat
emerald bead necklace, a garland-style parure of faceted pink topaz and
diamonds, two multi-strand torsade bracelets with pearl and diamond
clasps, one of natural black and the other of white cultured pearls. To an

A 21.25-carat canary diamond ring
in a gold wire coronet mount with
small round diamonds. The ring
was designed for Babe Paley and
worn by her in this photograph by
Horst (*Vogue*, March 1948).

A pair of natural black and white pearl torsade bracelets with pearl and diamond clasps created for Babe Paley who was often referred to as Verdura's muse.

interviewer asking what kind of woman wore jewelry to best advantage, Fulco responded (probably thinking of Babe): "Tall and dark." And what about the others? "They do their best."

It was also an exhilarating time to be in Italy and, according to Count Rudy Crespi, "it started in those wonderful, crazy Fifties." A brilliant public relations impresario for the country's nascent fashion industry, the Brazilian-born socialite and his American wife Consuelo—later to become Italian *Vogue's* most influential editor—paradoxically embodied the best of Italian style. "Everything had gone wrong for so long. The Italians had been repressed under fascism, beaten in the war, humiliated, occupied. Then the Marshall Aid money came in and there was a lot of money. Upper class Italians were suddenly the gayest and best-dressed people in the world." The success of the 'Italian look'—first featured in the March 1953 issue of American *Vogue*—was instant and durable. The combination of opulent materials and classically proportioned cuts intended, unlike French designs, to last more than one season, was flattering to women who were not professional clothes horses.

Fashion, however, was never the main attraction for Fulco, who organized his Italian holidays around lengthy stays in Sicily, wrapped as ever in its "heavy cloud of sadness and madness." During the year, Mamà's letters—almost illegible documents crossed in the Victorian manner—provided him with weekly reports. A friend cured of a nervous

Verdura, Bill Paley, Tony Mortimer, and Carter Burden pose after a swim off Gianni Agnelli's yacht in the early 1960s.

breakdown thanks to the telepathic intervention of a psychic, a wave of mysterious orchid thefts, an heirloom painting long believed to be by Lippi disappointingly re-attributed to Vivarini: bizarre phenomena put down to the *scirocco*, a disorientating, hot wind out of Africa, laden with red dust. Cracking her whip over "the bears"—her servants—Mamà continued to read voraciously and to lead socially exclusive spiritual exercises. Although even his closest friends were not allowed inside the shabby labyrinth of Casa Verdura, Fulco happily took visitors trawling through Palermo's "weird sprawling mixture of Byzantine, Norman, Arab, Spanish baroque, Mussolini's Italy and Brooklyn's slums." There were *palazzo* parties, soirées on the Niarchos yacht *Creole* and pilgrimages to "Cerda, the cradle of a noble race." On one such reckless drive, two blown tires resulted in 14 hours on the road; Fulco survived "a terrible struggle to mend the inner tubes by the flickering light of a hurricane lantern and the exertions of a dwarf mechanic. Also the luggage rack blew away with half our luggage..." House parties at Fulco's rented cottage in Taormina drew the likes of Beaton and Capote, Duff and Diana Cooper, the Trees, and exuberant Roosevelt offspring whose dalliances with local fishermen provoked a *frisson* among their elders. Judith Montagu often presided as hostess: Judy was not only a surrogate sister, but a soulmate who fueled Fulco's dangerous sense of fun, shared his love of the absurd and reciprocated his letter-writing "Sévigné moods" during the many months of the year they were apart. The *très haute et puissante Dame Judith*, affectionately known as Jude or even Goose, introduced Fulco to her cousin Nancy Mitford, who embraced him instantly as a "great new friend," drawing on his store of gossip to enliven her brittle *romans à clef*. One such episode in *The Blessing* featured an Englishwoman on a guided tour through a Paris mansion, discovering in a secret boudoir none other than her roguish French husband with his teenage mistress.

By 1954, Fulco's traveling schedule had become very regular. He divided his time between New York, where he spent most of the winter and part of the summer, and Paris, where he stayed always in his own apartment in order to direct operations in his shop. His holiday periods consisted of the customary visits to Sicily, where he went two or three times a year to see his mother, and Italy, where he would stay either with his sister in Rome or with Domitilla Herculani or friends in the country.

In the summer of 1954, he went to stay with his old friend Princess Ferdinand Liechtenstein, born 'Dumpy' Oelrichs; member of a well-known American family, she was the sister of the wife of the popular band leader Eddie Duchin. At the Villa Fioretina next door, the beautiful home of Lady Kenmare and her son Rory Cameron, there was a large party, including a tall, handsome Englishman called Tom Parr. At this time Tom was just about to open a shop in London in partnership with David Hicks, to be known as Hicks and Parr. This business was to last for six years, when Tom left to join the most highly esteemed interior decorating firm of Colefax and Fowler, where he worked and eventually became chairman until his retirement in 1995.

From the time of this meeting in the South of France, Tom and Fulco became great friends, and this friendship lasted until Fulco's death in Tom's apartment in London in 1978. As a result of their meeting, Fulco added London to his regular ports of call. He always stayed with Tom in Eaton Square, and it was there that he saw his old friends from the theater, such as Joyce Carey, Dorothy Dickson, Irene Worth, and a large group of Italians who gathered mostly in the welcoming house of Ascanio Marina Branca, and often saw Carlo the son of his old friend Olga di Robilant.

Weekends would be spent with Michael and Anne Tree at Merriworth Castle, their splendid Palladian house in Kent and with Caroline and David Somerset in the cottage where they lived in the shadow of the big house until the Duke of Beaufort died and David eventually succeeded to the Dukedom. Fulco also enjoyed visits to Lady Juliet Duff and her friend Simon Fleet at Bulbridge House in Wilton; and in London he had a bevy of friends, including Marion Sainsbury and the Glendevons, John and Liza, who was the daughter of Somerset Maugham.

Fulco was often high-spirited, boasting of "health triumphant, age regressing, temper lagoon-like, charm overwhelming." But even his most successful years were veined by melancholy. "Life seems to go on in its own rickety way," he wrote to Judy. "One gets older, pretending to get wiser, realizing that one has remained the same old fool and covering up this dismal discovery with a threadbare mantle of so-called sophistication." Mamà sent him prayerful missives, doubtless intended to raise his spirits. In December 1954, she wrote: "As Christmas approaches, I think of you even more intensely (if possible), especially before the Holy

Two pairs of paisley earclips: peridot and diamonds; pink tourmaline and diamonds.

Child. May He heap upon you His blessings. *Sursum Corda!* Let us wait upon Him with trust, let us pray for Him to come to console us and reassure us and give the world peace." Sharp practical advice would follow: "I exhort you to abandon your hermit-like existence, and to accept some invitations."

Religious themes appear more frequently in Verdura's work at this time. One outstanding example is the pin featuring a crucifix with a diamond-encrusted cloth draped over the crossbar (a two-tone gold pendant version was also available). The fabric represents Veronica's Veil, believed to have been miraculously imprinted with Christ's likeness when a woman used it to wipe his brow as He passed her on the road to Calvary. Artists traditionally painted the relic unfolded, so as to display the Holy Face. Verdura transformed the symbol, assimilating it to other motifs in early Christian and medieval iconography in which the Cross is shown together with the seamless tunic or the winding sheets.

Linda Porter's death in 1954 had come as a blow to her friends, despite her protracted illness. Her last commission was a case patterned with interlocking Cs, to be presented to Cole on the gala night of *Can-Can* in May 1953, which her illness prevented her from attending. The twinned Cs—an obvious reference to the names of the musical and its author—also drew on historical precedent: aside from Chanel's famous interlocking logo, there were the jeweled emblem of Charles the Bold, the combined monogram of Catherine de' Medici and her son, the future Charles IX of France, not to mention the vast rococo repertory of double-letter motifs. At the opening night of *Silk Stockings* two years later, Cole's oldest friends continued Linda's tradition, presenting him with a special box. The lid was inset with a Russian gold coin framed by a sunburst; the inscription within read: *In memory of Linda*, followed by the signatures of Jean Howard, Preston Sturges, Nicky de Gunzburg, Natalie Paley, and Fulco. In 1956, Cole ordered his celebratory box himself, for the première of the movie *High Society*. The black enamel case was scattered with a lustrous constellation of thirty-eight old mine diamonds of various sizes that came from an heirloom brooch of Linda's. She was mourned as the last of the legendary beauties to have bridged the gap between "the worlds of fashion and glitter and the pantaloon world of the theater."

Although these worlds were now spinning farther and farther apart, some stylists were energized rather than disoriented by the changed social environment. One was Chanel; after several years of taking potshots at Dior from the safety of retirement, the *couturière* made a surprise comeback in February 1954. Initially dismissed by European critics as a retrospective—at best irrelevant, at worst embarrassing—her sporty yet elegant line caught on quickly in the United States where women were eager for high fashion that was also wearable. Within a year, sales of Chanel clothes on both sides of the Atlantic were skyrocketing. Once again, magazine writers recommended accessorizing Chanel's

Opposite A pink sapphire cross with diamond encrusted scarf representing Veronica's Veil.

Verdura's sketch for the gold cigarette case that Linda Porter gave to Cole Porter when his musical *Can-Can* opened in New York in 1953. The exterior is in a wavy reeded motif and the *Can-Can* monogram (interlocked 'C's) is centered on the cover.

A rope bracelet drawing, 1940s. Opposite: a diamond and gold rope necklace.

outfits of "enormous casual chic" with Verdura jewels. And for those who could not afford authentic Verdura, Fulco's original semi-precious creations from the Thirties—notably the Maltese Cross bracelets—were put back into production in France as Chanel costume jewelry.

Another designer who came to the fore was Jean Schlumberger. Society writers magnified the rivalry between Verdura and Johnny Schlum, who had moved in the same social circles in Paris before the war. In fact, when Schlumberger first moved to New York, Fulco offered him the use of his apartment. The two master jewelers were supposedly engaged—as Letitia Baldrige recalled—in a "heated race to supply the biggest, most exciting brooches to the most prominent women." She enjoyed a view from the grandstand, first as Clare Luce's assistant at the American Embassy in Rome, then as Director of Public Relations for Tiffany & Co.

Although both designers shared a keen interest in floral motifs and precious *objets*, Schlumberger tended towards sharply defined pieces with a certain volumetric cubist flair (Fulco criticized them for being 'spiky'), while Verdura's manner reflected the softer, illusionistic qualities of baroque art. Their personal styles couldn't have been farther apart. Eight years younger than Fulco, Schlum—the scion of a textile manufacturing family prominent in Alsace—had a certain Protestant reserve that enabled him to interact easily with America's industrial élite. In 1956, he was recruited as Tiffany's house designer. Since his debut in couture with Lelong and Schiaparelli, Schlumberger had always been accustomed to catering to a wider clientele, while Verdura was known mainly for 'bespoke' pieces. One outstanding such creation was the massive 'commodora' brooch, made for Anne Kinsolving Brown to mark her husband's election as Commodore of the Newport Yacht Club: four diamond stars nestled among sapphires encircled with thick gold twine. Verdura continued to extend the range of his rope jewels, updating ancient motifs as well as inventing contemporary models with an appealingly improvised look. The sections of a four-strand pearl choker are linked by gold Heracles knots, inspired by the reef knots that embellished Hellenistic jewelry. Diamonds drip from a macramé-style knotted gold rope bib.

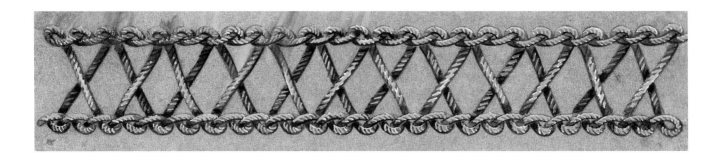

"Diamond is king" was the watchword in the Fifties. In retrospect, Diana Vreeland gave a more nuanced view: "People only remember diamonds." Although much has been made of Verdura's special way with semi-precious stones, he found the challenge of diamonds irresistible. He would quash a client's unreasonable demands with a haughty "You don't take liberties with diamonds." His creations could be as naturalistic as the golden horse-chestnut brooch with a pavé diamond slit inspired by Thirties *bijouterie*—or as imposingly *ancien régime* as a garland-style necklace with 289 old-cut diamonds supporting a fringe of pear-shaped diamonds and three large ruby-and-diamond cluster pendants. For Washington hostess Marjorie Merriwether Post, Fulco remounted an outdated brooch as a distinctive bracelet that still exudes glamor. Thanks to her fabulous wealth, Marjorie Post had become not merely a collector, but a real connoisseur. When her father C. W. Post left her $100 million, he explained that as a result she would never be able to trust anyone, but would have to rely solely on her own expertise. She therefore developed an appetite, as voracious as it was informed, for items of historical relevance that led her to amass Fabergé eggs by the dozen, Habsburg regalia and the jewels of Marie Antoinette. As he sat with his discerning client, Fulco let his pencil rove across the paper until inspiration struck: interlocking gold and diamond crescents inspired by the headdress of Diane de Poitiers, as illustrated in a painting at the Louvre. The royal favorite, first of François I, then of his son Henri II, adopted as her own the lunar emblem of Diana, goddess of the hunt, using it profusely throughout her castle at Anet. This substantial piece was particularly pleasing to Mrs. Merriwether Post who had an aversion in jewelry to anything 'constipated', i.e. small in scale.

As early as 1953, the historian Joan Evans, who was both a connoisseur and a collector of historical gems, remarked that "it is not easy to see the future for the art of jewellery; it may even be considered that as an art it has not a future. For all the centuries of recorded time it has existed as an art in which style and fashion were set by the taste of an aristocracy." As patrons changed, and full-dress ceremonial occasions became ever more scarce, the custom of wearing certain kinds of jewels—such as tiaras—became less frequent. In Britain, however, tiaras actually returned to fashion after the Coronation of Queen Elizabeth II in 1954. Verdura's sprightly American Indian Tiara was commissioned by Jock Whitney for his wife when he was appointed Ambassador to the Court of Saint James. It was not designed to compete with the diamond tiaras worn by European ladies and was meant to emphasize her American and therefore republican background. It was much admired at the 'courts' when Mrs. Whitney would introduce American debutantes and on other social occasions that merited such a headdress. It bristles with irregularly spaced feathers, curling upward and slightly forward, diamond alternating with gold. The jewel is sometimes mistakenly described as

Two brightly colored 'candy' rings designed in the 1940s, one in pink tourmaline, the other in blue topaz.

Overleaf Gold and diamond American Indian Tiara designed by Verdura for Betsey Whitney. As wife of the U.S. Ambassador to the Court of St James, she wore it for her presentation before Queen Elizabeth II in 1956.

composed of laurel leaves, patterned after the laurel wreaths worn in ancient Rome as a symbol of victory and adopted during the neoclassical period as an emblem of excellence. Josephine Bonaparte wore a diadem of golden leaves set with diamond and ruby berries for her Coronation as Empress in 1804. Empress Eugénie had the motif copied by Bapst in 1855; so popular was the laurel-leaf style throughout the Second Empire that Mellerio designed a diamond version. Half a century later, the Duchess of Sutherland was portrayed by Sargent crowned with golden laurel leaves. At the request of the Duchesse de Cadaval, the former Olga di Robilant, Fulco agreed to remount the historic Cadaval tiara, made of eighteenth-century rose-cut diamonds reputed to be the first to reach Portugal from Brazil. The result was an elaborate beribboned concoction that could almost pass for an heirloom of the period—or perhaps an Edwardian replica.

Certain quirky models of the recent past continued to intrigue Fulco, and his attempts to revive them had varying degrees of success. Not surprisingly, there was little enthusiasm for filigree 'fingernail rings' similar to those Etienne de Beaumont devised in 1938, inspired by the discovery of a hoard of pre-Columbian gold funeral ornaments. However, demand was strong for Verdura brooches in the form of a single ivory hand—encased in a net glove, adorned with a bowknot, cuff or ring, clasping a single black pearl or ruby heart. These were throwbacks to a motif popular in both the arts and fashion of the Thirties. Schiaparelli's 1934 hand-shaped purse-clasp, Cartier's onyx and coral hand-shaped pins, Flato's Hand of God pendant and his set of twenty-four black enamel hands forming the letters of the alphabet in sign language, were contemporaneous with the tiny cast of intertwined hands shown in Man Ray's portrait of Dora Maar as well as his punning *Main Ray* sculpture of a milk-white hand holding a golden orb. Fulco was also familiar with earlier iconography, from the hand-shaped bronze votive relics unearthed in Gallo-Roman sanctuaries, to sixteenth-century silver hand pendants from Spain, to the suggestive coral hands that still serve as talismans against the evil eye throughout southern Italy. By the end of the nineteenth century, such amulets were highly sought after by ethnologists like Giuseppe Pitrè, whose extensive collection had been displayed at the Villa Favorita from 1935 onward.

Verdura *objets* and accessories continued to be promoted as fashion essentials, such as a lady's cigarette-holder tipped with pink quartz to mimic a lipstick-stained filter. His compacts served as portable conversation pieces. One in the shape of a wicker basket filled with tiny tourmaline and turquoise 'eggs' resembles a child's Easter prize. A rough fossil set in the lid of an octagonal gold *poudrier* contrasts unexpectedly with a lustrous black pearl button. In a revival of late eighteenth-century modes, gold pillboxes are surmounted by delicate moss agate 'pictures'. A spectacular tour-de-force is the oval powder case on which Verdura

Two of Verdura's flower jewels: a pansy brooch with a large 43 carat peridot and tanzanites; below: an iris brooch with a large 18 carat vivid yellow diamond and cabochon sapphires.

Opposite A collar necklace made up of 357 carats of cabochon sapphires and ribbons of baguette diamonds.

arranged twenty-four American Eagle gold coins with Indian chieftains' profiles on their obverse: the $1 gold pieces form the base of the carefully balanced heap, which is topped by $2.50 pieces.

Harking back to the Art Nouveau *femme-fleur* theme, flowers were making "fashion news...on everything from grand evening dresses to raincoats," according to *Vogue*. Singled out for praise was Verdura's double narcissus brooch, "realer than real, with emerald stems, diamond petals, centres of canary diamonds." Thanks to an ingenious mechanism, it could be divided in two, or worn as one. For the Baroness Alain de Rothschild, Fulco remounted a necklace of rough emeralds, to create two stylized diamond-centered blossoms linked by double strands of beads. He called them *les ferrets de la Reine*, after the diamond cloak clasps given by Louis XIII to Anne of Austria in Dumas's novel *The Three Musketeers*. Although he made lavish orchid, hibiscus, and arum lily pins, Verdura preferred using precious and semi-precious stones to reproduce single sprays and bunches of wild and garden flowers, such as the 'emerald-eyed' pansy brooch with pavé amethysts and diamonds. Verdura blooms were generally life-size, one notable exception being the iris earclips he designed for Jock Whitney's sister, Mrs. Charles Whitney Payson. In this tour-de-force, 182 sapphires of varying hue, thirty-six emeralds and twenty-eight canary diamonds were set in 18-carat gold to reproduce the blossoms in the famous Van Gogh painting that graced her family's Manhasset residence.

The brilliant palette that was already recognized as a Verdura trademark is best exemplified in the necklaces known as 'collars of color'. So extravagant were these pieces that they were often mistaken for fakes. At a New York dinner party, one of Verdura's clients wearing a diamond and star sapphire necklace and bracelet was pained to overhear another guest whisper to her partner: "Don't you think it's perfectly awful to go out to dinner wearing plastic?" These subtly proportioned, tapered bibs seem almost to float, as stones of differing size and hue are clustered to create a shimmering, painterly effect, rather than emphasize

a single gem; fresh green peridots are mixed with yellow zircons, for example, or amethysts with rubies. In the more elaborate 'ribbon necklaces', yellow diamond trim might wind through massed amethysts and emeralds; or pavé diamond and calibré-cut sapphire streamers crisscross a diamond-dusted collar of cabochon sapphires ranging in color from misty gray to deepest violet. A circular-cut white and yellow diamond ribbon is softly looped around a graduated square-cut amethyst line neck chain—from which hangs a magnificent cushion-shaped 99.88-carat Siberian amethyst pendant.

The introduction of enameling further extended Verdura's chromatic scale. While American firms tended to avoid the use of enamel in fine jewelry, Verdura yearned to restore a tradition that had become virtually extinct after the heyday of Lalique and Fabergé. The loss of a technique that had once been regarded as essential worried many European jewelers. Only a few years earlier, the Worshipful Company of Goldsmiths had convened at Goldsmith's Hall in London in the presence of Her Majesty Queen Mary, to debate the question of "How far the traditional craft of the enameller will be applicable to present-day conditions." When he was approached by André Chervin, Fulco welcomed the opportunity to experiment with a master craftsman. Chervin, a young French enameler, who had unsuccessfully been making the rounds of the major New York companies, was delighted at last to find a client "unafraid of doing fine jewellery in enamel and of charging high prices for it." And Verdura had finally found a skilled artisan able to interpret his painterly renderings *à la française*. Together they developed novel effects. Red enamel could be striated to resemble invisibly set calibré-cut rubies; in floral pieces, champlevé details were inserted to suggest the spidery veining of petals. In a modified lotus necklace, the green-and-blue enamel ground enhanced the luminosity of sapphire and emerald cabochons.

Chervin was passionate about every aspect of his trade. When a long-time supplier located near Paris announced that, after several centuries in business, the family firm was finally closing down, Chervin toured the factory, alert for bargains. Peering inside a half-open desk drawer, he noticed a mound of grayish powder. "You won't be able to do anything with that," the proprietor said. "It's all that remains of the blue enamel that was once used for Versailles porcelain." Chervin decided nonetheless to dump a kilo of the unpromising dust into a plastic shopping bag. Upon his return to New York, he processed and purified the granules—"to the point where I had tears in my eyes"—eventually reducing two pounds to a mere three ounces. The result was a superlative royal blue enamel that Marie Antoinette probably once loved and that Verdura used—for as long as it lasted—to embellish yellow gold knotted rope bracelets worn by the Duchess of Beaufort and Baroness de Rothschild. A more modest example of Verdura's enamel work found its

Opposite A lotus-form necklace with diamonds and enamel designed for Mrs. Albert Lasker.

way to Buckingham Palace. Jock and Betsey Whitney were invited to lunch with Queen Elizabeth and Prince Philip, where the conversation unpredictably turned to the lost art of enameling. To illustrate a point, the ambassador removed his enamel tie clip. So keen was the Duke of Edinburgh's enthusiasm for the piece that Whitney insisted he keep it. He was amused to receive a note from the Prince, graciously enclosing one of his own "in exchange"—a safety-pin.

Another addition to Verdura's professional entourage was Lois Lee, a young Parsons School of Design graduate with a bent for fashion illustration. A family friend, convinced that her exquisite draughtsmanship was ideally suited to jewelry rendering, arranged for her to meet Verdura, who hired her as his assistant. Lee eventually went on to a successful career with a major American firm, and in 1976 won first prize in the De Beers design competition for a bracelet of heart-shaped links brimming with diamonds. With her fine features and trim figure, the fair-haired Lee also served as house mannequin, obligingly slipping into a black velvet dress with a boat neckline whenever clients needed to see a piece modeled. However, it was her skill as an *animalier* artist that had most impressed Fulco; animal charms had lost none of their popularity since Flato first launched the mode for pet portraiture in jewelry. On one of her first assignments, Lee captured the attitudes of Vincent Astor's poodle in a series of lively pencil and watercolor vignettes: lion- or lamb-cut, begging, seated, pouncing, at play, at rest, in profile, with crimson bow, gilt coronet or emerald collar.

Verdura also begot nobler beasts. Unlike the Cartier panther glamorized by the Windsors during the Forties, Verdura's crowned leopard with jeweled collar partook less of the *fauve* than of the *gattopardo*. This heraldic creature, lifted from the Lampedusa coat-of-arms, appeared in Verdura's repertory as his cousin Giuseppe was finishing *Il Gattopardo*, and as Fulco was starting to compose his own later published memoirs, unbeknownst to the many friends who were constantly urging him to record his witty Palermitan anecdotes. Letters flew back and forth across the Atlantic, as Fulco and Maria Felice reminisced over deliciously cruel childhood sport, and the genealogy of the various Angelinas at Villa Niscemi.

Some of Verdura's endearing animal jewels: a poodle in platinum and diamonds; and a dachshund in diamonds and enamel. Opposite: a leopard brooch in gold, platinum, rubies, diamonds, and cabochon emeralds, 1957. The mouse comprises an opal, pavé diamonds, emeralds, and rubies, c. 1950.

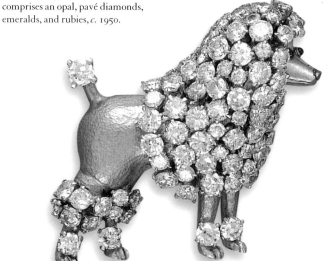

*Fashion is the self-portrait of society,
and the horoscope it casts of its own destiny.*
- E. Flaiano

9 New Ways

A 60-carat aquamarine brooch
wrapped in diamonds.

Opposite Verdura at work.

As the Fifties peaked, taste and the very concept of style underwent a radical transformation. Almost overnight, diamonds began to look 'tacky' on anyone under 40—at least according to Holly Golightly, the sprightly heroine of Capote's *Breakfast at Tiffany's*. As Diana Vreeland remarked at the time to Beaton, it seemed society was no longer relevant: only youth mattered. Fashion magazines gave up publishing full-page color portraits of immaculately groomed society ladies, because "today only personality counts, with very few exceptions unless it is a 'new beauty'." Ironically, only a couple of years earlier, Carmel Snow at *Harper's Bazaar* had been rebuked for trying to publish a photograph of Marian Anderson: "We are not an anthropological journal," was the publisher's explanation.

The ostentatious pursuit of elegance was not instantly wiped out, however, least of all in Manhattan, which remained the international arena for conspicuous consumers. But now the question most anxiously debated by the experts was just how much jewelry a woman might tastefully display during the daytime hours. To be worn with "the foot-long handbag, the expert glove, [there was] *the focal pin*: Verdura's 18-carat gold rope star blinking with seventy diamonds—enough jewel for one look, for one wardrobe really." Echoing Chanel, *Vogue* declared that "anybody could wear jewelry in the evening, there's no trick to that: all you have to do is to own the jewelry, but to wear important jewels in the daytime—that's the interesting thing—that's what takes the know-how." The ideal choice would always be a Verdura decoration pin, "made with wheeling gold spokes and ribboned very narrowly with diamonds," which the writer described as having been "worn for more years than I care to remember by one smart woman and...copied twice, once in emeralds and in diamonds for another." Or a design inspired by a military order, such as the bombé diamond starburst commissioned by Nicholas Brown to celebrate the publication of his wife's English-language edition of *Anatomy of Glory*, Henri Lachouque's definitive study of Napoleon's Garde Impériale.

Verdura's early enthusiasm for semi-precious translucent stones such as amethyst, citrine, tourmaline, and aquamarine had heralded the trend toward informality. Even mundane rose quartz could be transformed into a glamorous Heart brooch, surmounted by a pensive golden cherub, chin cupped in hand after the *putti* in Raphael's *Sistine Madonna*. As the unconventional became more acceptable, Verdura launched a "wholly individual new approach" to other less expensive

Drawing for a necklace in turquoise with bow knots of diamonds and navy blue enamel.

Opposite A similar necklace made with baroque pearls replacing the turquoise.

Overleaf A hummingbird brooch of black opal, enamel, and white and yellow diamonds, together with Verdura's original drawing, 1964. Below: a bee brooch made of diamonds, coral and onyx, c. 1961. Its wings are four large etched antique Indian diamonds. Opposite page: a yellow and white diamond, ruby and black enamel dragon brooch.

A pair of pink tourmaline and gold cornucopia earclips.

stones, turquoise and coral, once considered appropriate only for ethnic or dressmaker ornaments verging on costume jewelry. According to the French fashion magazine *L'Officiel*, a "Renaissance of the turquoise" was in full swing: a stone for all seasons, it enhanced blond as well as brunette complexions. Verdura scrambled turquoise with amethysts and diamonds, devising colorful brooches that could be worn with casual outfits. Dressier pieces include stylized blossom brooches or girandole earrings, formed of large turquoise drops framed in gold rope. Three butterflies, made of rubies, sapphires, and yellow diamonds, flutter above a large turquoise heart studded with diamonds. To Anglo-Saxon eyes, the image is an exquisite Victorian valentine; in Latin cultures, however, the butterfly is a symbol of the immortal soul, although it also suggests flirtatiousness or even inconstancy. One of Verdura's most delightfully feminine concoctions was a short string of large turquoise beads separated by plump blue enamel bowknots lined with diamonds—a throwback to the grand painted enamel jewelry of the seventeenth century.

Clare Boothe Luce had Fulco transform a set of ancient Italian coral pieces into stylish souvenirs for her staff at the American Embassy in Rome. Mounted as brooches or hatpins, tiny carved birds and blossoms were encrusted with diamonds and turquoise, cherubs embellished in the manner of *camées habillées* with earrings and other ornaments. He strung branches of pallid angel-skin coral together to form a naturally lacey, ruff-like collar. For Maria Felice, Fulco designed his most magnificent coral piece, a brooch in the shape of a Medusa head. Diamond eyes glitter in the Gorgon's mask-like visage, crowned with a gold diadem; pearls hang from the twisted locks. The Medusa motif, which Fulco had treated many years earlier with Dalí, appears frequently in traditional Sicilian jewelry: in *The Leopard*, Prince Salina wears a distinctive Medusa cravat stickpin. The powers of the mythological creature, capable of turning her adversaries into stone, were not merely destructive. Legend has it that the blood flowing from the decapitated head of the vanquished Medusa turned seaweed into coral.

Verdura's American clients were starting to feel more comfortable with his exotic bestiary: a new cultural sophistication was in the air, a certain receptiveness to foreign-flavored fantasies, such as Giancarlo Menotti's opera *The Unicorn, the Gorgon and the Manticore,* which had its premiere in Washington in 1956. Pieces reminiscent of sixteenth-century pendants in the shape of mythological beasts— particularly unicorns and stags, crowned or winged—were flaunted as personal emblems by individualists such as Diana Cooper, Clare Luce, and Ailsa Mellon. Amusing novelties also had cachet: green-scaled salamanders glinting with canary diamonds, pearl-bellied mice, and playful kittens. Sportsman Laurence Rockefeller ordered a flying fish brooch, and Betsey Whitney, an avid gardener, wanted a black opal humming-bird, enriched with forty-one diamonds and eighty emeralds.

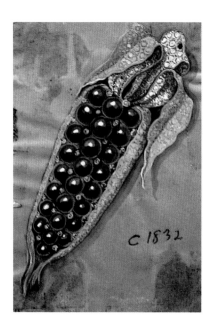

Drawing for an ear-of-corn brooch
of black pearls and yellow and
white diamonds.

Opposite Ruby and diamond
pomegranate brooch, 1960.

Verdura continued to be fascinated by flowers—as well as fruit
and vegetables—from his native and adopted lands. The widest range of
precious and semi-precious gems were combined to obtain a painterly
effect. A pomegranate brooch, crafted in gold and enamel, is made of
pavé rubies and canary diamonds, as well as zircons and olivenes. The
emerald skin of another over-ripe fruit is split open, to reveal diamond
rivulets running down the juicy ruby flesh within. Verdura's American
black corn brooch has rows of black pearls nestled in a gold husk lined
with diamonds. A jack-in-the-pulpit pin is crafted in different shades of
gold and trimmed with diamond pith. Floral brooches continued in high
demand, notably the invisible-set pansies and violet posies with yellow
diamond hearts, glistening with white diamond dew. There were paired
sapphire thistle pins, and a reprise of the famous lilac brooch, featuring a
cluster of fifteen amethyst hearts with yellow diamond centers, wreathed
by forty-three cabochon emerald leaves.

Fulco also created a series of floral *objets*: flowering plants and
sprigs set in carved bases or faceted aquamarine vases brimming with
sapphire, ruby, and diamond blooms. For Mrs. Paul Mellon, he designed
an espaliered apple tree as well as a tiny strawberry bush, rooted in
rough-hewn rock crystal. An enchantingly tangled bouquet of
wildflowers—daisies, marigolds, poppies, and bluebells—was composed
for Mrs. Laurence Rockefeller, using yellow, white, and blue diamonds,
sapphires and emeralds. For the Baronne Elie de Rothschild, Fulco
devised a unique memento with a special luster that was both aristocratic
and sentimental. The Baroness had already begun to amass a collection,
inspired by her given name Liliane, of elegant, lily-shaped ornaments.
Improving upon the mawkish nineteenth-century tradition of mounting
baby teeth in jewelry, Verdura designed a gold spray of lily-of-the-valley,
with blossoms made of the milk teeth of her three children. The plant
was set in a hardstone base carved to resemble a humble terracotta
flowerpot. He pleased the Baroness by using the same ruddy porphyry
that served for Napoleon's tomb at the Invalides. An inlaid gold crest
displays the Rothschild shield and five arrows, with the initials of the
Baroness's offspring: N, N and G. To admirers exclaiming "Why, it's just
like Fabergé!" Fulco would retort: "No, it's just like Verdura." A few
years later, the Baroness ordered a lily-of-the-valley brooch with green-
enameled gold leaves cradling nine *tremblant* buds made of pearls ringed
with diamonds. "When Fulco finished it," the exacting Baroness noted,
"there were many more flowers—too many, actually—so I made him
prune a few."

Hardstone had always fascinated Fulco, and over the next
several years he inaugurated a new range of magnificent *objets de vertu*
that would not look out of place in an Italian Renaissance palace or the
rococo *salons* of a French château. These were "objects of no functional
use whatever, existing only for the pleasure of the eye," as Verdura

explained in one catalogue; "things one would like to touch, things that could bring into a room an intimate message of beauty; a feeble echo of the magnificence that once was." Fulco responded to the challenge of three-dimensional design by developing an even more finely nuanced palette in which translucent gems were offset by opaque stones. "It has been of great interest and pleasure to me, after so many years of thinking in terms of jewels, to broaden my view, and also look towards the *pietra dura* and make diamonds, rubies and emeralds merge with porphyry, malachite and lapis lazuli." Roman sculpture of the late Imperial era inspired the polychrome bust of a Caesar; there was also a pair of porphyry obelisks embellished with topaz suns. Antique Blue John vases are wrapped with golden vines laden with pearls. A rose quartz dog rests upon a gilt-tasseled malachite cushion; a gold-crested rock crystal heron grips a tiny fish in its beak. Verdura's colorful menagerie runs the gamut from a coral tortoise and an amethyst and obsidian hedgehog to a dusky sodalite rhinoceros with fierce ruby eyes.

Fulco revived yet another lost genre: *paesini*, or little landscapes. "I have endeavoured to bring back to life the almost forgotten art of painting on calcareous lime tablets, trying to follow the shapes suggested by the designs of the stone." When sliced thin, stones like moss agate, milky chalcedony, red carnelian, striped jasper and specular selenite can appear to contain miniature landscapes. Until the Enlightenment, they were believed to be supernaturally formed representations of the natural world. *Paesini* were often retouched by such masters as Antonio Carracci—dotting horizons with tiny figures and monuments, underscoring dramatic cliff lines, highlighting storm-tossed seas. There was a surge of curiosity about these strange, dream-like images when Surrealist André Breton devoted an essay to *les pierres imaginées* in 1957. The following year, Fulco exhibited a series of *paesini* at the Arthur Jeffress Gallery in London. An aesthete who divided his life between a London home decorated in Charles X style and a Venetian *palazzo* where the servants wore yellow silk liveries, Jeffress liked neo-Romantics such as the Russian scenographer Eugene Berman and Cecil Beaton, whose schoolmate he had been. Fulco's show was a success. The day after the opening, Douglas Fairbanks, Jr, sent Fulco a letter: "Each time I turned around to gaze at your fascinating exhibition last night, I found that someone would beat me to it in selecting the one I wanted. I was dizzy with frustration and making too slow a choice." He finally placed an order for a Venetian scene as a birthday gift for his wife Mary Lee. He added: "It is always so wonderful to have friends who grow in value through the years. It is even nicer to have those friends enjoy great gifts— and it is even more agreeable when those gifted friends blossom out into still another avenue of talent, which is widely recognized by their contemporaries." Diana Cooper started to refer to her old friend teasingly as "the Sicilian Duke who made good."

A Verdura table *objet* depicting a rhinoceros in sodalite, rock crystal and gold.

Overleaf Left: a gold shell form compact, together with a gold striated compact with a large faceted sapphire mounted upside down in the lid, *c.* 1945. Right: a pair of hardstone and gold *bonbonniers* made for Betsey Whitney, 1968.

Fulco was the embodiment of the "international nomad," a term coined by his friend, the social arbiter Lanfranco Rasponi, for "the new breed of fast-moving, socially-minded wanderers." In England, Fulco was astonished when, at a party, Clarissa Eden thanked him for supporting her husband the Prime Minister: "My God, if they care about the opinion of a bloody little Italian like me, things must be bad." In Paris, whenever he was overcome by an urge to "feel like a Viking," he would go and see the Patiños. He was an early supporter of the Festival of the Two Worlds, launched in 1958 by Gian-Carlo Menotti. Like Fulco, the Italian-born composer had found his professional niche in the United States, but yearned to bring New and Old World cultures closer together. This annual summer event aimed to present the best classical and avant-garde in art, theater, dance, and music from around the world in Spoleto, a diminutive Umbrian hill-town. *Time*'s Italian correspondent, Eric Amfitheatrof, relished the sense of "enormous class mixed with the quicksilver inventive casualness of a happening. Though the festival's hard-pressed organizers were often in a state of panic, the atmosphere around them was pleasingly indolent. International society would meet at the piazza during the day and gather at night after the last performance at Menotti's or at Countess Spalding's palazzo for midnight suppers that lasted into the wee hours." Countess Consuelo Crespi remembers the women at these *soirées* indulging in a little game of one-upwomanship in which Verdura compacts were indispensable accessories. "At one end of the table, a lady would set it off by pulling out her *poudrier*, and within minutes another lady, at the other end of the table, would pull out hers." These proved to be the next best aid to coquetry since the invention of the fan. French fashion experts rejoiced: "One can brandish it, handle it, play with it, open it, place it on the table—but one cannot treat it with indifference. The precious cases give us a new countenance in the evening. The woman whose delicate hands are burdened with this bauble adopts a fragile attitude, she demands protection of a man. At the same time—and this is the essence of flirtatiousness—she knows herself to be strong, since she has all she needs in hand. In a world without certainties, she is assured of all beauty's munitions." Countess Crespi took pleasure in handling her own compact which, "with aquamarine and gold piping all around, felt very substantial, yet extremely sensuous." Men could play at this game too: "the gentlemen all had their cigarette boxes, which they laid down nonchalantly at their places." Verdura cases ranged from elegant and discreet models—engraved with leaf and feather patterns, or enameled in black and tied with diamond-set bowknots—to more fanciful creations. One gold box has polished hematite studs that shine like Paris cobblestones under the rain.

From the start, Fulco established himself as one of Spoleto's more flamboyant habitués, immortalized as Fulke Greville in Alberto Arbasino's Proustian *roman à clef*, *Fratelli d'Italia*. Still dark-haired except

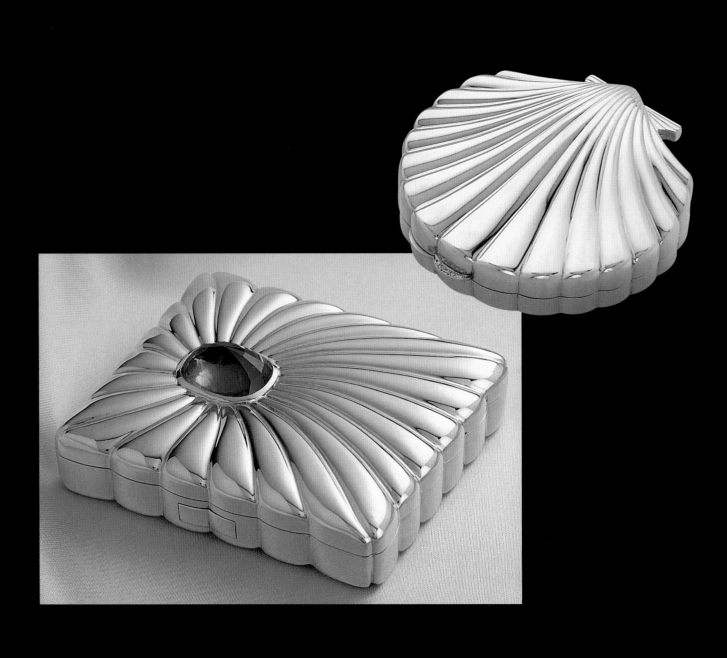

for a single shock of gray, Fulco resembled a "lively, aged Anglo-Sicilian youth, whom everyone treats as if he were very young." Arbasino was host in his villa to Domietta Hercolani, the same woman whom Fulco had cast as Winter in his entrée at the Beistegui Ball. Fulco, who shared the villa, organized impromptu tango competitions and relentlessly promoted a picturesque, bohemian ambience. Bustling about in a Sulka Indian print robe tied with a curtain cord, whiskey glass firmly in hand, he decorated a 'Beaton corner' with an Etruscan *krater* surrounded by wicker furniture to evoke Brighton (or "to be frank, Bath!"). This was followed by other corners devoted to Tennessee Williams, to Lyda Borelli, to Queen Margherita, and—"Let's not forget Giuseppe!"—to Lampedusa, with a symbolic leopard skin tossed over an unsprung sofa.

When it was published in 1958, *The Leopard* was recognized as a masterpiece and hailed as Italy's first international bestseller. Its disenchanted vision of the compromises forced by the Unification of Italy—"everything must change, in order for everything to remain the same"—was considered an indirect indictment of the entire political class. Cardinal Ruffini of Palermo publicly condemned Lampedusa's novel as one of the three factors contributing to the dishonor of Sicily—the other two being the Mafia and the social activist Danilo Dolci. Initially, Fulco was hurt and outraged at his cousin's portrayal of Granmamà as a vulgar *parvenue* whose father's stinking moneybags had bought her way into the aristocracy. It was not long before less fastidious relatives were claiming for themselves the prestige of descent from the original Prince of Salina. Eventually, it transpired that the author had based Salina on himself, and the dashing Tancredi on his adopted son, the musicologist Gioacchino Lanza Tommasi. Fulco came to accept that Lampedusa's work, while grounded in historical reality, was an extraordinary feat of literary imagination.

Within three years, production was under way of a film based on *The Leopard*, a nostalgic and lavish epic that is often described as the Italian equivalent of *Gone with the Wind*. The cast featured Burt Lancaster as Prince Salina, Claudia Cardinale as the gorgeous Angelica, and Alain Delon as Tancredi. The real star, however, was director Luchino Visconti, a friend of Fulco's since the late Twenties when they had both been protégés of Chanel. The young Milanese nobleman had spent several years in Paris vacillating between a job in textile design and a career in the nascent film industry. Uncompromising in his quest for absolute historical authenticity, Visconti always insisted on shooting on location: now, he traveled to Palermo with an army of 150 builders, 120 make-up men, hairdressers and seamstresses, twenty electricians, fifteen florists, and ten cooks, plus an assortment of friends with their pets. Visconti needed the comfort and reassurance of a tribal entourage, which embraced not only actors and other professional associates, but especially glamorous young people blessed with beauty, breeding and taste—on

A portrait of Luchino Visconti, who directed the movie version of *The Leopard*. The picture was taken by Horst, Paris, 1936.

this, as on many other occasions, exemplified by Domietta Hercolani. Fulco, who shared Visconti's rapturous vision of times past, was recruited to advise on Sicilian arcana, from court etiquette and Bourbon genealogy to how the aristocracy danced the quadrille.

Fulco had not been in Sicily since his mother's death on 2 February 1961 at the age of 91. Departing Casa Verdura after the funeral, Fulco had vowed never to return and thrown his keys down the courtyard well in despair and disgust. But now he was back, ransacking the ancestral treasure house for antique portraits, furniture, and bibelots to make Visconti's real sets even more real. Much filming took place in the Mirror Gallery of Palazzo Gangi, which Fulco had described for the readers of *Harper's Bazaar* in 1937: "a long room entirely covered with mirrors in fantastic rococo gold frames, and then a ceiling which opens into a central cupola surrounded by minor irregular ones. From these bulb-like cavities, lazy Olympians reclining on clouds look down through immense Venetian chandeliers into the gold world below. The floor is made of tile with a single enormous pattern... representing a leopard hunt in a wood. It gives the impression of a strange, shiny tapestry." When not providing props and background material, he served up hilarious stories of turn-of-the-century Palermo. Scriptwriter Enrico Medioli nicknamed Fulco *Tusitala*—the title the Samoans gave Robert Louis Stevenson—meaning 'teller of tales'. He remembers Fulco at one particularly effervescent dinner, interrupting a stream of *bon mots* to goad a sluggish waiter: "After all, we are not here to amuse ourselves!" In the final ballroom scene of *The Leopard*, Visconti paid tribute to Fulco by introducing a namesake character—perhaps his great-grandfather.

When he returned to New York, Fulco moved to a brownstone house at 17 East 82nd Street. He added to his two-room apartment another one on the same floor, thus creating a modest enfilade that nonetheless exuded *palazzo*-style luxury. The most imposing feature in the decor was a vast seventeenth-century portrait of Antonia Eguidyuz del Darco by the Spanish painter Juan Amigo; on other walls, floor-to-ceiling bookcases alternated with clusters of Old Master drawings and engravings. Palm trees and gilt Baroque figures loomed over an array of Louis XVI, Empire and Second Empire furniture. A curious two-sided sofa was upholstered in blue-and-yellow striped upholstery, copied after Delacroix's 1833 oil sketch of the Comte de Mornay's study.

It was well known that Fulco's passion for his native country went deep, and that he was sentimental about the beauties and wonders of Italy. Tom Parr recalls that one evening when he and Fulco were sitting after dinner in the New York apartment, there was a knock at the door. Claus Virch, who was then Curator of European Paintings at the

Metropolitan Museum of Art, told them they must come immediately to the Museum, which was one block away, and see something extraordinary. They hurried along, entered through a back door and back passages until they came to a balcony. There below, hanging on a wall, was the *Mona Lisa*, spotlit and guarded by two Marines in full-dress uniform. The picture had just arrived, brought by Claus from the Louvre in Paris for an exhibition of Italian works of art that was held at the Met. For anyone this would have been a moving sight, but for someone who loved his country so intensely it was indeed extraordinary.

Fulco's American lifestyle was as various and unpredictable as his European existence. On one night he might accompany Visconti and Cardinale, with Jean Seberg and Warren Beatty, to the New York premiere of *The Leopard* at the Plaza Theater. On another, he could be seen queuing democratically for a special exhibition at the Metropolitan. Among his eclectic list of American friends, there were many people from the theater. Most of them he met during his friendship with Cole Porter. The Lunts, Alfred and Lynn Fontanne, were among this group, known lovingly as the Olympians by another of its members, who was an intimate friend of Fulco's, Madeleine Sherwood, the widow of Robert Sherwood. Then there was the actress Hope Williams, who had appeared in *Anything Goes* and whom Fulco adored and saw frequently, and Anita Loos, a great favorite of his, with whom he lunched regularly on Wednesdays. Thursday dinner was reserved for Cole, by now a virtual recluse as a result of his riding accident in 1937 and the subsequent amputation of one of this legs.

He enjoyed weekends at William and Babe Paley's country house, Kiluna Farms. Babe's sister, Minnie Cushing Astor and her new husband, James Whitney Fosburgh, convinced that Fulco needed looking after, would invite him to their house in Katonah, New York, for bouts of heavy drinking in fine company: Leonard Bernstein, Irene Selznick, the Lunts, John Richardson, Princess Margaret, Kitty Carlisle Hart.... Fulco continually told the rapturous newlyweds that "when happiness is that nakedly apparent, one puts a fig leaf on it, it becomes cumbersome to the bystander."

A former Second World War pilot, Fosburgh was a painter, art historian and collector who lectured at the Frick Collection for over two decades. Jacqueline Kennedy appointed him to the Fine Arts Committee that succeeded in acquiring 150 American masterpieces for the White House. "The excitement was up all over the country," one of the First Lady's aides recollected: "Everyone was interested and in the next two years there wasn't a painting of first-class quality... which we didn't get or have offered to us." After a trip to the West Coast in the Spring of 1962 with Jackie, Fulco allowed himself to be persuaded to part with one of his precious flea market finds: a folio volume, bound in tooled and gilt red leather, containing the 120 lithographs of the McKenney-Hall *History of*

Design for a baroque pearl, diamond, and turquoise Native American brooch made for Doris Duke in 1957.

Below A drawing for an enamel, sapphire and ruby frog brooch, 1961; the pair of snail brooches with putti astride consists of diamonds, rubies, and enamel, *c.* 1965.

the Indian Tribes of North America (1837–44). These rare hand-colored plates were done after copies of portraits of Native American chiefs, originally executed by Charles Bird King and other artists *c.* 1821–30 at the behest of the Bureau of Indian Affairs. 'Redskin' motifs creep into Verdura's repertory at this time: for heiress Doris Duke, he produced a lavish brooch paradoxically inspired by the lowly five-cent coin. An irregular Baroque pearl, mounted in gold and platinum, embellished with diamonds and turquoise, was transformed to resemble the thunderbird profile on the reverse of the nickel. Duke was so pleased with the gem that she ordered a duplicate in which the single pearl was replaced by pavé diamonds.

A jewel worth owning, according to *Vogue*, must now possess some "telling personal significance" resulting from a "combination of the jeweler's art and a woman's awareness of it." Verdura's frog brooches had this elusive quality; described as "frankly blockbusting," they captivated the Duchess of Windsor: frogs had always figured largely, though enigmatically, in the Windsors' baby-talk. The first specimens, crafted by Chervin in sapphire and emerald cabochons, were soon followed by a frosty brilliant-set variety. Verdura's competitors were quick to adopt the unusual motif, which first came into favor during the Renaissance. The young David Webb in particular made a speciality of enameled frog bangles and clips. When Fulco appeared at a show of Webb's work, the young jeweler rushed forward to greet his mentor *malgré lui*, exclaiming: "I do so admire your work!", to which Fulco responded dryly: "So I've noticed."

Chief among the professional Verdura enthusiasts was the Paris firm of Darde & Cie, who were reproducing his ever-popular shell gems for the Duchess of Windsor. Costume jeweler Kenneth J. Lane fabricated an accessible version of the Verdura look, simply by winding colored metal wire around snail shells, which he then mounted as brooches and

Verdura's detailed drawing for a clamshell compact. Opposite: the actual *objet* with sapphire and diamond seaweed applied to the lid.

A pair of shell, coral, and gold earclips.

cufflinks. Lane made a point, however, of purchasing items for his personal use from Verdura, who always expressed genuine puzzlement. "But why do you even bother?" he would enquire amiably. "While Schlumberger did mind my copying," Lane recalls, "Fulco was just amused." More than anything, this was based on Fulco's fondness for Lane.

Verdura's shell jewelry became increasingly fanciful as he enhanced his palette, often through the use of enamels. A nautilus might be 'lined' with turquoise enamel, echoing the brilliant blue of the Mediterranean, before being wrapped in spiraling strands of gold seaweed. Twin scallop shells were coated a delicate shade of pink, each ridge picked out with diamonds. Lavish three-tier gold and diamond fantasy shell brooches were inspired by a scalloped Baroque furniture motif. A rough Cohogue clam picked up on a beach was set in gold, awash with diamond foam and blue sapphire bubbles. In a witty reprise of an ancient Roman decorative motif, two golden *putti* are perched like jockeys astride a pair of green and blue snails with ruby-tipped diamond horns.

Verdura also revisited the wing motif that had been so popular in the Thirties and Forties, drawing on Biblical and art-historical sources to achieve a novel, more complex pattern. Six blue, red, and violet pinions, edged with diamonds, frame the central stones of earrings and brooches,

A bracelet of cabochon sapphires and diamond stars, *c.* 1940.

Opposite A peridot and yellow diamond pendant necklace.

or the face of a watch. This motif, described in the Book of Isaiah, was the emblem of the seraphim, the first and most zealous rank of heavenly host: "each one had six wings: with twain he covered his face, and with twain he covered his feet and with twain he did fly." The airborne angelic figures appear in religious art, from the tenth century onward; Fulco had long been familiar with the brilliant mosaic examples in the Cathedral of Cefalú in Sicily and in the Basilica of Saint Mark in Venice.

In 1961, the photographer Irving Penn had documented the "look of unruffled neatness, serenity and composure; [the] total personal elegance" of Mainbocher's evening fashions accessorized with jewels by Verdura: a four-strand graduated pearl necklace, a diamond and gold necklace, a black seed pearl *torsade* bracelet with a foliate clasp of pavé diamonds. By the mid-Sixties, Rasponi confirmed that it was still customary "in the chic restaurants, [for] middle-aged women to wear exceedingly dressy feathered hats along with diamond bracelets, pins and rings in the middle of the day. In no other city do women need so many evening clothes. Dinners are often on a large scale and the charity events succeed one another relentlessly..." He offered reassurance that "although the tendency all over the world is for chic wealthy women to wear little jewelry, in New York the opposite is true. Since there are so many dressy parties, women have many chances to show off their jewels and competition still exists between the well-established ladies and those on their way up." In *Answered Prayers*, Truman Capote described the polished look of a woman lunching at the Côte Basque, "very handsomely set up inside a brown Balenciaga suit with a brooch composed of cinnamon-coloured diamonds fixed to the lapel."

These were the years in which Verdura mounted seven dozen emerald-cut pink topazes in a garland-style parure; another sumptuous set featured nineteen graduated emerald-cut kunzites in a gold foliate setting, scattered with round diamonds. One of his more extravagant collars of color in diamonds and peridots with matching earrings and bracelet was modeled by Sophia Loren, swathed only in floor-length Russian sable. When Capote was planning his epochal 1966 Black and White Ball at the Plaza Hotel, worried "that the multi-hued sparkle of rubies, sapphires or emeralds might destroy his austere design, he considered adding a stern 'Diamonds Only' to the bottom of the invitations."

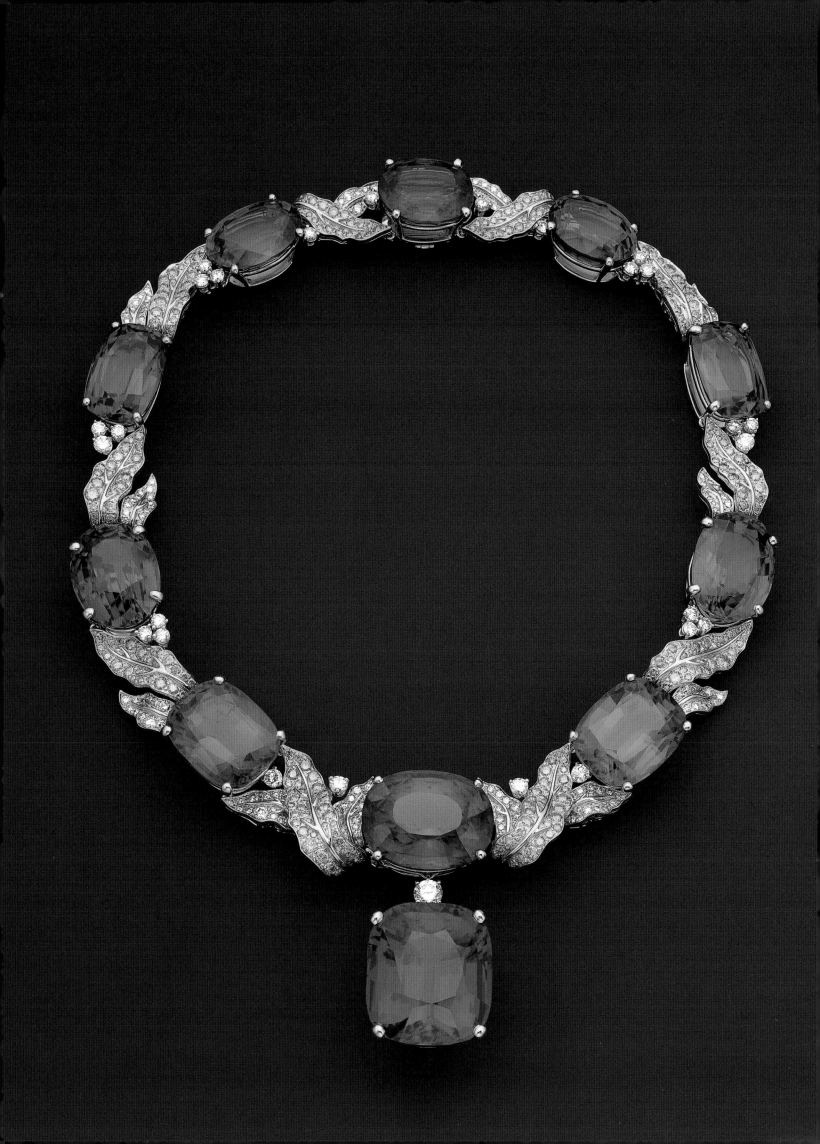

A Verdura miniature painting of a deserted beach.

The reverse of the miniature painting opposite, which was commissioned by Betsey Whitney in 1966 as a Christmas present for her husband Jock. Depicting some of the works in the Whitneys' private collection, it was mounted on a gold easel with a cabochon finial.

At this time, Fulco's miniatures acquire an increasingly contemplative air. There are serene still-lifes: a brown crusty loaf of bread on a white linen cloth, a *radicchio di Treviso* with ruffled, purple leaves, its roots still caked with soil; green laurel against a sharply contrasting orange ground; a batch of London Sunday papers—*The Observer* and *The Telegraph*—tossed onto a green baize-covered table. Even his landscapes and interiors have a subdued, introspective quality: a view of a deserted beach, with folded bleachers and furled umbrellas; a study of an amber-eyed cat stalking a canary in a cage; an illustration of Leopardi's famous poem *L'Infinito*, inscribed with the famous first verse: *Sempre caro mi fu quest'ermo colle.* Fulco took pleasure in devising special mementos for close friends. For Caroline Somerset, whose husband was the future Duke of Beaufort on the death of his cousin, he designed a bookplate around the Beaufort emblem of the portcullis, with a little stone parapet in the foreground on which her embroidery and gardening shears rest: "Scissors are such an important part of my life." Fulco had originally planned to include a sketch of Badminton, but her husband felt such ostentation could be vulgar.

For Marella and Gianni Agnelli, who invited him each year to stay with either Maria Felice or Tom at Villar Perosa, their eighteenth-century house outside Turin, he made a tiny double-face painting. On the recto, a classical *veduta* shows the loggia of this house overshadowed by the cupola of its nearby church of San Pietro in Vincoli. On the verso, in *trompe l'oeil*, he painted a fuzzy black-and-white snapshot that appears to be held by tacks; it portrays a penguin which Gianni had famously rescued from certain death as a summer attraction on the Adriatic shore near Rimini.

In 1966, as a Christmas gift for her husband Jock, Betsey Whitney asked Fulco to illustrate the masterpieces in his collection—a

Van Gogh self-portrait, as well as works by Gauguin, Toulouse-Lautrec, and Renoir —using the same formula. This he did in a small easel painting inspired by art-historical models dating back to the eighteenth century, in which a wealthy connoisseur's pictures are displayed as a mosaic-like composition. On the verso could be seen wooden stretchers, a note from Betsey and a sprig of holly. The next year, on the couple's twentieth wedding anniversary, Whitney gave Betsey a golden tree set in a rose quartz hillock. Its branches are hung with round and oval miniatures framed in sapphires and diamonds, showing all the Whitney homes—Greentree on Long Island, the stud farm in Kentucky, the estates in Georgia, on Fisher's Island, and in Saratoga. Betsey would point to one or the other, enquiring sweetly: "Where is *that* house, darling?"

Verdura's jewelry designs of the Sixties and Seventies display the amazing vitality and inventiveness that often mark an artist's maturity. He introduced a series of abstract shapes, often executed in unadorned polished gold: x-es, squiggles and wavy lines. These slender, wonderfully supple pieces are crafted in diamond-encrusted white, yellow, or rose gold; inspired by South American voodoo cord bracelets, they offer an understated alternative to the ubiquitous diamond line bracelet. For Baroness Alain de Rothschild, Fulco mounted a flawless diamond in an innovative, prongless setting in which the stone is caught between two curving, pavé diamond ribbons. The engagement ring for the young fashion editor Mary McFadden featured a superb 10-carat blue diamond in a bold diamond and lapis lazuli turban setting.

Some of Verdura's gems can be taken as metaphors for old age. In his final, highly elaborate version of the pine cone motif, a disintegrating cone reveals the delicate tracery of its inner structure. Perhaps his most eloquent piece is the 1972 furled orange hart's-tongue leaf, accented by a fine diamond vein: the design was taken from a magnified image published in Verdura's own copy of a pioneering study in photography by K. Blossfeldt, *Art Forms in Nature* (1935).

An offer came from Cartier, interested in forming a stable of celebrity designers such as Tiffany developed with Schlumberger, then Paloma Picasso and Elsa Peretti. Fulco would have total artistic licence and a permanent, prestigious showcase: the Verdura Window on Fifth Avenue. He was flattered, but refused; though times had changed, he felt as unsuited as ever to the corporate environment. As word of his possible retirement spread, collectors rushed to place what they feared might be last orders. For his new fiancée, Pamela Digby Churchill Hayward, Averell Harriman commissioned an unusual engagement ring that could be worn on informal as well as formal occasions. This time the stone was real: a superb emerald cabochon in a massive gold setting inspired by jewels of the Italian Renaissance, startlingly offset by glossy black enamel. Other clients opted for classical Verdura. Mary McFadden, about to embark on a new career as a stylist, commissioned a lion's paw shell

Opposite A pine cone brooch of pavé-set diamonds, *c.* 1950.

brooch dripping with diamonds and sapphires. Another connoisseur purchased a classical Forties-style long-stemmed ruby rose brooch. "The goose is mine," an outdoorsman from Columbus, Ohio, wired Verdura when he received a brochure illustrating an unusual bird brooch. There was a Minnesotan advocate of East-West rapprochement who wanted an enameled Imperial Dragon brooch to mark President Nixon's trip to mainland China. Nicholas Brown was captivated by the rendering for an extravagant Baroque pearl jewel featured on the cover of Verdura's Christmas catalogue—a golden *putto* wearing a pearl turban and emerald sash sitting astride a ruby-eyed dolphin with gold and diamond fins, a pear-shaped diamond pendant hanging from its lip—and had it made up as an engagement gift for his future daughter-in-law, Constance Mellon, who was engaged to J. Carter Brown. One last major commission for Paul Mellon marked a return to the Baroque extravagance of the Dinglinger tradition: a grand vermeil *dessus-de-table* richly enameled to resemble an Oriental carpet, with elephants and camels amid jeweled flowers, palm trees, and fountains.

Fulco was now spending more and more time abroad, cruising with Tom and Cecil Beaton in the Windward Islands, holidaying in Tripoli with Countess Cicogna, vacationing with the Trees at Spetsos, sailing in the eastern Mediterranean with Alain and Marie de Rothschild in their three-masted Greek caique, the *Saita*.

The Rothschilds liked to sail in the Turkish and Greek waters of the Adriatic, and often began or ended their cruise in the port of Venice. On one such occasion, they decided to go sightseeing with Fulco and chose to explore the old Ghetto district. While there, they came upon what appeared to be a very old synagogue, which was closed. Fulco knocked at the door, and finally a rabbi appeared. Fulco asked whether they could come in and see the synagogue. The rabbi, scrutinizing the three of them, said to Fulco, "You can come in, but I'm afraid your friends cannot." Though Fulco was not at all ashamed of his large nose, it was a marked feature of his face, and this had led the rabbi to make his decision.

He and Tom were regular visitors to the Salzburg music festival, where he feuded happily with his favorite diva, Leontyne Price. They watched the world go by in Venice, staying at Ca' Giustinian as guests of the Brandolinis; however, their favorite vantage point was at the Gritti Hotel, where they could enjoy the spectacle of tourists staggering on and off gondolas.

Fulco was increasingly inconvenienced in his work by the contraction of a nerve in his right hand, due to Dupuytren's disease, which had to be operated. More devastating than this was the road accident in which he was involved. One evening he, Tom, and their friend Emma Yorke were dining with Daisy Fellowes in her Belgrave Square apartment. On leaving the apartment house, Fulco stepped out

Four Verdura miniature paintings of the Whitney residences, each round frame surrounded by diamonds and sapphires, suspended from a gold tree on a pink quartz and gold base, 1967.

Drawing for a baroque pearl and diamond boy-on-a-dolphin brooch.

into the street, and was knocked down by a passing car. Carried back into Daisy's apartment, he noted her evident distress as he bled onto her Aubusson carpet, and could not resist a caustic *bon mot* (referring to the houseproud character in the novel *Rebecca*): "Thank you, Mrs. Danvers." Later, when Tom diplomatically shaved five years off his age in response to the ambulance medic's queries, Fulco murmured approvingly: "Thank you, dear boy." As a result of his injuries, he had to spend two months in hospital and another month recuperating. There is no doubt that this contributed to the deterioration of his health.

On his seventy-fourth birthday, it was clear that the party organized in New York by Louise Grünwald at the 21 Club, with Bobby Short at the piano playing Cole Porter, was going to be his farewell to New York. Fulco had by now settled comfortably into a flat above Tom Parr's at 72 Eaton Square, London, surrounded by his collection of eighteenth-century Chinese porcelain animals and the antique Italian porcelain Cole had left him. He could still be coaxed out to attend costume balls. In response to an Oxfordshire invitation to 'dress operatic', he showed up as a prompter, a metal hood over his head and shoulders, his face illuminated by little lights within, and a rich red velours curtain falling to his feet. He continued to correspond with Nancy Mitford, who delighted in his politically incorrect jokes: "St Peter to the assembled throng: 'You are about to see God and there are one or two things I want to tell you—in the first place she's black.'" He insisted that the last London *salon* where decent conversation still flourished was the greengrocer's, Justin de Blank, where the prices were "also very highfalutin: there you meet every morning all the local gentry and exchange *lieux communs* in the midst of Israeli melons, French *asperges* and Italian prosciutto." His friends teased him that the only reason he had moved to Britain was that his charlady would call him 'Your Grace'. The real reason, aside from the fact that Tom's work was based in London, was that England had always felt like a second home to Fulco, both socially and culturally. He rejoiced when E. F. Benson's Mapp and Lucia books, gently satirizing English country life, were brought back into print. Hearing that the daughter of David Hicks and Pamela Mountbatten had been christened India, he suggested helpfully that the next child might be called "Suburbia, after the father's side." He patronized old Mr. Anthony Cleverley, cobbler by appointment to the great and good, as well as the rich and famous, who paid house calls armed with his fabled 'book of shoes', from which Fulco invariably ordered embroidered black evening slippers with red heels.

Although he would moan, "No virgin island or secluded vale left!", exotic destinations still exerted a powerful attraction. There were trips with Tom to stay with Jimmy Davison and Nicky Haslam in the high desert in Arizona, sailing on the Nile with Caroline Somerset, Marella Agnelli and her sister-in-law Suni, and Barry Sainsbury. They spent one Christmas holiday in Rajputan, India, including a visit to the Ajunta caves, where Fulco was borne aloft in sedan chairs by four bearers. Ever the monarchist, he fulfilled what he considered to be his avuncular obligations by escorting Maria Felice's grandson Alessandro to Cascais in Portugal for a private audience with his old friend Umberto of Savoy whom, on this solemn occasion, he addressed as *Maestà*.

In 1975, Verdura was prevailed upon to design a silver rose to be donated by his many friends to the Royal Opera House, in memory of Raimund von Hofmannsthal, son of Hugo, who provided the libretto of Richard Strauss's *Der Rosenkavalier*. The intention was that this silver rose should be used in perpetuity at every performance of the opera at Covent Garden. Fulco was thrilled for several reasons: it had been "love at first sight" when he was introduced to the opera as a boy at the Vienna Hofoper, and Raimund had been a close friend, as the husband first of Vincent Astor's sister Alice, then of Diana Cooper's niece Lady Elizabeth Paget. The rose was presented to the director of the Covent Garden Opera House, Sir Claus Moser, by Diana's son Lord Norwich at the performance on 10 December of a production originally staged by Visconti, in which Brigitte Fassbaender sang Octavian and Gwyneth Jones the Feldmarschallin. The wonderfully naturalistic 25 cm-long blossom was executed in the workshops of Annabel Jones from renderings by Verdura, in the tradition of the *rosa aurea*, the golden 'rose of virtue', traditionally bestowed by the Pope upon the consorts of monarchs.

Friends of Fulco had for some years been writing memoirs, often thinly disguised as novels, such as *Oublier Palerme* (Forget Palermo) by Edmonde Charles-Roux, editor-in-chief of French *Vogue*, about a European discovering the New York fashion world. Closer to home, Gianni Agnelli's sister Susanna (Suni) wrote the autobiographical *Vestivamo alla marinara* (We Wore Sailor Suits), about her childhood in Turin. Succumbing to the blandishments of the London publisher George Weidenfeld, Fulco devoted more time to recording his youthful memories of Sicily. The title he chose—*The Happy Summer Days*—was drawn from a passage in Lewis Carroll's *Alice in Wonderland*, quoted on the title page: "…with many a strange tale, perhaps even with the dream of a Wonderland of long ago; and how she would feel with all their simple sorrows, and find a pleasure in all their simple joys, remembering her own child-life, and the happy summer days." Prince Salina's deathbed reflections probably echoed in Fulco's mind: "the significance of a noble family lies entirely in its traditions, that is in its vital memories; and he was the last to have any unusual memories, anything different from other families."

When the book was published in 1976 it was well received. Reviewing it for *The Spectator*, Alastair Forbes suggested Fulco's "utterly enchanting and characteristically humorous account of his own very

Fulco being carried on a litter while on a visit to India.

unusual Sicilian begetting and childhood" could be regarded in the light of a postscript to *The Leopard*. Fulco translated the book into Italian and it was published a year later by Feltrinelli, the firm that had published Lampedusa's book. Fulco was touched by a letter from Giovanna Pipitone, the wife of the chief gardener at Villa Niscemi, who marveled at how "signor Fulco remembered all the facts down to the least details. Villa Niscemi! Who can forget it? How can one who has lived there so many years forget it? The sick swan, the arrival of the camel..." He dodged questions about a sequel with the disingenuous remark: "Nothing ever happened after I was fifteen years old." There were offers for a sequel, but Fulco didn't want to write "just another name-dropping memoir." He was planning a biographical work, devoted to the tastemakers who had exerted the greatest influence upon him: Cole Porter, Daisy Fellows, "who invented eye contact," Prince Youssoupov, Mimì Pecci Blunt as champion of the avant-garde, and Chanel. The working title, borrowed from Cocteau, was *Les Monstres Sacrés*.

After a year of ill-health, which he refused to allow to interfere with his style of life, Fulco died on 15 August 1978. If he dreaded death, he never showed it, thanks to his faith and the good manners that dictated that he should never bore people. "Frail and stooped, but very valiant," is how Lady Airlie remembered Fulco. "Death is at home in Sicily," was

A sketch by Fulco of his proposed
holiday with Tom Parr, arriving at
John Betjeman's house in Cornwall,
southwest England.

Opposite Fulco's 1955
Christmas card.

one of his favorite sayings. He scribbled cheerily in the margin of an
illustration of the twelfth-century Church of Sant'Orsola on the outskirts
of Palermo, where the family vault is located: "The family chapel is here
—I will be buried in the shadow of this church!" The graveyard seemed
to him "a peaceful place full of flowers and birds, where I am sure I will
one day feel at home surrounded by relations and friends." He looked
forward to sharing a berth with his stillborn brother Garibaldi. Even as
he faced imminent death, he executed a wobbly pencil sketch of an
eagerly anticipated holiday in Cornwall, with Tom valiantly carrying
their two bags and Fulco leaning on his cane, as they proceeded up the
drive to the house that John Betjeman had promised to lend them.

In September, Tom carried Fulco's ashes to Sicily. There was a
stop in Pisa, where the loyal friends who were staying at the Pecci Blunt
estate, Marlia, near Lucca—including the daughters of the house and
Johnny de Faucigny-Lucinge—had gone to meet Tom at the airport and
pay their respects to Fulco. As Tom was passing through customs,
bearing his precious parcel, he was stopped and asked what the parcel
contained. Tom answered in English, "Ashes." Taking this to mean
hashish, the officers in high alarm called for carabinieri and police dogs.
The mêlée this caused was fortunately short-lived, as Camilla Pecci Blunt
leapt over the barrier and explained.

Fulco would have loved the story of this misunderstanding.

with my best wishes

Fulco

Christmas 58

NOTES

All unattributed quotes regarding Fulco's life are taken from his autobiographical *The Happy Summer Days* (London 1976) or translated by the author from *Estati felici* (Milan 1977). Quotes from G. Tomasi di Lampedusa's *The Leopard*, first published by Feltrinelli in 1958, are translated by the author from the definitive 1969 edition.

CHAPTER 1

p. 12 "Ducrot, a local firm...," from the October 1903 *Studio*, quoted in Pirrone, G., *Palermo, una capitale dal Settecento al Liberty* (Milan 1989), p. 268.

p. 14 "The marquisate...," San Martino de Spucches, F., *La storia dei feudi e dei titoli nobiliari di Sicilia dalle loro origini ai nostri giorni* (Palermo 1927), v. V, pp. 253–55.

p. 14 "As agreeable, as you are to women...," *Caporal Terribile*, Palermo, (30 August 1900).

p. 15 "*Dictons Pornographiques...,*" Pornographic Sayings of a Churchgoing Woman.

p. 16 "There were inlaid marble floors," for a brief history of the Villa, see Ruggieri Tricoli, M. C., *La Villa Niscemi*, (Palermo 1989); in 1987 the property, officially recognized as "a living and unspoilt testimony to a luminous past," was purchased by the City of Palermo for representation and use as exhibition space.

p. 17 "In later years, Baron Farvara," for Favara's wealth and education, see Maniscalco Basile, L., *Accadde in Sicilia* (Palermo 1987), pp. 144–45; for other biographical details, Vitello, A., *Giuseppe Tomasi di Lampedusa* (Palermo 1987), pp. 267–71.

p. 20 "in order that he might suffer the same fate as his comrades." Tancredi was an amalgam of Corrado, Francesco Brancaccio di Carpino, and Lampedusa's own adopted son Gioacchino Lanza Tomasi, according to Gilmour, D., *The Last Leopard* (London 1988), p. 165. Another relative, Giuseppe Caravita e Tomasi, was suggested as a model in Caravita di Sirignano, F., *Memorie di un uomo inutile* (Milan 1981), p. 14. For Corrado's arrest, see Brancaccio di Carpino, F., *The Fight for Freedom: Palermo, 1860* (London 1899), p. 107. Alexandre Dumas *père* witnessed the patriotic activities in 1860 of several of Fulco's ancestors—Corrado, Giuseppe Santostefano della Cerda, Giulio Benso, Duca della Verdura—which he reported, sometimes uncomprehendingly, in *Les Garibaldiens* (Paris 1861)

p. 20 "majestic maternal figures," Lo Valvo, O., *L'ultimo ottocento palermitano* (Palermo 1937) 1986, p. 395

p. 22 "this Aida was 'the most complete...'," *La lince*, (Palermo, 1 April 1907). For a complete history of the Teatro Massimo, see Maniscalco Basile, L., *Storia del Teatro Massimo di Palermo* (Florence 1984).

p. 24 "It was a matter of course," Pomar, A., *Donna Franca Florio* (Florence 1985); for the Florio milieu and style, see Giuffrida, R. and Lentini, R., *L'età dei Florio* (Palermo 1986); for Donna Franca's wardrobe, see the Palazzo Pitti exhibition catalogue, *Il guardaroba di Donna Franca Florio* (Florence 1986); for fashion in Palermo, see the Museo del Costume R. Piraino catalogue, *Abiti d'Epoca 1700–1940* (Palermo 1992).

p. 26 "A street-sweeper," *Capitan Fracassa*, (22 August 1913).

p. 26 "Life was easy and protected then," Verdura, F. di, "Siciliana," *Harper's Bazaar* (New York, December 1937), p. 97.

p. 27 "Even Pius X," *Caporal Terribile*, (Palermo, 1 February 1914), p. 2, and 8 March 1914, p. 2.

p. 28 "A letter from the Princess," for the details of the Niscemi di Valguarnera inheritance, see *Maniscalco Basile*, (Palermo 1987), pp. 142–50, and *Vita di un avvocato* (Palermo 1993), pp. 56–59.

p. 29 "And beyond the Verdura portals," Verdura, F. di, "Siciliana," p. 136.

CHAPTER 2

p. 34 "In my day, we only ever," *Don Camillo*, (Palermo, 21 December 1922).

p. 34 "leaving nary a trace," a contemporary description of the work, probably by Lampedusa, quoted in Gilmour, p. 125. In 1977, in accordance with the wills of Agata Giovanna, Casimiro and Lucio, the Villa was inaugurated as Piccolo di Calanovella Family Foundation, awarding annual prizes in literature and agriculture and displaying Casimiro's paintings.

p. 35 "Mamà wants you," Servadio, G., "Gattopardini a Palermo," *Tuttolibri*, (Palermo, 21 January 1978).

p. 35 "she drank to Mark Antony's health," "The Nan Garcia Show," *WOR*, (New York, 1957).

p. 36 "vulgar beyond words," K. Clark cited in Bradford, S., *Sacheverell Sitwell. Splendours and Miseries* (London 1993), p. 124.

p. 36 "society gypsies," *Vogue* (Paris, July 1918), p. 25.

p. 36 "the kind of thing you shudder at now," "Pebbles of Verdura," *The New Yorker* (New York, 24 May 1941), p. 15.

p. 36 "scabrous events and bizarre individuals," Giardinelli, G. di, *Una Gran bella vita* (Milan 1988), p. 86.

p. 37 "just plain Elsa Maxwell," quoted in Maxwell, E*., I Married the World* (New York 1955), p. 151.

p. 38 "This Palermo has so many beautiful examples," Eells, G., *The Life that Late He Led* (New York 1967), p. 68.

p. 38 "every listener made them his own," Giardinelli, *op. cit.*, p. 31.

p. 39 "Maria Felice had suffered as a girl," Scintilla, "I più caldi innamorati della spiaggia," *Corriere della spiaggia* , (13 July 1919).

p. 39 "heedless of danger," Giardinelli, p. 87.

p. 39 "How not to love someone," Faucigny-Lucinge, J.-L., *Un Gentilhomme Cosmopolite* (Paris 1990), p. 84.

p. 40 "The gondoliers are threatening," Kochno and Beecham quoted in Gill, B., *Cole* (New York 1971), p. 75.

p. 40 "Beaton hated being a nobody," Vickers, H., *Cecil Beaton* (London 1985), p. 75.

p. 40 "Beaton reserved special disapproval," Beaton, C., *The Wandering Years; Diaries 1922–1939* (Boston 1961), p. 124.

p. 42 "Bricktop burst into tears," Bricktop with J. Haskins, *Bricktop* (New York 1983), p. 111.

p. 43 "The nobles will not become advocates," quoted in J. Parris's introduction to *Brancaccio di Carpino*, p. 7.

p. 43 "euphemism for worse things," Tomasi di Lampedusa, G., *Racconti* (Milan 1961), p. 29.

CHAPTER 3

p. 46 "We were a young couple," Faucigny-Lucinge, p. 53.

p. 46 "the 'Nothing Doing Bar'," for a history of the nightclub and its patrons, see the Artcurial exhibition catalogue, *Au temps du boeuf sur le toit,* (Paris 1981).

p. 46 "the crossroads of destiny," Hugo, J., *Avant d'oublier 1918–1931* (Paris 1976), p. 131.

p. 46 "a chic and comfortable Congo," Acton, H., *Memoirs of an Aesthete* (London 1948), p. 155.

p. 49 "a personage of great influence," Ballard, B., *In My Fashion* (New York 1960), p. 72–73.

p. 49 "vague idea that a man may remain," Fry, R., (London 1910).

p. 50 "the clotted blood of the Romanovs," Liaut, J.-N., *Une Princesse déchirée. Natalie Paley* (Paris 1996), p. 75.

p. 50 "it was never shown," Horst, H., *Salute to the Thirties* (New York 1971), p. 181.

p. 51 "so much money all around you," Bricktop, p. 95.

p. 51 "a grand-niece of Pope Leo XIII," for Countess A. L. Pecci Blunt's involvement in the arts, see exhibition catalogue, *Una Collezionista e mecenate romana,* (Rome 1991).

p. 52 "like a Samurai mask," *cf.* 1957 WOR radio interview on *The Nan Garcia Show.*

p. 52 "Ilia Zdanevitch," for I. Zdanevitch's life and work, see Centre Georges Pompidou exhibition catalogue, *Iliazd,* (Paris 1978). For Chanel's textile production, see Abbaye de Royallieu exhibition catalogue, *Tisserands de légende. Chanel et le tissage en Picardie,* (Compiègne 1993).

p. 55 "insolence that is always on the alert," Morand, P., *L'Allure de Chanel* (Paris 1976), p. 127.

p. 57 "concept of sacrificing to beauty," For an illustrated account of some of these balls, see Faucigny-Lucinge, J.-L., *Fêtes Mémorables, Bals Costumés 1922–1972,* (Paris 1986).

p. 58 "Palermo means beauty," account excerpted from McMullin, J., "The Palermo Balls," *Vogue* (London, 15 May 1929), pp. 68 *ff.*, illustrated by M. Ogilvie-Grant. Additional details taken from *Vogue* (Paris, June 1929), pp. 7 *ff.* For Beaton's photographs, see *Vogue* (Paris, July 1929), pp. 74–75.

p. 60 "Rome before the fall," Walton, S., *William Walton. Behind the Façade* (Oxford 1988), p. 81.

p. 62 "Women were covered with jewels," Mona Bismarck Foundation, *Mona Bismarck. Cristobal Balenciaga. Cecil Beaton* (Paris 1994), p. 32.

CHAPTER 4

p. 64 "The point of jewelry," Madsen, A., *Chanel* (New York 1990), p. 197.

p. 64 "a little more manganese, or less chromium," Coquet, J. de, "Coiffures nouvelles et parures à la mode," in *Fémina* (Paris, December 1927), pp. 7–10.

p. 66 "turquoises and various stones," Bayard, E., *L'art de reconnaître les bijoux anciens* (Paris 1924), pp. 225 and 230.

p. 66 "in every length and size," excerpted from Ballard, pp. 54–55.

p. 67 "golden chains, though 'ancient in design'," *Fémina* (Paris, November 1927), p. 11.

p. 67 "Misia Sert was Beaumont's closest associate," Morand.

p. 67 "neither one nor the other," Sert, M., *Misia par Misia* (Paris 1952), p. 106.

p. 68 "magically lucid hands," Colette quoted in Gold, A. and Fizdale, R., *Misia* (New York 1980) 1992, p. 291.

p. 68 "through spontaneous generation," Castellane, B. de, *Mémoires* (Paris 1986), p. 340.

p. 68 "which were of no great value," M. Haedrich quoted in Mauriès, p. 43.

p. 68 "semi-precious stones that had been gaining in favor,"

Clouzot, H., Supplément artistique, *Le Figaro* (Paris, 14 July 1929), pp. 685–88.

p. 68 "a company badge," Fouquet, G., Supplément artistique, *Le Figaro* (Paris, 13 June 1929), p. 607.

p. 68 "pink tourmalines and pink sapphires," Christie's, *Sale of Fine Jewelry* (New York, 25 April 1990), p. 142, lot 229; Mauriès, ill. 90.

p. 70 "up the glass-walled staircase into the great salons," *Vogue* (London 23 July 1930), p. 41.

p. 70 "on all the Chanel suits," *Harper's Bazaar* (New York, November 1939).

p. 70 "of a primitive effect," such as those by Rivaud; see *Fémina* (Paris,1 April 1919), p. 34.

p. 70 "one of Chanel's entourage," Sachs, M., *Au Temps du Boeuf sur le toit* (Paris 1939, ed. 1987), p. 235.

p. 71 "a 50 per cent decrease," Delbourg-Delphis, M., *Le Chic et le Look* (Paris 1981), p. 170.

p. 72 "Paris correspondent Janet Flanner," Flanner, J., *Paris Was Yesterday* (New York 1972), p. 67.

p. 76 "five smaller rectangular and oval green glass stones," see Christie's, *Sale of the Personal Collection of Chanel* (London, 2 December 1978), lots 1, 8 and 15.

p. 76 "nothing so much resembles a fake jewel...," Morand, pp. 116–18.

p. 76 "I wanted to cover women with constellations," Chanel quoted in Mauriès, pp. 22–25.

p. 77 "Luxury is a need," Iribe, P., *Défense du luxe* (Montrouge 1932).

p. 77 "whose cost was inferior to their beauty," see Fouquet, G., *La Bijouterie, la joaillerie, la bijouterie fantaisie du XXème siècle,* (Paris 1934).

p. 77 "erudite barbarism," *Vogue* (Paris, September 1933), p. 39.

p. 77 "preserved at Palazzo Verdura," "Capitoli della Compagnia di San Francesco dell'Opera di San Lorenzo," manuscript illuminated *c.* 1584–1600 by P. Brasuè, now in the G. Volpi collection, Rome; see Natale, M. C. di (ed.), *Ori e argenti di Sicilia dal Quattrocento al Settecento* (Milan 1989), pp. 28–29.

p. 78 "summarized in *Vogue,*" *Vogue* (London, 11 July 1934), pp. 44–45.

p. 78 "bracelets and earrings of barbarian inspiration," *Vogue* (Paris, March 1934), p. 41.

p. 78 "Merovingian barbaric splendours," *Vogue* (London, 27 June 1934), p. 92.

p. 80 "as gay as this evening," *Vogue* (Paris, August 1934), pp. 14–15, 56.

CHAPTER 5

p. 82 "will make a name for himself on the screen," see Cendrars, B., *Hollywood,* (Paris 1936) 1973, pp. 235–42.

p. 82 "never really came his way in the New World," Lawford, V., *Horst: His Work and His World* (New York 1984), p. 129.

p. 84 "Diana Vreeland...introduced him to Paul Flato," sources include Paul Flato's written responses to the author's queries, as well as unpublished quotes generously supplied by P. Proddow and M. Fasel. See also Christie's, *Fine Jewels* (Los Angeles, 2 November 1995), pp. 44–47; Proddow, P., Healy, D. and Fasel, M., *Hollywood Jewels* (New York 1992), pp. 92–99 and 108–13.

p. 86 "All this does not smell good," Mugnier, A., *Journal de l'Abbé Mugnier, 1879–1939* (Paris 1985), p. 560.

p. 88 "Chanel box of the same period, probably also by Verdura," *cf.* ill. 78 in Mauriès.

p. 90 "after midnight, at El Morocco," American *Vogue,* quoted in Grafton, D., *Red, Hot and Rich! An Oral History of Cole Porter* (New York 1987), p. 86.

p. 92 "our old car which was constantly breaking down," Giardinelli, p. 87.

p. 92 "always King of Sicily," excerpted from Verdura, F. di, "Siciliana," pp. 96 *ff.*

p. 92 *"Toujours présent,"* Always present, rarely presentable, never presented.

p. 93 "the Serbian Prince Bojidar Kargeorgevic," *cf.* biography by Pavlowitch, S., *Bijou d'art* (Paris 1978).

p. 96 "until 1935 by Cartier," see Nadelhoffer, H., *Cartier Jewelers Extraordinary* (New York/London 1984), p. 76, and Gere, C. and Munn, G., *Artists' Jewellery* (Suffolk 1989), color pls. 2, 71 and 72, pls. 99 and 100.

p. 96 "gold wing earclips and paired wing brooches," *Vogue* (Paris, April 1934), p. 29.

p. 96 "Joan Evans," Oxford 1922.

p. 96 "On precious stones and metals," *Harper's Bazaar* (London, February 1939), pp. 68–69, 82.

p. 98 "like a heart on a sleeve," *Harper's Bazaar* (London, August 1939), pp. 58–59.

p. 98 "buying up all the old pieces," *Harper's Bazaar* (London, October/November 1939), pp. 46–47.

p. 98 "caught in a net of gold," *Harper's Bazaar* (New York, December 1940), p. 33.

p. 100 "pre-nuptial Mediterranean cruise," Culme, J. and Rayner, N., *The Jewels of the Duchess of Windsor* (London 1987), pp. 129–31, nos. 97 and 98.

p. 100 "diamonds, rubies, emeralds, and sapphires," Hapsburg, G. von and Lopato, M., *Fabergé Imperial Jeweller* (London 1993), pp. 378–79.

p. 100 "always a surprise to him," see Parke-Bernet Galleries, Inc., *Presentation Cigarette Cases & Boxes from the Collection of the Late Cole Porter*, (New York 1967).

p. 102 "the heart of the place," see Letson, N., "The Peerless Verdura," *Connoisseur* (March 1983), pp. 52–62.

p. 102 "formidable personal distinction," Lawford, p. 185.

p. 103 "Caresse Crosby," for her own account of the *années folles*, see Crosby, C., *The Passionate Years* (New York 1953).

p. 103 "his toenails lacquered gold," *Ibid., p. 125.*

p. 103 "and a *Life* photographer," "Life Calls on Salvador Dalí," *Life* (New York, April 1941), pp. 98 ff.

p. 103 *"Deux Cochons Noirs sur la Neige,"* Effect of Seven Negroes, a Black Piano and Two Black Pigs on Snow-

p. 104 "in-honor-of-the-arts events," Levy, J. *Memoir of an Art Gallery* (New York 1977), p. 252.

p. 104 "the Zodiac syndicate," Gala's ingenious scheme, by which patrons maintained Dalí year-round for the privilege of being allowed to make annual selections from his work.

p. 104 "diamond-encrusted and ruby-tipped," the brooch, acquired by Mrs. Thomas H. Shevlin, was photographed by L. Dahl-Wolfe in *Harper's Bazaar* (New York, June 1940), pp. 40–41, 90. In 1958, Dalí presented an adaptation of this motif in his own collection of "leaf-veined" jewels and *objets*, suggestive of hands that "reach out into the future." See Dalí, S., *A Study of His Art-in-Jewels* (Connecticut 1970), pp. 34 and 44, pls. XI, XVII and XVIII.

p. 106 "printed in *Harper's Bazaar*," Fulco's version excerpted from Verdura, F. di, "Massa Dalí in Ole Virginny," *Harper's Bazaar* (New York, May 1945), pp. 89 *ff.*

p. 106 "Freudian jewels by the *New Yorker*:," "Pebbles of Verdura," *The New Yorker* (New York, 24 May 1941), p. 15.

p. 106 *"Araignée du soir, espoir,"* the title is from a French proverb suggesting that to see a spider in the evening is a good omen.

p. 106 "statuette of Saint Sebastian," purchased by John B. Ryan

for his wife, the former Margaret Kahn.

p. 106 "an Apollo and Daphne brooch," the Medusa and Apollo and Daphne brooches were bought by Verdura's former colleague at Flato's, Millicent Rogers.

p. 107 "the deity of the Seventh Door," see Aeschylus, *Seven against Thebes*.

p. 107 "Avida Dollars," André Breton's anagram of Salvador Dalí.

CHAPTER 6

p. 110 "Pauline Potter," exerpted from *Harper's Bazaar* (New York, 1 March 1941), p. 55.

p. 110 "Joe Alfano," these quotes are taken from the unpublished transcript of an interview conducted by Judith Landrigan on 14 November 1988.

p. 110 "on both lapels," see Linzeler, R., "Bijoux des Indes," *Vogue* (Paris, June 1938), pp. 34–35, for E. De Wolfe; photograph of Princesse de Faucigny-Lucinge, *Vogue* (Paris, July 1939), p. 24.

p. 112 "chased and inlaid with gold," for the Spanish king's ornaments, see Hackenbroch, Y., *Renaissance Jewellery* (New York 1979), p. 411; for Cellini's rings, see Cellini, B. (trans. A. MacDonell), *The Life of Benvenuto Cellini, Written by Himself* (London 1960), p. 47.

p. 112 "indispensable elements of Art Déco style," for snail shell motif by R. Templier, see Duncan, A., *Paris Jewellers. 1895–1914* (Suffolk 1994), II, p. 232; for 1928–37 shell designs by Boivin, see Cailles, F. (trans T. Leslie), *René Boivin Jeweller* (London 1994), p. 269.

p. 114 "snuffboxes and *bonbonnières*," shells from protodynastic Ur (2500 BC), conserved at the British Museum, ill. in Rossi-Osmida, G., *Un'arte per la bellezza* (Padova n.d.), nos. 94–96; shells from 4th–3rd century BC Southern Italian sites, at the Museo archeologico nazionale, Taranto, ill. in Branchetti, M. G., *Boîtes* (Paris 1994), p. 13. For eighteenth-century pieces, see Tait, H., *The Art of the Jeweller. A catalogue of the Hull Grundy Gift to the British Museum* (London 1984), no. 483, and Snowman, K., *Eighteenth-Century Gold Boxes of Europe* (London 1966), nos. 213 and 214.

p. 118 "Mary Queen of Scots's mother-in-law," at Windsor Castle; see Victoria & Albert Museum, *Princely Magnificence* (London 1980), pp. 57–58.

p. 118 "To mysteries and knowledge more sublime," I am grateful to D. Scarisbrick for the quote from G. Wither (*Emblemes*, 1635), as well as for the *Henry VI* reference (Part 2, Act III, scene ii), in her unpublished ms. *Fulco di Verdura: Historical Precedents for His Designs and His Place in Twentieth Century Jewellery*, p. 47–48.

p. 118 *"Sa beauté m'attire*', Her beauty attracts me; ill. in Branchetti, p. 40.

p. 118 "as well as carnal passion," see Gere, C. and Munn, G., *Artists' Jewellery* (Suffolk 1989), pp. 136 and 138.

p. 120 "originating in the Bronze Age," see British Museum, Williams, D. and Ogden, J., *Greek Gold* (London 1994), p.163; Mascetti, D. and Triossi, A., *Earrings from Antiquity to the Present* (London 1990), pp. 10, 11.

p. 120 "late nineteenth-century Italian and German models," for F. Kreuter's 1873 arrow model, see Mascetti, D. and Triossi, A., p. 79.

p. 120 "Virgil's *Eclogues*," see VIII, 73–75.

p. 123 "in rococo France," Pouget, J. H., *Traité des Pierres Précieuses* (Paris 1762), pls. 1 and 3; transformable diamond brooch/circlet of the second half of the nineteenth century at the British Museum, ill. in Tait, H. ed., *Seven Thousand Years of Jewellery* (London 1986), p. 185.

p. 123 "Boucheron and Debut in the 1880s," see Vever, H., *La bijouterie française au XIX siècle* (Paris 1906), III, pp. 412, 425 and 440.

p. 127 "as well as by Fabergé," eighteenth-century feather-patterned snuffbox, ill. in Snowman, no. 361, possibly related to Fabergé's loving cup with peacock feather motif, see Hapsburg, G. von, *Fabergé* (Geneva 1988), no. 161.

p. 127 "estates belonging to the family," see Vitello (1987), p. 255.

p. 128 "in his right hand seven stars," Book of Revelation, 1:16 and 20.

p. 128 "Julienne's Milky Way parure," Vever, II, p. 240.

p. 128 "suites of crowned heads," this set of heads was eventually acquired by Andy Warhol; see Sotheby's, *The Andy Warhol Collection. Jewelry and Watches* (New York, 4 December 1988), lot 688.

p. 128 "eighteenth-century French hat-shaped jewels," Pouget, pl. 7.

p. 132 "on the inside of the lid," after Porter's death, the box was acquired by the actress Lauren Bacall, who later sold it; see Christie's, *Sale of Fine Jewelry* (New York, 5 December 1990), lot 16.

p. 132 "like a badge of pride," quotes from Martin, R., *Henry and Clare: An Intimate Portrait of the Luces* (New York 1991), pp. 286 and 288. Both Maltese Crosses were sold by Sotheby's, *The Jewelry and Objects of Vertu of The Honorable Clare Boothe Luce* (New York, 19 April 1988), lots 613 and 614.

p. 133 "Even the simplest dress must not look timid," Mainbocher and Valentina quoted in Ballard, pp. 67 and 165 respectively; Selznick quoted in Vickers, H., *Cecil Beaton* (London 1985), p. 313

p. 136 "acerbic talkers I know," Coats, P., *Of Generals and Gardens* (London 1976), p. 201.

Chapter 7

p. 140 "pink glass for their money?," Gordon, R., *Ruth Gordon.: An Open Book* (New York 1980), pp. 128–30 and 355.

p. 140 "a projection of themselves," excerpted from S. Blum's introduction, in Costume Institute, Metropolitan Museum of Art, *American Women of Style* (New York 1975).

p. 141 "the Tudor jeweled swan pendants," for examples at the Hermitage and the Metropolitan Museum of Art, see Scarisbrick, D., *Tudor and Jacobean Jewelry* (London 1995), p. 69, and Hackenbroch, p. 249. More recent swan jewels include the Swan Egg and 1906 baroque pearl pendant by Fabergé, ill. in Snowman, K., *The Art of Karl Fabergé* (London 1962), p. 145.

p. 141 "that which they have never seen," *cf.* Chastel, A., *La Grottesque* (Paris 1988).

p. 146 "with *belle époque* opulence," Verdura's design is reminiscent of Vever's 1892 diamond scallop shell which has a single large pearl balanced on its lip, dripping with diamond water; this *fin de siècle* design was inspired by rococo shell trophies such as that ill. in Pouget, pl. 4.

p. 146 "an Imperial commission in 1867," see Koch, M. *et al.*, *The Belle Epoque of French Jewelry 1850–1910* (London 1990), pp. 171 and 197–98 for examples by Vever and Mellerio; for Rouvenat, see Vever, II, p. 289, and Evans, J., *A History of Jewelry 1100–1870* (London 1970; New York 1989), p. 173.

p. 148 "as Capote put it," Capote quoted in Clarke, G., *Capote* (New York 1988), p. 275.

p. 148 "how to make her a duchess," quoted in *The Sunday Times Magazine*, (London, 6 November 1989).

p. 150 "a hundredfold its original price," Sotheby's, *The Jewels of the Late Duchess of Windsor* (Geneva, 2–3 April 1987), lot 103.

p. 154 "procurator of the Venitian republic," quotations from Alsop, S., *To Marietta from Paris* (New York 1975), pp. 184–87; *cf.* also interviews with Countess Sheila de Rochambeau, Countess Consuelo Crespi, Princess Laudomia Del Drago.

Chapter 8

p. 156 *"Working as it does...,"* Bainbridge, H. C., *Peter Carl Fabergé* (London 1949; New York 1979), p. 157.

p. 158 "to Picasso and Peter Arno," Maxwell, E., *How to Do It* (Boston 1957), pp. 181–85.

p. 158 "sketchy attempt at interior decoration," Beaton, C., *Self-Portrait with Friends: The Selected Diaries of Cecil Beaton, 1926–1974* (London 1979), p. 298.

p. 159 "while *you* were kicked out," see Mosley, C. (ed.), *Love from Nancy: The Letters of Nancy Mitford* (London 1993), p. 267, and Bryan, J. and Murphy, C.J.V., *The Windsor Story* (New York 1979), p. 555.

p. 160 "that borders on surrealism," *Art Digest* (New York, 15 December 1953), p. 23.

p. 160 "souvenirs of grand tours past," M. Ayrton, "Minutiae within Minutiae" in *Vogue* (New York, June 1955), p. 56.

p. 161 "Fulco's friend Arturo Lopez," representation *c.* 1580 of zoological rarity soon thereafter to become extinct; see Hackenbroch, Y., *Renaissance Jewellery* (New York 1979), p. 248, and lot 23 (erroneously described as a turkey) of the Lopez-Willshaw sale at Sotheby's, London, 10 June 1974.

p. 161 "a pair of roundels in its claws," for examples of crowned eagle pendants, see Natale, M.C. di (ed.), *Ori e argenti di Sicilia dal Quattrocento al Settecento* (Milano 1989), pp. 102–03; for iconography relating to the Eagle of the Palermitan Senate, see D'Amico, E., "Le parate dell'effimero e la committenza del Senato Palermitano," in *Immaginario e Tradizione* (Palermo 1993), p. 117, fig. 1.

p. 161 "Order of the Elephant," the 12th-century order, featuring a white elephant with blue trappings, surmounted by a tower, was revived in 1464 and survives to this day.

p. 161 "Residenz in Munich," probably by Hans Riemer according to Tillander, H., *Diamond Cuts in Historic Jewellery 1381–1910* (London 1995), p. 106

p. 161 "Dalí's later surrealist landscapes," as illustrated in the *Temptation of Saint Anthony*, 1946; Dalí produced a jeweled Space Elephant Clock in 1961.

p. 161 "the Liotru fountain in Catania," 1736, by G. B. Vaccarini.

p. 164 "East of Persia or Byzantium," *Vogue* (London, May 1933), p. 46.

p. 164 "otherwise, she was perfect," Clarke, G., *Capote* (New York 1988), p. 280.

p. 167 "They do their best," see transcript of Garcia, N., *The Nan Garcia Show* (WOR), 1957.

p. 167 "best-dressed people in the world," Amfitheatrof, E., *The Enchanted Ground. Americans in Italy, 1790–1980* (Boston 1980), p. 172.

p. 169 "his teenage mistress," see Mitford, N., *The Blessing* in *The Nancy Mitford Omnibus* (1951; London 1986): ch. XIV, pp. 411–15.

p. 169 "mantle of so-called sophistication," letter dated 11 January 1954.

p. 170 "the seamless tunic or the winding sheets," see Kuryluk, E., *Veronica and Her Cloth* (Oxford 1991), pp. 47–48, 193, 197, 231, 255.

p. 170 "repertory of double-letter motifs," see Pouget, J., *Dictionnaire de Chiffres et de Lettres ornées* (Paris 1767), pl. 1767.

p. 170 "pantaloon world of the theater," Moss Hart quoted in

Gill, B., *Cole* (New York 1971), p. 129.

p. 172 "enormous casual chic," *Vogue* (New York, 15 September 1995), p. 97.

p. 172 "encircled with thick gold twine," at the end of Nicholas Brown's tenure, the gem was generously passed on for subsequent "commodoras" to enjoy but eventually disappeared.

p. 174 "inspired by Thirties *bijouterie*," Becker, V., *Fabulous Costume Jewelry* (Atglen, PA, 1993), p. 132.

p. 174 "set by the taste of an aristocracy," Evans, J., *A History of Jewellery 1100–1870* (London 1953, 1970; New York 1989), p. 183.

p. 175 "or perhaps an Edwardian replica," Hughes, G., *Modern Jewelry. An International Survey* (New York 1963), p. 285.

p. 175 "Beaumont devised in 1938," for Beaumont's sets, designed to cover each phalange and finger tip, see *Vogue* (Paris, April 1938). Wide coverage was given in 1932 to the discovery near Oaxaca, Mexico, of the Monte Albán Treasure, that included Mixtec culture (1250–1500) funeral jewelry.

p. 175 "at the Villa Favorita from 1935 onward," for Spanish charms, see Tait, H. (ed.), *Seven Thousand Years of Jewellery* (London 1986), p. 212; for Sicilian charms, see Museo Regionale Pepoli di Trapani, *Coralli, talismani sacri e profani* (Palermo 1986), pp. 212 and 420.

p. 175 "moss agate pictures," see 1789 piece by A. Vachette in Snowman, K., *Eighteenth Century Gold Boxes of Europe* (London 1966), nos. 412–13.

p. 178 "topped by $2.50 pieces," see Sotheby's (New York, 14 April 1992), lot 616.

p. 182 "enclosing one of this own 'in exchange' – a safety pin," Grafton, D., *The Sisters: The Lives and Times of the Fabulous Cushing Sisters* (New York 1992), pp. 112–13.

CHAPTER 9

p. 184 "it is a 'new beauty'," Vickers, H., *Cecil Beaton* (London 1985), p. 497.

p. 184 "for one wardrobe really," *Vogue* (New York, 15 March 1958), p. 71.

p. 186 "enamel jewelry of the seventeenth century," see French necklace *c.* 1670 with blue bowknots edged in black (Victoria & Albert Inv: 95–1909); ill. in Somers Cocks, A., *An Introduction to Courtly Jewelry* (London 1980), p. 43–44.

p. 186 "Medusa turned seaweed into coral," Ovid, *Metamorphoses*, Book IV (750) and Book V (415).

p. 186 "stags, crowned or winged," see stag pendants in Hackenbroch, Y., *Renaissance Jewelry* (New York 1979), p. 251.

p. 190 "mounting baby teeth in jewelry," Toulouse-Lautrec's mother had four of his *dents de lait* set into a ring.

p. 190 "just like Fabergé," *cf.* the 1898 Lily of the Valley Easter egg by Fabergé.

p. 192 "*les pierres imaginées* in 1957," Baltrusaitis, J., *Aberrations. Les perspectives dépravées* (Paris 1995), pp. 67–149.

p. 193 "things must be bad," Alsop, S., *To Marietta from Paris* (New York 1975), p. 294.

p. 193 "into the wee hours," Amfitheatrof, E., *The Enchanted Ground. Americans in Italy 1790–1980* (Boston 1980), pp. 183–84.

p. 193 "all beauty's munitions," excerpted from *Vogue* (Paris, June 1935), pp. 45–46.

p. 193 "*Fratelli d'Italia,*" by Arbasino, A. (Milan 1993), pp. 451 *ff.* The name is an evocative composite, derived from a character in Giordano Bruno's *Cena delle ceneri* and Robert Fulke Greville, the early-19th century owner of a fabulous gem and mineral collection, who was a protector of Emma Hamilton.

p. 197 "readers of *Harper's Bazaar* in 1937," Verdura, F. di., "Siciliana," *Harper's Bazaar* (New York, December 1937), pp. 96 *ff.*

p. 197 "perhaps his great-grandfather," descriptions of Visconti's filming in Palermo and Fulco's involvement from Arbasino, A., *op. cit.,* p. 660; Servadio, G., *Luchino Visconti* (New York 1983), p. 175; Stirling, M., *A Screen of Time: A Study of Luchino Visconti* (New York 1979), p. 165.

p. 198 "we didn't get or have offered to us," Thayer, M. van R., *Jacqueline Kennedy: The White House Years* (New York 1971), p. 333.

p. 199 "*Indian Tribes of North America...,*" information supplied in 20 May 1996 letter from The White House. See also *Art in The White House. A Nation's Pride* (Washington, D.C., 1992), pp. 85–86.

p. 199 "a woman's awareness of it," *Vogue*, April 1961.

p. 202 "with twain he did fly," Ch. VI, verse 2.

p. 202 "succeed one another relentlessly," Rasponi, L., *The International Nomads* (New York 1966) p. 108.

p. 202 "those on their way up," Rasponi, L., *The Golden Oases* (New York 1968), pp. 115-16.

p. 202 "fixed to the lapel', Capote, T., *Answered Prayers* (New York 1987), p. 152.

p. 202 "bottom of the invitations," Clarke, G., *op. cit.*, p. 370.

p. 204 "*Sempre caro...,*" It was always dear to me, this solitary hill...

p. 209 "in the first place she's black," Mosley, C., *op. cit.*, p. 497

p. 210 "upon the consorts of monarchs," see sixteenth- and seventeenth-century examples ill. in Brunner, H., *Schatzkammer der Residenz München* (Munich 1970), p. 127. The Verdura rose was used in all performances of the opera until the night of 21 January 1991, when it mysteriously disappeared. The next day, an unidentified Cockney caller alleged he had been offered the rose by two Scotsmen, but after several subsequent telephone conversations, in which the possibility of a reward was discussed, there was no further contact. The piece, with a high in-house valuation, was eventually reproduced by Annabel Jones's silversmiths working from photographs, since Verdura had modified his original drawings during execution.

p. 211 "a postscript to *The Leopard*," Forbes, A., "A prince among writers," *The Spectator* (London, 26 November 2988), p. 42.

ACKNOWLEDGMENTS

I am extremely grateful to all those who kindly shared their memories of Verdura with me, and allowed objects in their possession to be reproduced in this book: Senatore Giovanni and Donna Marella Agnelli, the Countess of Airlie, Principessa Lina Alliata di Pietratagliata, Sir Hardy Amies, Mrs. Vincent Astor, Eve Auchincloss, Letitia Baldridge, the Duchess of Beaufort, Comte Henri de Beaumont, Gorges Bernier, Marilyn Bertone, Conte Manolo Borromeo d'Adda, Luc Bouchage, Mr. Billy Boy, Marina Branca, Contessa Cristiana Brandolini d'Adda, J. Carter Brown, Nicholas Brown, Stephen Calloway, John Cavanagh, The Hon. Mrs. Paul Channon, Edmonde Charles-Roux, Contessa Consuelo Crespi, James Davison, James Douglas, John Seymour Erwin, Mrs. Angela B. Fischer, Paul Flato, Mrs. Afdera Fonda, Alastair Forbes, Principessa Gabriella di Giardinelli, Christopher Gibbs, Giovanni Grasso, Mrs. Gordon Gray, Jean-Pierre Grédy, Madam Germaine Gripoix, Mrs. Henry Grunwald, the Hon. Pamela Harriman, Nicholas Haslam, Principessa Laudomia Hercolani del Drago, Derek Hill, Jean Howard, Horace Kelland, Eleanor Lambert, Kenneth Jay Lane, Marchese Wenceslao Lanza di Villanrutia, Maestro Gioacchino Lanza Tomasi, Walter Lees, Avvocato Luigi Maniscalo Basile, Anna Gendel Mathias, Romana McEwen, Enrico Medioli, Lady Alexandra Metcalfe, Bernard Minoret, Principe Pietro di Moncada, Charlotte Mosley, Florence Muller, Geoffrey Munn, Cavaliere Quintino di Napoli, Viscount Norwich, Baronessa Laura Oddo, Baronessa Maria Bianca Pasqualino, Architetto Giorgio Pes, Michael Pearman, Raffaele Pirajno, Barone Alberto Pucci, Marquise Isabel de Ravenel, Mrs. Richard Redmond, John Richardson, Comtesse Sheila de Rochambeau, Baronne Alain de Rothschild, Baronne Elie de Rothschild, Mrs. Barry Sainsbury, Gaia Servadio, Michele Silvestri, Babs Simpson, Lady Anne Tree, Hugo Vickers, Claus Virch, Margaret Vyner, Lord Weidenfeld, Baronessa Renata Pucci Zanca, Architetto Francesco Zito.

Documentation regarding various aspects of Verdura's life and career was provided by Michael Chelk, Property and Insurance Manager, and Jane Jackson, Archivist, Royal Opera House (London); Judy Rudoe, Curator of the Modern Collection, Department of Medieval and Later Antiquities, British Museum (London); Lydia Tederick, Curatorial Assistant at the White House (Washington D. C.); Annie Barbera, Librarian, Palais Galliéra Musée de la mode et du costume (Paris); Lisa Brody, Archivist *Vogue* (London); Diana Edkins *Vogue* (New York); Dennis Golonka, *Harpers Bazaar* (New York).

Permission to quote from Verdura's correspondence with Nancy Mitford was generously granted by the Duchess of Devonshire; Milton Gendel authorized the use of letters to Judy Montagu Gendel. Mrs. Earl McGrath graciously allowed reproduction of her photographs of Verdura.

Many family reminiscences came from Verdura's relatives, his cousins Princess Alexander Romanoff and Maita di Niscemi, and in particular his great-nephew Alessandro Koch-Lequio.

I am indebted to jewelry historians Diana Scarisbrick, Vivienne Becker, Marion Fasel and Penny Proddow, who shared much unpublished material. Eric Valdieu of Christie's (Geneva) supplied details of Verdura pieces sold at auction.

Lois Lee Alloy and André Chervin contributed essential information regarding Verdura's showroom and the realization of his designs. I would like to express all my gratitude to Grace, the Countess of Dudley, for introducing me to Verdura. Special thanks to Roderick Coupe for his constant, constructive critcism to the work-in-progress. Thomas Parr, in addition to providing numerous introductions, also offered to read the manuscript and helped avoid many pitfalls. My editor Stanley Baron must be credited for his unfailing patience, as well as his unique expertise in jewelry and fashion history.

Harry Fane of the Obsidian Gallery, London, arranged for photography of jewels and miniatures in various European collections.

The project could not have been completed without the assistance and encouragement of Verdura, Inc. I benefited immensely from Maria Kelleher's knowledge of Verdura's style and draughtmanship; and from Brigid Leary's meticulous review of his registers and albums. Deepest gratitude must go to Judith and Edward Landrigan, who have devoted years to the study of Verdura's œuvre: if this book conveys something of its excitement and individuality, it is due to their learning, enthusiasm and unstinting support.

PATRICIA CORBETT

Picture Credits

Index